DILEMMAS OF SOLIDARITY: RETHINKING REDISTRIBUTION IN THE CANADIAN FEDERATION

Edited by Sujit Choudhry, Jean-François Gaudreault-DesBiens, and Lorne Sossin

Since the rise of the Canadian welfare state in the aftermath of the Second World War, the politics of social policy and fiscal federalism have been at the centre of federal-provincial relations. More recently, political, social, and economic developments in areas such as taxation, health care, and constitutional law have given impetus to the federal and provincial governments to re-examine present fiscal arrangements. In 2002, the Quebec Commission on Fiscal Imbalance (the Séguin Commission) released its report, which introduced the term 'vertical fiscal imbalance' into the vocabulary of Canadian politics. Essentially, the commission determined that a disjunction between revenue-raising capacity and expenditures involving different orders of government – vertical fiscal imbalance – was an urgent problem that must be addressed.

In *Dilemmas of Solidarity* editors Sujit Choudhry, Jean-François Gaudreault-DesBiens, and Lorne Sossin bring together a group of respected legal and political scholars to reflect on the Séguin Commission's findings. Their contributions examine current debates surrounding Canada's equalization program and suggest various approaches to the problem of fiscal imbalance. While taking into account the particulars of different policy debates, the authors concentrate on basic questions regarding redistribution, thus providing a highly informed, yet focused, discussion of the issues.

SUJIT CHOUDHRY is an associate professor in the Faculty of Law and the Department of Political Science at the University of Toronto.

JEAN-FRANÇOIS GAUDREAULT-DESBIENS is an associate professor in the Faculty of Law at the University of Toronto.

LORNE SOSSIN is an associate dean and associate professor in the Faculty of Law and the Department of Political Science at the University of Toronto.

Edited by Sujit Choudhry,
Jean-François Gaudreault-DesBiens,
and Lorne Sossin

Dilemmas of Solidarity

Rethinking Redistribution in the Canadian Federation

UNIVERSITY OF TORONTO PRESS
Toronto Buffalo London

© University of Toronto Press 2006
Toronto Buffalo London
utorontopress.com

ISBN 978-0-8020-9126-0 (cloth)
ISBN 978-0-8020-9407-0 (paper)

Library and Archives Canada Cataloguing in Publication

Dilemmas of solidarity : rethinking redistribution in the Canadian
federation / edited by Sujit Choudhry, Jean-François Gaudreault-DesBiens
and Lorne Sossin.

ISBN-13: 978-0-8020-9126-0 (bound)
ISBN-13: 978-0-8020-9407-0 (pbk.)
ISBN-10: 0-8020-9126-1 (bound)
ISBN-10: 0-8020-9407-4 (pbk.)

1. Income distribution – Canada.   2. Canada – Economic conditions –
Regional disparities.   I. Choudhry, Sujit   II. Gaudreault-DesBiens,
Jean-François, 1965–   III. Sossin, Lorne Mitchell, 1964–

HC120.I5C46 2006   339.5′2′0971   C2006-903352-8

The publication of this book was sponsored by the Forum of Federations.

University of Toronto Press acknowledges the financial assistance to
its publishing program of the Canada Council for the Arts and the
Ontario Arts Council.

University of Toronto Press acknowledges the financial support for
its publishing activities of the Government of Canada through the
Book Publishing Industry Development Program (BPIDP).

Contents

Comments

Part Three: The Spending Power and the Constitutional Architecture of Redistribution

Comments

Acknowledgments

This book came together around a symposium held at the Faculty of Law, University of Toronto in February 2004. The symposium began with opening remarks delivered by the Honourable Benoît Pelletier, minister responsible for the Secrétariat aux affaires intergouvernementales canadiennes of the Province of Quebec. In addition to the contributors to this volume, a number of leading voices on Canadian federalism enriched the discussion at the symposium, including Barbara Cameron, Tom Courchene, Mark Freiman, Ken McRoberts, David Schneiderman, Robert Young, Jean Leclair and John Whyte.

This symposium would not have been possible without the generous financial support of our sponsors: the Privy Council Office, Government of Canada; Secrétariat aux affaires intergouvernementales canadiennes, Province of Quebec; the Bureau du Québec à Toronto; the Ministry of Intergovernmental Affairs, Province of Ontario; the Law Foundation of Ontario; the Forum of Federations; and the Faculty of Law, University of Toronto. At each of these institutions, key individuals deserve special thanks. Patrick Fafard, Director General of Strategic Policy and Research, Intergovernmental Affairs at the Privy Council Office, supported this project from the outset. Fareed Amin, former Deputy Minister, Ministry of Intergovernmental Affairs, Province of Ontario, Claude Longpré of the Secrétariat aux affaires intergouvernementales canadiennes of the Province of Quebec, Ghislain Beaudin of the Bureau du Québec à Toronto, David Macdonald at the Forum of Federations, and Mary Brown at the Law Foundation of Ontario were equally supportive. Finally, at the Faculty of Law, University of Toronto, former Dean Ron Daniels, and Interim Dean Brian Langille, were enthusiastic supporters of this project, and Jennifer Tam worked her usual organizational magic to make the symposium run smoothly.

We are indebted to Virgil Duff and the staff of University of Toronto Press for their support of this project and to Zimra Yetnikoff who has provided superb research assistance. Finally, we are grateful to Iris Antonios and Robert Leckey for excellent editorial assistance.

DILEMMAS OF SOLIDARITY:
RETHINKING REDISTRIBUTION IN
THE CANADIAN FEDERATION

Introduction: Exploring the Dilemmas of Solidarity

SUJIT CHOUDHRY, JEAN-FRANÇOIS GAUDREAULT-DESBIENS, AND LORNE SOSSIN

Since the rise of the Canadian welfare state in the aftermath of the Second World War, the politics of social policy and fiscal federalism have been at the centre of federal-provincial relations and constitute a perennial topic of academic study. Recent events have given impetus for scholars to re-examine and interrogate some basic aspects of the institutions and policies of the 'Social Union,' a term coined by Keith Banting and others to emphasize that the Canadian welfare state had to adapt to the reality of federalism.

The immediate impetus for this volume was the publication of the report of Quebec's Commission on Fiscal Imbalance, chaired by Yves Séguin, in 2002 (the Séguin Commission).[1] The commission argued that because of demographic pressures, the provinces face growing expenditures in areas of provincial jurisdiction, such as health care and education, but lack access to sufficient sources of revenue to meet these needs. The federal government, by contrast, will enjoy surpluses for years to come. The commission suggested that the disjunction between revenue-raising capacity and expenditures involving different orders of government – vertical fiscal imbalance – poses a number of serious problems. Unless steps are taken to ensure that provinces have adequate fiscal means to match their areas of policy responsibility, provincial autonomy will be severely undermined. And federal transfers that close the fiscal gap undermine provincial autonomy if they impose conditions, are changed arbitrarily, or do not take into account actual levels of demand for public services. The concept of vertical fiscal imbalance was quickly seized upon by all provinces to frame their arguments and make common cause against the federal government. The Health Accord of September 2004 can be viewed as one policy file where the provinces successfully deployed arguments regarding vertical fiscal balance to increase the levels of federal transfers to the provinces.

The Séguin Commission conceptualized the problem of fiscal federalism as the realignment of revenue-raising and taxing powers between the federal and provincial governments, either through a direct transfer of taxing authority, or through transfer payments to offset any such misalignment. But the recent debate surrounding Canada's equalization program suggests that this is not the only way to approach the issue. The formula used for equalization claws back from equalization payments a significant proportion of revenues from non-renewable resources. Nova Scotia and Newfoundland argued that the formula created the equivalent of a welfare trap for the provinces, and they successfully demanded that they receive 100 per cent of resource revenues without any decline in equalization payments. Not surprisingly, other provinces that receive equalization (Saskatchewan and New Brunswick) immediately indicated that they too would be seeking enhanced equalization payments.

But far more surprising and significant is Ontario's response, which has been highly critical of these new arrangements. Ontario makes an argument that has hitherto not been made by the 'have' provinces: that since the equalization program is financed principally by taxpayers in Ontario, enrichments to equalization come at Ontario's expense. Indeed, Ontario has gone further and has launched a campaign to reduce the $23 billion gap between federal tax revenue raised from Ontario and federal expenditures in that province. Ontario's lurking fear is, in essence, to become a 'have-not' province, a fear that is being fuelled by a recent report of the Ontario Chamber of Commerce.[2] These arguments about the level of vertical fiscal imbalance have been joined by another – that inter-regional transfers largely funded by Ontario have been ineffective in reducing disparities in economic performance between have and have-not provinces.[3]

To complicate the debate even further, Alberta's huge budgetary surpluses and unsurpassed revenue-raising capacities have recently been characterized by Tom Courchene as posing a potential threat to Canadian unity unless that province agrees to share its surpluses and the revenues it gets from its natural resources.[4] The crux of Courchene's argument is that Alberta's wealth, if it were not shared, could be used to produce a combination of extremely high-quality public services (e.g., in the areas of health care and higher education) and low taxation rates, which would irremediably undermine the competitiveness of other provinces by eroding their capacity to retain their most productive and dynamic citizens. Predictably, the Alberta government has refused to subscribe to this thesis.[5] In doing so, Alberta was supported by the government of Quebec, a province which, while much poorer than Alberta, understands that, as a producer of energy – in its case hydroelectricity – any logic of 'compelled sharing' would also apply to what it perceives as its own and exclusive resources.

As a result of these debates, Canada must now juggle the following variables: both have and have-not provinces want a better alignment between expenditures incurred and revenue-raising capacities; some have-not provinces (Newfoundland and Nova Scotia) want to reap the entire and exclusive benefit from new sources of revenues without losing their status as 'have-not' provinces under the equalization program; one have province (Ontario) increasingly sees a nexus between its contribution to the federation and what it perceives to be its concomitant impoverishment; another have province (Alberta) is adamantly opposed to sharing its ever-increasing wealth beyond the contribution it makes to the equalization program; and, last but not least, a relatively wealthy federal government has yet to show any thirst for fully examining any principled and structural solution to the problem of redistribution.

At their very core, these debates are about redistribution within the Canadian federation. But as our brief description makes clear, there are fundamentally different ways of conceptualizing what the appropriate character and scope of redistribution should be.[6] And disagreement over these basic questions of principle generates disagreement on particulars. Thus, while the mantra of vertical fiscal imbalance allowed the provinces to maintain a united front against the federal government, debates over equalization illustrated how provincial interests in redesigning redistribution are not aligned. Clearly, horizontal fiscal imbalance is as much on the policy agenda as vertical fiscal imbalance. And at a deeper level, these debates turn on different visions of the type of political community Canada is. Indeed, the dilemmas of solidarity raised by redistribution within the federation are, in the end, dilemmas about Canada itself.

Thus, although this volume was prompted by the publication of the report of the Séguin Commission, our goal is to stand back from the particulars of these policy debates and to enable the contributors to reflect on basic juridical, political, economic, and philosophical questions regarding redistribution. It is hoped that this volume will inform a more nuanced and wide-ranging debate among both academics and policy practitioners than has occurred in the past. In order for this forward-looking debate to commence, however, it is necessary to better understand how fiscal federalism in Canada has evolved.

Fiscal federalism is said to be the glue that binds Canadian social policy.[7] It comprises the network of taxation, expenditures, and transfers that characterizes the fiscal relationships between the federal and provincial governments in Canada.[8] Major programs in health care, education, and social assistance have all come about through often complex fiscal arrangements between the different levels of government. While fiscal federalism helped provinces support growing social programs in the years after the Second World War, federal involvement in the provision of social services has always been controversial. The Constitution Act, 1867 gives the federal government the capacity to generate revenues for spending but is widely thought to give the legislative authority for the development and distribution of social services to the provinces. At Confederation, this division of powers had little practical effect because government involvement in health, education, and welfare was minimal.[9] However, as social programs grew and became more central to political agendas, this division of powers became unworkable. Tensions began to mount between the federal and provincial governments over social service policy and delivery.

It is important to emphasize that not every dimension of fiscal federalism is equally problematic. Indeed, since a significant number of the most important social programs that fiscal federalism serves to fund lie within provincial jurisdiction, it is not so much the legal grounds upon which provinces can exercise their power in areas covered by fiscal federalism as their actual capacity to deliver services in areas over which they have jurisdiction that is at stake in contemporary debates.

The situation is different with respect to the federal government's ability to influence social programs that normally fall within provincial jurisdiction – a central feature of fiscal federalism since the creation of the Canadian welfare state. This ability rests on several constitutional sources, all of which have been, and still are, controversial. The first source is the federal power to legislate over matters affecting 'the peace, order and good government of Canada.' The second source is the federal spending power. The third source is the constitutional provision governing equalization. Each will be briefly discussed in turn.

First, the federal government's involvement in pan-Canadian social programs can be supported by its power to legislate for the peace, order, and good government of Canada (POGG) under section 91 of the Constitution Act, 1867. Parliament may use this power to adopt temporary legislation if a national emergency arises.[10] However, this hardly provides the federal government with a foundation strong enough to establish long-lasting, pan-Canadian programs. Parliament can also act under this power to regulate matters that concern the federation as a whole. In *R. v. Crown Zellerbach*, the Supreme Court of Canada confirmed the test for determining when the POGG power would justify federal legislation when a concern has attained a 'national dimension.'[11] For a policy area to meet this test, it must obviously transcend merely local and private concerns. Moreover, the item regulated 'must have a singleness, distinctiveness and indivisibility that clearly distinguishes it from matters of provincial concern and a scale of effect on provincial legislation that is reconcilable with the fundamental distribution of legislative power under the Constitution.' The Court further suggested that 'in determining whether a matter has attained the required degree of singleness, distinctiveness and indivisibility that clearly distinguishes it from matters of provincial concern it is relevant to consider what would be the effect on extra-provincial interests of a provincial failure to deal effectively with the control or regulation of the intra-provincial aspects of the matter.'[12] Sujit Choudhry has argued that the national dimensions test actually encompasses two different sets of situations: a situation of extra-provincial externalities, where the regulatory decisions of a province (e.g., lax environmental laws) impose costs on extra-provincial interests; and situations of interprovincial and federal-provincial collective action problems, in which the risk of interprovincial and federal-provincial non-cooperation leads to regulatory races to the bottom. Needless to say, such broad functionalist or efficiency-based interpretations of the POGG power are controversial.[13] In any event, both the difficulty of applying the test for determining whether a concern has a national dimension, as reflected in the majority and dissenting reasons in *Crown Zellerbach* itself and in subsequent cases,[14] as well as the impact such a determination may have on the balance of powers within the federation transform any federal impulse to base a pan-Canadian social program solely on Parliament's power to legislate for the peace, order, and good government of Canada into a hazardous enterprise.[15]

Second, deeper federal involvement in social services may be achieved through the spending power. In other words, while the federal government cannot legislate how the provinces deliver social services within provincial jurisdiction, it can provide funding for such services and can impose conditions on that funding. The case of *Winterhaven Stables v. Canada*[16] provides the most extended discussion on the legality of the federal spending power. In that case, the applicant challenged several federal social service programs as being *ultra vires* Parliament. It complained that the federal government was collecting taxes from the provinces and then spending that money on matters that fell within provincial jurisdiction. In essence, the claim was that the federal government was using its financial powers unconstitutionally to coerce the provinces to participate in programs established and regulated by the federal government. The Alberta Court of Appeal rejected this argument and held that using the spending power to attach conditions to social programs was constitutionally valid. Parliament is entitled to spend the money it raises on any matter it so chooses. The court noted that one consequence of this may be that the federal government can pressure provinces to pass legislation that complies with federal requirements. However, the court concluded that providing funding does not mean that the federal government is intruding on provincial jurisdiction.[17]

Gaudreault-DesBiens has argued that the reasons of *Winterhaven Stables*, as well as most traditional defences of an absolutely unfettered federal spending power, are highly formalistic. They rely on a dubious distinction between legislation and contract as the means to create legal obligations, and fail to address, from a federative perspective, the main problem of federal constitutional spending in areas of provincial jurisdiction – that is, doing indirectly what cannot be done directly and thus tangibly ignoring the provinces' legislative and executive autonomy in these areas.[18] However, this case confirms the constitutionality of a practice that has not been frontally challenged in court by any provincial government since the advent of the Canadian welfare state.[19] In fact, it is as if the constitutionality of conditional federal spending in areas of provincial jurisdiction was something no one wanted to submit to courts of law and, ultimately, to the Supreme Court.[20] Maybe this is so for fear of an undesired outcome or because the relative comfort provincial governments enjoy under the current scheme induces them to accept their legal fate with some indifference, to paraphrase filmmaker Denys Arcand.[21] But politically the field of federal spending power undeniably remains heavily mined.

The third justification for federal involvement in fiscal federalism's redistribution game is the equalization program, which finds its source in section 36 of the Constitution Act, 1982. Under this provision, the federal government has the ability to make equalization payments 'to ensure that provincial governments have sufficient revenues to provide reasonably comparable levels of public services at reasonably comparable levels of taxation.' These payments differ from other federal-provincial transfers in that they are wholly unconditional. While the purpose of the equalization program is to ensure the implementation of basic standards across the country, it also respects provincial autonomy by providing each province with the capacity to deliver comparable programs. This program relies to some extent on federal-provincial arrangements but is first and foremost a federal program, as the funds for equalization come from the federal budget, collected from individual taxpayers across the country. This means that individuals in the poorer provinces receiving equalization payments also contribute to the program, albeit not on a net basis.

Until recently, the equalization program was relatively uncontroversial, at least in respect of its main orientations. But this is rapidly changing. The recent agreements, crystallized in the 2005 federal budget, between the federal government and the provinces of Newfoundland and Labrador on one hand, and Nova Scotia on the other, reveal a significant shift in the politics of equalization. These bilateral agreements, which in practice allow these provinces to retain all the revenues stemming from off-shore energy resources without having to suffer any clawback under the equalization program, are seen as a means by which these provinces will extirpate themselves from chronic poverty. Under that view, pan-Canadian solidarity expressed through equalization payments is certainly helpful, but insufficient to allow recipient provinces to enjoy a lasting and meaningful financial autonomy. This approach thus privileges empowerment over solidarity. And since the situation of each province is different in that respect, no one-size-fits-all solution can be considered. Asymmetry now becomes the name of the game.

However, such asymmetrical access to sources of revenues is noticeably different from the side deal Quebec was able to strike with the federal government in the context of the Health Accord of September 2004, to the extent that this side agreement can really be characterized as genuinely asymmetrical.[22] Indeed, the Quebec deal concerns only what, arguably, is already under that province's jurisdiction. Moreover, other provinces could have requested a similar agreement and Quebec would not have opposed such a request. Last, it hardly affects the jurisdictional and financial position of other provinces. In sum, this agreement is far more limited in nature, scope, and potential impact on third parties than those concluded about off-shore resources by Newfoundland and Nova Scotia with the federal government, especially given that government's acceptance not to impose clawbacks on equalization payments to these provinces. Indeed, to the extent that one considers that redistribution is a norm in the Canadian federation, these deals could herald a major change in the understanding and implementation of that norm.

The emergence of these two different levels of intensity of asymmetry must be acknowledged in debates about redistribution in the Canadian federation, for both are likely to frame further discussions on this issue. These discussions will surely involve the usual constitutional actors – the federal government and the provinces – but they might also implicate new actors such as the autonomous Aboriginal governments that could be created in the future.[23] Such an eventuality, which should become a reality if Canada takes seriously its commitment towards Aboriginal peoples, will inevitably complicate the politics of redistribution and render the dilemmas of solidarity faced by this country even more acute.

Constitutional debates surrounding fiscal federalism do not take place in the abstract. The history of fiscal federalism in Canada reflects the constitutional challenge of the federal government having the resources but not the jurisdiction to deliver social programs and the provincial governments having the jurisdiction but not sufficient ability to raise the needed resources without federal assistance.

Federal-provincial fiscal arrangements for social programs began to emerge in force after the Second World War, when Canada, like all other Western democracies, embarked on constructing a Keynesian welfare state. Before medicare, medical services were available on the market just like any other service and were subject to the vagaries of supply and demand. The amount and quality of health care services a person could access thus depended on the individual's ability to pay. In 1948 the federal government established cost-matching and block grants for provincial activities in health care. In 1951 it began transferring per capita grants to universities. Arrangements to provide social assistance to seniors and to disabled, blind, and unemployed people soon followed. These arrangements required provincial governments to spend money in compliance with federal conditions in order to receive federal grants.

In 1957 the equalization program made its first appearance. This program entitled the federal government to make unconditional grants to the poorer provinces in order to help finance their public services.[24] Equalization payments are established by a legislative formula which has varied over time, both in terms of the number of provinces used to calculate the national average to which other provinces were equalized (two in 1957, ten in 1962, two in 1964, ten in 1967, and finally five in 1982) and in the components of that formula (e.g., actual revenues versus revenue-raising capacity, and the relative weightings given to different revenue sources). The current formula attempts to measure each province's revenue-raising capacity and compare it to the average per capita revenue-raising abilities of five provinces (Ontario, Quebec, British Columbia, Saskatchewan, and Manitoba). Revenue-raising capacity is determined by a province's ability to raise revenues in each of thirty-three revenue sources, which include personal income tax, corporate tax, property tax, fuel taxes, and revenues from natural resources. Equalization payments are then made to provinces with revenue-raising capacities below the average amount in order to bring their fiscal capacity up to standard. When a province's abilities to raise revenues increase, its entitlement to equalization declines accordingly.[25]

The year 1957 also marked the beginning of federal involvement in the health care arena, with the introduction of the Hospital Insurance and Diagnostic Services Act. The act authorized the federal government to contribute 50 per cent of the cost of provincial hospital services, as long as the provinces made insured services available on the same uniform terms and conditions to all residents. The main problem with the scheme was that non-hospital services were not covered. Saskatchewan was the first province to go beyond the requirements of the act and extend its plan to cover all medical treatment. Saskatchewan proposed its new plan in 1959, and it was to come into force in 1962. In 1960, in an attempt to prevent Saskatchewan's model of comprehensive health care coverage from spreading to the other provinces, the Canadian Medical Association (CMA) requested that the federal government study the problem of health insurance. In response to this request, Prime Minister Diefenbaker created the Royal Commission on Health Services in 1961. The royal commission, reporting back in 1964, recommended the implementation of universal, comprehensive health insurance across Canada. This recommendation was enacted as the Medical Care Act in 1966, which provided for federal funding on a 50/50 cost-sharing basis. The act provided coverage for non-hospital care and laid down specific provincial eligibility criteria. These included operation on a non-profit basis by a public authority, reasonable access by persons across the province according to uniform terms and conditions, coverage of no less than 95 per cent of the provincial population, and portability of coverage between the provinces. These criteria were eventually incorporated into the Canada Health Act's five principles of health care.

In the 1960s the provinces, especially Quebec, began to challenge the federal government's senior position in federal-provincial arrangements. They relied on their primary constitutional authority over social welfare policy and delivery and also cited a greater competence in forming and administering social programs, based on a better understanding of their regions and electorates. The federal government accordingly entered into an agreement with Quebec, whereby it provided a tax point transfer for university funding instead of direct payments, which was regarded as more intrusive. A few years later, in response to similar provincial pressures, the federal government offered tax points in place of existing social transfers, including those targeted towards social assistance and hospital insurance. However, only Quebec accepted this offer.

The next significant change in fiscal federalism was the establishment of the Canada Assistance Plan (CAP) in 1966. The CAP collapsed previous federal-provincial welfare arrangements into one harmonized program, based on an equal sharing of costs between the two levels of government. In exchange for federal funding, provincial social assistance programs had to comply with a set of national standards, including that every 'person in need' be eligible for social assistance at a level 'that takes into account the basic requirements of that person,' that there be no residency requirement for the receipt of social assistance, that there be an administrative appeals mechanism for decisions regarding applications for social assistance, and that all of these national standards be found in provincial law.

The next major change to the architecture of shared costs programs came with the Established Programs Financing Act (EPF), introduced in 1977. The EPF provided a block grant for health care and postsecondary education, composed of equal parts of tax points and cash grants. The cash transfer portion of the arrangement was set to increase annually according to economic and population growth. However, the EPF soon demonstrated weaknesses. The federal government found the annual increases in cash transfers unacceptably high, and maintained that the provinces were failing to keep up their spending on health care and education.

Towards the end of the 1970s, the integrity of the Medical Care Act was also suffering due to extra-billing and user charges, both of which amounted to extra charges for patients. Public outcry over these direct charges led to the appointment of a special commission, led by the Honourable Emmett Hall, to review medicare coverage. In his report, delivered in 1980, Hall concluded that direct charges were undermining reasonable access to health care. The federal government's response sparked a battle that pitted the federal government against the health care profession and the provinces. The provinces resented the incursion into their jurisdiction, while the CMA considered Hall's recommendation a direct assault on its freedom. Despite these vociferous objections, the federal government adopted the Canada Health Act (CHA) in 1984. With the CHA, in order to qualify for cash contributions from the federal government, the provinces must comply with the five principles of health care: public administration, comprehensiveness, universality, portability, and accessibility.[26] The CHA reflected the position that health care is a national issue, not just a personal, community, or provincial one. Access to health care based on need and not the ability to pay became a defining Canadian characteristic and one of the most important aspects of Canadian social citizenship.[27]

But the consolidation and extension of the legislative framework for federal involvement in health care occurred alongside declining federal funding, which began in 1977, with the shift away from 50/50 cost-sharing to a block grant (the Established Programs Financing or EPF grant) consisting of a mixture of cash and tax points, with the cash component tied to an escalator based on growth in per capita gross national product (GNP). In 1982, the escalator was applied to the entire EPF entitlement, not just the cash component, making the EPF cash transfer strictly residual. The escalator was then eliminated in stages, first in 1986 (when it was reduced to GNP less 2 per cent), then in 1990 (when the EPF per capita transfer was frozen).

The reduction in federal contributions under the EPF was accompanied by reductions in federal contributions under CAP. Perhaps the most famous of these was the 'cap on CAP,' whereby federal contributions to Alberta, British Columbia, and Ontario were capped in 1990, irrespective of the levels of demand for social assistance in those provinces. The sudden and severe reduction of transfers led to a provincial budgeting crisis, which put a significant strain on intergovernmental relations.

These limits on transfer payments stemmed largely from the persistent and growing federal deficit and debt. Given that the transfers represented a large portion of federal spending, reducing the transfers became part of the federal deficit reduction strategy. The provinces particularly resented the fact that they had set up their social services to conform to federal requirements, only to have the federal government unpredictably cut funding to those services.[28] Between 1989 and 1992 provincial deficits rose from $1.5 billion to $22.8 billion. British Columbia went so far as to challenge the legality of the federal government's unilateral decision to cap CAP.[29] While British Columbia lost its case in the Supreme Court, the action reveals the degree of animosity the provinces felt towards the federal government because of the transfer cuts.

In 1995 the federal government announced that CAP and EPF would be combined to produce the Canada Health and Social Transfer (CHST). Under the CHST, the federal government reduced funding for health, welfare, and postsecondary education from $29.7 billion in 1995–6 to $25.1 billion in 1997–8. The reduction in cash transfer payments was even more dramatic, falling from $18.5 billion to $12.5 billion. However, as a quid pro quo for reduced federal funding, the CHST also imposed fewer conditions on the provincial governments and gave them more independence in determining social policy. While national standards for health care under the CHA remained, all conditions for social assistance were removed with the exception of the prohibition on a minimum residency requirement.

Initial reaction to the CHST was overwhelmingly negative. Without the condition that provinces spend money on those most in need, and with block funds replacing matching grants, provinces had less incentive to spend money on their poorest inhabitants. Instead, they were free to fund whichever 'deserving' applicants they chose. In particular, the CHST allowed provinces to redistribute public funds away from welfare to more popular health and postsecondary education plans. Another criticism of the CHST was that it would destroy the cohesion of Canada's national social system by giving the provinces the freedom to differentiate their social programs. Equalization payments had been designed for the purpose of ensuring that provinces were able to provide comparable services. With the prospect of greater provincial differentiation, the very reason for equalization would be undermined.[30] On the other hand, in a federal state, unity can hardly be synonymous with uniformity, and diversity in programs in areas which constitutionally fall under provincial jurisdiction can reasonably be seen as an inevitable incident of such a regime, even though that diversity might be deplored from a pan-Canadian nationalist perspective.

Although the limits to federal-provincial transfer payments affected all areas of social services, the concerns focused mainly on health care. In particular, it was feared that the reduction of cash grants would limit the federal government's ability to enforce the Canada Health Act. According to section 15 of the CHA, the governor in council can withhold federal transfers from provinces that fail to comply with the act's terms. With the reduction in transfer payments, the leverage the federal government had to enforce the CHA appeared weak. However, it is unclear whether the federal government had much leverage over the provinces in any event. Sujit Choudhry has noted that there is a large gap between the federal government's rhetoric supporting national health care and its enforcement of the CHA, since it is largely unaware of the degree of provincial non-compliance with the act. In cases of suspected non-compliance, the federal government's negotiations with the provinces have been kept secret.[31] In the auditor general's report of 1999, numerous instances of provincial non-compliance with the CHA were mentioned. Six of the cases were resolved without the use of financial penalties, while the other cases were not resolved at all. Enforcing the CHA is also discretionary. According to section 14, on finding that a provincial plan violates one of the act's five principles, the governor in council *may* direct that cash contributions to that province be reduced or withheld. This discretionary enforcement mechanism has never in fact been used.[32]

Nevertheless, the concerns that the federal government would be less able to uphold national standards of social services have, to some degree, been borne out. Some provinces began initiating direct patient charges in plain contravention of the CHA. Other provinces instituted more subtle changes by de-insuring previously covered health services, thus making health insurance less comprehensive. Finally, some provinces indicated less willingness to insure fully residents who obtained services outside their home province, limiting the portability of public health insurance. These emerging disparities between provincial health care services have begun to weaken the ideal of truly national programs for the provision of social services. The recent Supreme Court decision in *Chaoulli v. Quebec*,[33] which struck down a provincial scheme prohibiting private insurance contracts in respect of medical services covered by the government, could further accelerate the demise of the public nature of the Canadian health care regime.[34]

In more recent years, the federal and provincial governments have attempted to build an effective partnership that would ensure adequate, stable, and predictable cash transfers, with less ambiguity and more transparency. Some of these sentiments were captured by the Social Union Framework Agreement (SUFA) of 1999, which was signed by all governments except Quebec.[35] The 1999 federal budget was advertised as a commitment to providing predictable health care funding to the provinces and introduced measures to eliminate provincial disparities.

Within the past five years, the federal and provincial governments have examined potential solutions to the funding of health care on several occasions. For example, the First Ministers' meetings of 2003 and 2004 have produced agreements that emphasize inter-governmental partnership even though they appeared to be brought about through inter-governmental strife.

The 2003 First Ministers' Accord on Health Care Renewal saw the federal government establish the Canada Health Transfer (CHT). This is supposed to correspond to provincial health care expenditures, previously accounted for within the larger category of provincial social spending under the CHST. The stated purpose of the CHT is to enhance the transparency of and accountability for health care funding, as well as to ensure predictable annual increases in health care funding.[36] The social spending envelope, formerly part of the CHST envelope, would now constitute a separate Canada Social Transfer (CST).

Through the 2003 accord, the federal government pledged a $17.3 billion increase to health care over three years. Of that money $16 billion was to go to a five-year Health Reform Fund to transfer resources to the provinces for investment in primary health care, home care, and catastrophic drug coverage. Implicit in the creation of this fund is recognition of the positive role the federal government can play through its use of the spending power. The structure of the fund recognizes that provinces are at different stages in the areas targeted for reform. The fund gives the provinces the flexibility to use the transferred money at their discretion, as long as the money is spent in the areas of reform the fund was established for. For its part, the federal government committed to ensuring that the level of funding provided through the Health Reform Fund will be rolled into the CHT by 2008.

In September 2004, in the face of continuing federal surpluses, provincial deficits, and health expenses far outpacing economic growth, the federal and provincial governments came to another accord to strengthen health care. The federal government committed to providing $41 billion over ten years for health care through the CHT. By 2009–10, the cash portion of the CHT is projected to be 45 per cent above current levels.[37]

Both the 2003 and 2004 accords were characterized by the federal government's attempt to set broader conditions for transfers while at the same time giving the provinces greater discretion in setting up and administering their health care programs. As noted, the 2004 accord also recognizes a form of asymmetrical federalism and Quebec's desire to retain its jurisdiction over health care. Under the agreement between Ottawa and Quebec City, Quebec may use transfer funds to implement its own plan for renewing the Quebec health care system.[38] Most importantly, these recent agreements reveal the relative effectiveness of the dynamic of interprovincialism that has characterized relations between provinces since the creation of the Council of the Federation in 2003 at the instigation of the government of Quebec. This new spirit of interprovincialism seeks to maximize the influence of provinces over the evolution of federalism in spite of their often divergent interests.[39]

The budget plan for 2004–5 also brought alterations to the equalization program. Changing economic and fiscal circumstances in the short term frequently led to volatility in equalization payments from one year to the next. For example, when Ontario's economy was growing rapidly relative to other provinces in the late 1990s, standard average raising-revenue capacity increased, causing equalization entitlements to increase. Similarly, when the Ontario economy is growing less rapidly, revenue-raising capacity gaps between high- and low-income provinces decreases, which leads to lower equalization payments. In order to make equalization payments more stable and predictable, the 2004 budget proposed to make payments based on a three-year moving average. Equalization entitlements for each fiscal year are thus made on the basis of average entitlements for the three years preceding the fiscal year.

In view of the above, it is easy to conclude that the social, political, and economic model that has prevailed in Canada in the past half-century or so is undeniably shaken and is probably bound to be substantially transformed. Although this is surely a source of concern for a good number of Canadians, it could also be envisaged as an opportunity to reinvent the country on a new, but possibly more solid, basis. Such an endeavour might imply sacrificing some sacred cows and breaking a few taboos, but we should not forget that states are contingent entities, as are their structures and methods of functioning. And to the extent that the plausibility of a significant, if not radical, transformation of the Canadian federation is acknowledged, then Canadians should strive to be proactive rather than merely reactive to the changes to come and the manner in which they may be implemented.

This book on the problems raised by redistribution within the Canadian federation is a report of past conversations. It is also a new conversation and an invitation to further discussions. It originated in a conference, held at the Faculty of Law, University of Toronto, to which David Boothe, Andrée Lajoie, and Richard Simeon contributed the principal papers. Most of what appear in this volume as comments on those papers were presented at the conference. The book is thus partially a record of the conference. Other comments were solicited afterwards. In that respect, the book is a fuller conversation than ever occurred in the flesh. The complexity of the problems under consideration could not be satisfactorily addressed through the lens of a single discipline. One merit of the book's format – principal papers each followed by several comments – is that it facilitates a common discussion by contributors from various intellectual fields. The interdisciplinary dialogue is focused by people from different backgrounds speaking to the same paper. The fields of origin of the contributors to this volume's conversation all usefully inform and deepen our reflection on the dilemmas of solidarity in the Canadian federation.

Part one of this volume addresses the politics of redistribution, and opens with Richard Simeon's paper, 'Social Justice: Does Federalism Make a Difference?' Simeon explores the connection between federalism and social justice, and notes that this connection has traditionally been examined from two perspectives, one that focuses on the needs of individual citizens independent of their place of residence, and the other that seeks to protect the freedom of provinces to set their policies on redistribution. Simeon dispels several myths about the relationship between federalism and distributive justice, and concludes that this relationship is, at best, slightly negative. Indeed, he shows that federalism only marginally influences the welfare performance of a state, and that the commitment to equality instead depends on other cultural, economic, and political forces. Simeon closes by reflecting on the current debate on fiscal imbalance. Observing that neither order of government has constitutional grounds for claiming exclusive jurisdiction over social citizenship, he argues that it is best to recognize social citizenship as a value that must underpin the programs and policies of all governments.

Sujit Choudhry explores Simeon's focus on federalism and social justice in the context of the recent debate over vertical fiscal imbalance. He notes that, until recently, the debate over vertical fiscal imbalance had obscured the fact of horizontal fiscal imbalance – that is, that redistribution occurs on a net basis from the residents of some provinces to those of others. Choudhry examines whether the conception of Canada as a sharing community, entailing transfers of wealth between residents of different provinces, is threatened by emerging political trends. One threat lies in federal policies that would loosen the conditions imposed on recipient provinces. The elimination of national standards could undermine the political motivation of wealthier provinces to maintain their own commitment to pan-Canadian retributive policies. Two trends could accelerate this process. The first one is the 'cities agenda,' which seeks recognition on the part of upper governments of the particular responsibilities and challenges faced by Canada's urban centres. Since Canada's major urban centres have been principally viewed as places to redistribute from, the question is whether the cities' agenda will lead urban Canada to challenge the arrangements of fiscal federalism. The second trend is the ethno-cultural diversification of these centres. Choudhry suggests that ethnic immigrants feel little or no loyalty towards traditional conceptions of Canadian federalism, and tend to be concerned with redistribution in their own urban communities rather than on a pan-Canadian scale.

Alain Noël starts his analysis where Simeon leaves off, with the conclusion that federalism is more or less neutral towards redistribution. Noël extends the logic of Simeon's position and contends that distributive justice turns more on politics than on institutions. The key factor for Noël is 'the politics of justice itself, the enduring conflict between political and social actors of the left and of the right over the meaning of equality in a liberal society.' He opines that the most important changes that have taken place in Canada have concerned the scope and delivery modes of social programs rather than the commitment to redistribution itself. He thus argues that little empirical evidence supports Choudhry's contention that the cities agenda, coupled with new Canadians' disaffection or frustration toward federalism, have eroded the widespread support the Canadian redistributive model still enjoys. Moreover, emerging concerns for a greater solidarity of proximity and a concomitant adherence to a broader, pan-Canadian, solidarity should not be seen as contradictory. The main factor undermining the status quo remains the growing vertical fiscal imbalance in the federation, which 'undermines the capacity of provincial governments to maintain and develop the social programs for which they are responsible.' This fiscal imbalance is first and foremost a power imbalance that is amplified by the absence of clear and consensual rules governing federal-provincial transfers.

Part Two is intended to highlight differing perspectives on the use of the tax system to effect redistribution, from normative questions of distributive justice to political questions of provincial asymmetry to economic questions of optimal equilibrium. By shifting the focus from federal-provincial transfers to the progressive income tax, this section highlights the complexity of redistribution and the tensions between vertical and horizontal equity.

The principal paper for this part is Paul Boothe and Katherine Boothe's 'Personal Income Tax and Redistribution in the Canadian Federation.' In Boothe and Boothe's rich analysis of the progressive income tax (PIT), redistribution lies at the heart of the nexus between politics and markets in Canada. These authors' contribution to our knowledge about the extent and effect of redistribution through the progressive income tax system is noteworthy in at least two respects. First, they confirm that progressivity is not always what it seems in terms of redistributing income: in other words, steeper and steeper progressivity does not necessarily equal greater redistribution. Second, they highlight provincial disparities in vertical equity in Canada. Both observations have important implications for the nature and future of federalism in Canada.

The comments on this paper address both the arguments advanced by Boothe and Boothe and the arguments they choose not to advance. David Duff raises the issue of whether the redistributive effect of the personal income tax should serve as an instrument for distributive justice, and if so, whether this suggests a greater provincial or federal role in redistribution. Duff concludes that the answer as to how the PIT should redistribute is certainly not settled, and those who consider the progressive income tax to be an instrument for distributive justice are likely to be less sanguine than Boothe and Boothe about the direction of PIT reform in Canada over the last decade. Duff also discusses how the dynamics of constitutionalism interact with tax principles in the sphere of redistribution.

While Duff examines Boothe and Boothe's analysis on its own terms, Lorne Sossin challenges their premises from a different perspective. Sossin emphasizes the political dimension of vertical equity and questions the desirability of provincial convergence on redistributive strategies. He also questions whether the normative foundation of Canadian federalism can encompass concerns for equity and asymmetry. Sossin asserts that because the tax system is either unintelligible or unhinged from widely accessible norms of fairness and justice, Canadians lack a political vocabulary with which to make claims about why one degree of vertical equity is preferable over another. Consequently, arguments about the desired degree of vertical equity are more likely to be settled on economic grounds of the kind Boothe and Boothe advance. Sossin concludes that viewing the tax system through a political and not exclusively an economic lens will allow debates around redistribution to occupy the prominence thus far reserved for a contested view of 'tax competitiveness.' The search for a defensible and principled optimal degree of vertical equity, according to Sossin, should reflect a deeply political question – it is a challenge to the normative foundations of federalism.

Finally, François Vaillancourt highlights the link between the tax system and how the federal government spends its tax revenues. He argues that the federal government, flushed with surpluses, has abused its spending power and should be reined in by a new distribution of the progressive income tax field between provinces and the federal government which, coupled with more generous equalization, will make provinces responsible for raising the highest possible share of the monies they spend. Vaillancourt contends that the tendency since 2000 to see increases in federal transfers to provinces as the appropriate way to fund provincial spending, particularly in the health sector, has led first to the weakening of provincial autonomy in fields of provincial responsibility (by making it easier for the federal government to require more or less binding constraints) and second to the weakening of the interest of provinces in ensuring the proper management of public funds. This may be desired by those who believe that the federal government should be more present in these areas of public policy, but Vaillancourt asks whether the proper route to achieve this goal would not be to modify the constitutional division of powers.

The third part of this volume marks a shift from redistribution through the raising of revenue to redistribution through federal expenditures. This section revisits long-standing debates surrounding the constitutionality of federal expenditures in areas of provincial jurisdiction, through the so-called federal spending power. In the principal paper, entitled 'The Federal Spending Power and Fiscal Imbalance in Canada,' Andrée Lajoie argues that the constitutionality of the federal spending power is tenuous at best. She situates her discussion against the backdrop of a narrative of constitutional centralization, in which she argues that the principal culprit is the Supreme Court of Canada and the legal doctrines of modern federalism. Juxtaposed against this narrative of centralization, her point is that federalist scholars who have argued for the constitutionality of the spending power implicitly derive support for their interpretive project by drawing upon this larger body of jurisprudence. Lajoie's response, based on a careful reading of the case law, is that federal expenditures in areas of provincial jurisdiction are likely unconstitutional. The implication of this legal conclusion for the debate on vertical fiscal imbalance is as follows: that since one manifestation of that imbalance are federal expenditures in areas of provincial responsibility, removing the legal basis of those expenditures can in turn be used to redress fiscal imbalance.

Daniel Weinstock picks up on Lajoie's disclaimer that she is not interested in the question of whether conditional federal spending in areas of provincial jurisdiction complies with normative theories of federalism. He argues that Lajoie in fact views the federal spending power as inconsistent with the federal principle. His question is whether federalism condemns this practice. He argues that the answer to this question depends on which conception of federalism one holds. In particular, he suggests that overlapping federalism, which countenances overlapping jurisdiction, is both more normatively attractive and more receptive to federal expenditures in areas of provincial jurisdiction. By contrast, side-by-side federalism, which argues for mutually exclusive spheres of jurisdiction, and which is hostile to the federal spending power, is not as normatively attractive.

Peter Russell also challenges Lajoie's thesis, but does so on doctrinal rather than normative grounds. He questions, in particular, her reading of a Privy Council precedent on the federal spending power, the

Unemployment Insurance Reference.[40] He favours a narrow reading of that case, on the basis that it involved compulsory schemes of contributory social insurance which clearly invaded provincial jurisdiction over employment contracts, and therefore did not rule upon non-contributory social insurance. Moreover, he argues that a stronger constitutional basis for federal social insurance programs would be Parliament's power to legislate for the peace, order, and good government of Canada, which was construed narrowly in the time of the Privy Council, but whose interpretation has been broadened by the modern Supreme Court. Finally, he argues that vertical fiscal imbalance is unavoidable in federations, because of the impossibility of designing constitutions in advance to align perfectly revenue-raising capacities with new areas of federal expenditure.

Rejecting Manichean approaches to the federal spending power, Jean-François Gaudreault-DesBiens also challenges Lajoie on the constitutionality of this power, but does so in a more nuanced fashion. He argues that this issue must be examined through the lens of a normative legal theory of federalism, with the following components: inter-provincial and federal-provincial loyalty; the relative autonomy and equality of federal actors vis-à-vis each other; solidarity between parties to the federal pact; and federative arbitration to resolve disputes over the division of powers and intergovernmental relations in the courts. His argument is that conditional federal spending in areas of provincial jurisdiction is sometimes constitutional because it is mandated by the principle of federal solidarity. Direct grants to private parties provide an example of such a constitutional use of the spending power. However, given the impact that it may have on provincial autonomy, he suggests the adoption of the following conflict rule: when an order of government spends, through direct grants to private parties, in a field that is constitutionally allocated to the other, that spending should be constitutionally allowed so long as it does not substantially undermine a policy or program promulgated by the order of government which does possess primary constitutional jurisdiction over the matter, or conflicts with its purpose.

Federalism and redistribution represent the two dominant narratives of the Canadian polity and yet the relationship between these two ideas remains largely unexplored. Together, the three parts which make up this volume attempt to both broaden and deepen the debate over redistribution in the Canadian federation. The principal papers and comments address this debate through different disciplinary prisms but with a shared conviction that Canada's future will be determined by how the dilemmas of solidarity are resolved.

NOTES

1 Commission on Fiscal Imbalance (Yves Séguin, chair), *A New Division of Canada's Financial Resources. Report* (Quebec: Bibliothèque nationale du Québec, 2002).

2 Ontario Chamber of Commerce, *Fairness in Confederation. Fiscal Imbalance: Driving Ontario to 'Have-Not' Status* (Toronto: Ontario Chamber of Commerce, 2005).

3 Institute for Competitiveness and Prosperity, *Fixing Fiscal Federalism* (Toronto: Institute for Competitiveness and Prosperity, 2005).

4 Thomas J. Courchene, *Resource Revenues and Equalization* (Montreal: IRPP Working Paper Series no. 2005–04, 2005).

5 Jason Markusoff, 'Hands off, Klein Warns,' *National Post*, 26 August 2005.

6 As a result, any attempt at reforming redistribution policies and mechanisms will be fraught with difficulties. For example, even if the provincial and federal governments unanimously agreed on the appropriateness of sharing provincial revenues flowing from natural resources – a rather unlikely scenario – they would still have to define what exactly would be shared. Gross or net resource revenues? And through what type of mechanism? For a reflection on this, see Courchene, *Resource Revenues*, 20–3. Economist Pierre Fortin's approach to the problem of redistribution is even bolder than Courchene's. Examining the case of Alberta, Fortin first notes that all provinces benefit, or will eventually benefit, from the oil boom in Alberta. Given the small size of that province, it has to rely on workers and businesses from other provinces. Inevitably, he argues, this will help create jobs not only in Alberta but elsewhere as well. However, should a lasting oil crisis erupt and the price of oil dramatically increase, a major recession would probably hit oil-dependent provinces such as Ontario, Quebec, and British Columbia. Fortin is of the view that such a situation could force the federal government to intervene, even if it meant imposing upon Alberta a revamped version of the much-hated National Energy Program. Fortin observes in this respect that the rest of Canada helped Alberta when it experienced a crisis in the 1930s. Absent a show of goodwill on the part of Alberta, some form of 'compelled solidarity' could be inevitable. However, this would very likely provoke a new constitutional crisis. But there is

more. Returning to the criteria to be used in determining the amount of resource revenues to share, Fortin observes that although Alberta is four times less populous than Ontario, it has released 221 million tons of greenhouse gases in 2002, compared to 203 million for Ontario and 91 million for Quebec. The gases released by Alberta in exploiting the very resource that makes it wealthy thus impact on Canada's global environment. These emissions also largely explain Canada's performance as one of the worst of all industrialized countries under the Kyoto Protocol. Fortin concludes that this situation could legitimize a federal intervention, which would, again inevitably, provoke a major backlash in Alberta. See Pierre Fortin, 'Tout à l'Alberta, rien pour les autres?' *L'Actualité* 30, no. 15 (1 october 2005), 50, 51–2. This begs at least two questions. First, can, or should, the extra-provincial externalities caused by a province's exploitation of a resource provide a rationale for redistributing the wealth flowing from this resource? Second, do the general costs imposed on other provinces as a result of the pollution caused by this exploitation as well as the specific cost Canada incurs as a result of not being able to meet its international obligations under the Kyoto Protocol constitute sufficient grounds for warranting a federal intervention under the national concern branch of Parliament's power to legislate for the peace, order, and good government of Canada?

7 Paul Barker, 'Disentangling the Federation: Social Policy and Fiscal Federalism,' in Martin Westmacott and Hugh Mellon, eds., *Challenges to Canadian Federalism* (Scarborough, ON: Prentice-Hall Canada, 1998), 144.

8 Douglas M. Brown, 'Fiscal Federalism: The New Equilibrium between Equity and Efficiency,' in Herman Bavkis and Grace Skogstad, eds., *Canadian Federalism: Performance, Effectiveness, and Legitimacy* (Don Mills, ON: Oxford University Press, 2002), 59.

9 Barker, 'Disentangling the Federation,' 144–5.

10 *Reference Re Anti-Inflation Act*, [1976] 2 S.C.R. 373.

11 *R. v. Crown Zellerbach Canada Ltd.*, [1988] 1 S.C.R. 401. The test was initially elaborated by Justice Jean Beetz in his opinion in *Reference Re Anti-Inflation Act*.

12 *R. v. Crown Zellerbach*, at 431–2.

13 For a vigorous critique of such approaches, see Jean Leclair, 'The Elusive Quest for the Quintessential "National Interest,"' *University of British Columbia Law Review* 38 (2005), 353.

14 Indeed, the Supreme Court has shown itself to be rather lukewarm about an expansive use of the national concern branch of the POGG power as expounded in *R. v. Crown Zellerbach*. See *Friends of the Oldman River v. Canada (Minister of Transport)*, [1992] 1 S.C.R. 3; *R. v. Hydro-Quebec*, [1997] 3

S.C.R. 213. In *RJR-Macdonald Inc.* v. *Canada (A.G.)*, [1995] 3 S.C.R. 199 and *R. v. Malmo-Levine*, [2003] 3 S.C.R. 571, the court declined to address arguments based on the national concern branch of the POGG power and found that the federal power to legislate over criminal law provided a more specific constitutional basis for the federal laws impugned in these cases.

15 The concerns that the application of the national dimensions branch of the POGG power raises in respect of the 'scale of effect on provincial legislation' (to quote from *Crown Zellerbach*) of federal measures defended on that basis could possibly be partly alleviated if Parliament's second house, the Senate, was a truly federal chamber where provincial delegates would participate in the federal legislative process. This is notably the case in Germany, with the Bundesrat. This would obviously imply amending the constitution to reform the Senate, a quasi-impossible task as past experiences have shown.

16 *Winterhaven Stables Ltd. v. Canada (Attorney-General)* (1988), 53 D.L.R. (4th) 394 (Alta. C.A.), leave to appeal to SCC refused (1989), 55 D.LR. (4th) viii.

17 *Winterhaven Stables*, at 416, 432–5.

18 Jean-François Gaudreault-DesBiens, 'The Canadian Federal Experiment, or Legalism without Federalism? Toward a Legal Theory of Federalism,' in Manuel Calvo-García and William Felstiner, eds., *Federalismo/Federalism* (Madrid: Dyckinson, 2004), 81.

19 This points to the de-juridification of federalism-related disputes over the past decades or so in Canada.

20 Sujit Choudhry, 'Recasting Social Canada: A Reconsideration of Federal Jurisdiction over Social Policy,' *University of Toronto Law Journal* 52 (2002), 163, 198–200.

21 Denys Arcand, *Le confort et l'indifférence* (Jean Dansereau and Roger Frappier, producers, National Film Board of Canada, 1981).

22 It is asymmetrical in the sense that only Quebec signed such a deal. However, this deal merely reflects an acceptance by the federal government to not exercise its spending power conditionally in a field that is already constitutionally devolved to provinces.

23 On this, see Michael J. Prince and France Abele, 'Funding an Aboriginal Order of Government in Canada: Recent Developments in Self-Government and Fiscal Relations,' in Harvey Lazar, ed., *Toward a New Mission Statement for Canadian Fiscal Federalism* (Montreal and Kingston: Institute of Intergovernmental Relations, 2000), 337.

24 For a brief overview of the history of the equalization program, see Tom J. Courchene, *Renegotiating Equalization: National Polity, Federal State, International Economy* (Toronto: C.D. Howe Institute, 1998).

25 'The Budget Plan 2004, Annex 6: Renewing Equalization and Territorial Formula Financing,' online: Department of Finance, <http://www.fin.gc.ca/budget04/pdf/bp2004e.pdf>

26 David Cameron and Jennifer McRae-Logie, 'Cooperation and Dispute Resolution in Canadian Health Care,' in Harvey Lazar and France St-Hilaire, eds., *Money, Politics and Health Care: Reconstructing the Federal-Provincial Partnership* (Montreal: Institute for Research on Public Policy and Institute of Intergovernmental Relations, 2004), 79–134; Harvey Lazar, Keith Banting, Robin Boadway, David Cameron, and France St.-Hilaire, 'Federal-Provincial Fiscal Relations and Health Care: Reconstructing the Partnership,' in ibid., 251–88.

27 Although a public, needs-based, health care regime has indeed become part of the dominant Canadian identity narrative, notably as a means to distinguish Canada from the United States, this is less true in Quebec, where support for that regime is arguably not rooted in a particular conception of Canadian identity but rather in the social-democratic leanings of Quebec's political culture.

28 Antonia Maioni, 'Health Care in the New Millennium,' in Bavkis and Skogstad, eds., *Canadian Federalism*; 87, 95.

29 *Reference Re Canada Assistance Plan (B.C.)*, [1991] 2 S.C.R. 525.

30 Barker, 'Disentangling the Federation,' 152, 149.

31 Sujit Choudhry, 'Bill 11, the *Canada Health Act* and the Social Union: The Need for Institutions,' *Osgoode Hall Law Journal* 38 (2000), 39, 53.

32 Ibid., 52.

33 *Chaouilli v. Quebec (Attorney General)*, [2005] 1 S.C.R. 791.

34 For a variety of perspectives on the *Chaoulli* case, see Colleen M. Flood, Kent Roach, and Lorne Sossin, eds., *Access to Care, Access to Justice: The Legal Debate over Private Health Insurance* (Toronto: University of Toronto Press, 2005).

35 In line with its traditional policy, the government of Quebec did not want to legitimize in any way federal claims about the validity of conditional spending in areas of provincial jurisdiction or the legitimacy of federal monitoring of the delivery of programs under provincial jurisdiction. For Quebec perspectives on the SUFA, see Alain Gagnon and Hugh Segal, eds., *The Canadian Social Union without Quebec: 8 Critical Analyses* (Montreal: IRPP, 2000).

36 '2003 First Ministers' Health Accord,' online: Health Canada at http://www.hc-sc.gc.ca/hcs-sss/medi-assur/fptcollab/2003accord/fs-if_1_e.html.

37 'New Federal Investments on Health Commitments on 10-Year Action Plan on Health,' online: Health Canada at http://www.hc-sc.gc.ca/hcs-sss/medi-assur/fptcollab/2004-fmm-rpm/bg-fi_inv_e.html.

38 'Asymetrical Federalism that respects Quebec's Jurisdiction,' online: Health Canada at http://www.hc-sc.gc.ca/hcs-sss/medi-assur/fptcollab/2004-fmm-rpm/bg-fi_quebec_e.html.
39 On the Council of the Federation and on the possibilities and limits of inter-provincialism, see Jean-François Gaudreault-DesBiens, 'La transformation du fédéralisme canadien sous l'impulsion du Conseil de la Fédération?' *Revue belge de droit constitutionnel* 2 (2004), 243.
40 *Attorney General for Canada v. Attorney General for Ontario*, [1937] A.C. 355.

PART ONE

Social Justice and the Politics of Redistribution

Social Justice: Does Federalism Make a Difference?

RICHARD SIMEON

'Social justice' is a concept that is hopelessly general, has multiple meanings, and is highly contested. Federalism also has multiple meanings, varies hugely across systems, and is highly contested. These two observations suggest that no clear linkages, positive or negative, can be drawn between the presence or absence of federalism institutions and social policies that promote justice through more or less egalitarian, redistributive, or 'progressive' means. But it is worth exploring the relationship between federalism and social justice, not least because so many assertions – both favourable and critical – abound in the literature and in the public discourse about federalism. Globally, there is a bull market both in federalism ('a federalist revolution is now sweeping the world,' as someone has remarked) and in debates about social justice. So there is merit to subjecting them both to some critical analysis.

There are three possible answers to the question our title poses. First, that federalism promotes and enhances social justice, perhaps even that federalism is a condition of social justice. Second, that federalism inhibits, undermines, and limits the possibility of achieving social justice. Third, that federalism is probably neutral with respect to social justice. If a society has a strong commitment to policies that promote social justice, a way will be found to achieve them, whatever the institutional barriers. Federalism may have marginal effects, but it will be far less important than other cultural, social, and economic factors. How we answer the question will also depend on the conception of social justice that we have in mind.

In this chapter I focus on social justice in the sense of T.H. Marshall's 'social citizenship.'[1] That is to say that all members of the society have a right to full participation in its economic and social life, and thus are entitled to basic provisions for health, education, security, and a certain measure of equality of condition. The quantity or quality of social benefits should not depend on where you live, or on any other arbitrary distinction. Social citizenship is to be equally available to all members of the political community. Inherent in it is the concept of mutual sharing. The question is whether federal systems are more or less likely to engage in politics that promote such common national standards for equality, and to promote redistribution between richer and poorer, whether among individuals or regions. This points us to the huge literature on federalism and the welfare state.

Whether or not federalism impedes or facilitates a fulsome sense of social citizenship can be approached in at least two ways. The first focuses on the institutional characteristics of federalism – the division of powers, multiple decision points, many actors, and the like – and on the associated policy-making processes in decentralized systems. Here the question's focus is on whether or not such systems make innovation more or less difficult, agreement harder or easier to achieve, and redistributive policies more or less likely. Perhaps the most powerful arguments in this regard are those which argue federalism has delayed and minimized the welfare state and fostered a 'rush to the bottom' that reduces chances for redistribution.

The second approach places more emphasis on federal 'society,' and on the contested concept of community. Put most bluntly, the fundamental question is what community do we have in mind when we talk of social citizenship? Is it the country-wide, pan-Canadian community? Is it the provincial communities? Is it the 'national' communities of Quebec and the rest of Canada?

The first perspective implies that social citizenship must treat like persons alike, wherever they live; that there should be 'national standards,' applied equally across the country. Keith Banting puts it well: 'Stripped to its core, the logic of social citizenship holds that a sick baby should be entitled to public health care on the same terms and conditions wherever he or she lives.'[2] This is a Canada of undifferentiated citizenship, seen not only as a political and an economic union, but also, and perhaps most importantly as a social union. The term is embodied in the 'Social Union Framework Agreement,' and suffuses the Romanow Report on Health Care, where common standards are seen as essential components of Canadian citizenship. Even if one adopts this conception, there remain many questions. If there are to be national standards, who defines them, the central government, or governments acting collectively? Who enforces them, the central government, the courts, or public opinion and elections? Should such standards be detailed and precise, or broad and general? Do national standards apply to detailed program design and policy instruments, as well as to goals and values?

But what if we have a more provincialist, or bi-national, conception of community, and hence of citizenship? That opens the possibility that different communities will make different choices about what they mean by social citizenship, and how they will express it in their own social policies. Social justice, then, may have different meanings in different places. Again, Keith Banting puts it plainly: 'Stripped to its core, the logic of federalism holds that the public health benefits to which a sick child is entitled also depend significantly on the region in which he or she resides.'[3]

Thus, the fundamental debate is between the logic of national values, common citizenship, and equality on the one hand, and the variations in policy choices and outcomes on which federalism is largely predicated on the other hand. The debates here relate to the relative predominance of country-wide versus provincial, regional or ethnic identities, and the appropriate balance among them. To the extent that different communities have different values and preferences, is justice served by reflecting them in public policies? What principles do we invoke to argue that standards of social citizenship defined by one community must hold sway in a community otherwise defined?

Federalism can also be evaluated in terms of procedural social justice: in terms of its relation to democracy, participation, accountability, responsiveness, and transparency. As Sujit Choudhry points out, these different dimensions of the problem evoke three different conceptions of citizenship – civic, ethno-cultural, and economic – each embodying differing conceptions of political community.[4] But, as James Tully also argues, the three dimensions are related. 'Justice,' he says is about 'freedom, both in the sense of possession of rights and the ability to participate in civic life, about equality in terms of social and economic rights, and the equality of peoples.'[5] We must find balance both within each conception of social justice and between them.

If there is any consensus in the literature on the policy consequences of federalism it is this: that the size of government, and the commitment to social spending, tends to be lower in federal countries than in non-federal countries. In 1978 David Cameron found that federalism was the most powerful institutional factor accounting for variation in welfare state spending; three of the four lowest per capita spenders (Canada, Australia, and the United States) were federations.[6] Duane Swank puts it most clearly: 'decentralized policy-making authority (degree of federalism and bicameralism) has large and negative effects on welfare state effort.'[7] 'Decentralization has more powerful negative effects on social welfare spending than any other institutional variables.' The 'price of federalism' in the United States, says Paul Peterson, is greater regional inequalities. 'To recommend that the provision of welfare should be locally controlled and its marginal cost borne by state and local governments is to recommend that the poor be all but abandoned.'[8] Federalism in Australia, says Australian political scientist Graham Maddox, is a big impediment to the 'equitable provision of welfare.'[9] In Canada, Banting suggests, the complexities of federalism help account for the relative tardiness of the establishment of the welfare state, and accounts for many of the design and administrative features of Canadian social policy.[10] In Canada, the United States, and Australia, 'progressive' social groups have consistently and loudly argued against decentralization, and for a stronger federal presence in social policy. Similarly, Herbert Obinger attributes the 'late-comer position of the Swiss welfare state' to the 'high degree of institutional pluralism in the Swiss political system.'[11] Even a relative sceptic of this thesis, Alain Noël, concedes that the data show that 'other things being equal, the dispersion of policy-making through federalism, decentralization and other forms of institutional fragmentation is negatively associated with social expenditures as a proportion of GDP.'[12] Juan Linz and Alfred Stepan drive the point home: federations have higher Gini indices of inequality, less equal access to health care, and more children and older persons living in poverty than non-federal systems.[13]

There is an interesting convergence between left and right here. If 'progressives' condemn decentralization and seek greater central control in order to enhance the redistributive role of the state, neo-liberal writers on federalism such as Barry Weingast ('market federalism')[14] or Tom Courchene praise it precisely because it places constraints on government intervention. As Galligan and Walsh put it, the purpose of liberal federalism is 'to guarantee citizens and groups the right to pursue their own happiness, and to restrict governments from legislating happiness schemes.'[15] What one group sees as a vice of federalism, the other sees as a virtue.

What is the logic behind such findings? What explains them? I think it is useful clearly to differentiate among several possible explanations. First, at the simplest level, is the argument that getting things done in federal systems is typically more difficult than in unitary systems. There will be more hurdles to clear, and more veto points where recalcitrant minorities can block the majority will. This is one reason why conservatives tend to like federalism, separation of powers, and checks and balances. There is some evidence for this. A.H. Birch attributes the relative lateness of the completion of the Canadian welfare state to the 'complexities of federalism,' and Banting agrees.[16] The distribution of powers and financial resources meant that much of the welfare state in Canada required extensive federal-provincial cooperation.

On the other hand, in the end these difficulties did not prove insuperable. Through a few constitutional amendments, and the use of the federal spending power, the basic building blocks of the welfare state were put in place. While in the early postwar years this was accompanied by a tendency towards greater centralization, it is striking that the 1960s – the decade when we enacted medicare, the CPP and QPP, and other programs – was a period of rapid decentralization in fiscal and political terms, and of the growth of Quebec nationalism. Increased provincial shares of revenue and spending, the declining role of conditionality in transfer programs, increased provincial activism or 'province-building,' and the growth of asymmetry manifested in opting-out legislation and the adoption of separate pension plans for Canada and the rest of the country did not block the completion of the welfare state.[17]

In fact, the comparative literature shows that the associations between federalism and low or weak welfare spending and redistribution tend to be relatively small. Federalism may be one factor affecting welfare state spending, but it is by no means the most important one. Moreover, there is wide variation across federal systems. What Linz and Stepan classify as 'non-classical' federations (such as Canada, Germany, Spain, and Belgium) differ little or not at all from unitary systems in their welfare state policies. One is tempted to speculate that factors other than federalism – classical or not – are at work here.

There is also the possibility that the 'stickiness' resulting from multiple decision-makers and veto points that slowed the growth of the welfare state will operate differently in a period of welfare state retrenchment. Federalism may slow change in either direction. There is some evidence of this in provincial resistance to federal spending cuts in the 1990s, and in the response of US states recently to 'unfunded mandates' emerging from Washington. In a major reversal, Peterson points out, 'Democrats are discovering the blessings of state and local control ... while the GOP is discovering some of the reasons Hamilton wanted a strong national government.'

A second explanation comes from the perspective of fiscal federalism. The argument here is that in a federal system, interprovincial competition will tend to drive down both taxes on the wealthy and benefits to the lower-income groups. Wealthier regions or provinces will want to hold on to their resources and be unwilling to share them with others. Fiscal crisis leads to increased competition, inequality, and fiscally induced migration. This is the 'rush to the bottom' argument. In a system where people and capital are mobile, the wealthy and capital will move to low tax/low social welfare states, while high tax/high welfare states will become 'welfare magnets.' As states and provinces react to these incentives, the pressure to reduce redistributive welfare spending will grow. Intergovernmental competition for low taxes and spending will make it more difficult for a federal system to counter market forces in the interests of social justice. The more autonomy the local governments have, the greater these pressures. As Paul Peterson puts it, 'The smaller the territorial reach of a local government, the more open its economy and the less its capacity for redistribution.'[18] Hence welfare economists argue that in federations, redistributive policies (social security, pensions, and the like) should move to the highest level. Allocation may best be done locally; redistribution or sharing should be done nationally. National standards in social policy need to be set and enforced centrally.

More generally, there is a long line of argument, perhaps originating with Laski's article, 'On the Obsolescence of Federalism,'[19] which asserts a fundamental lack of fit between a political system in which decision-making is decentralized or localized, and a political economy with corporations and capital that are national, and now global. As Samuel Beer argued, modernization (as in the welfare state) and centralization go together.'[20] In Canada there is a similarly long tradition that has asserted that social progress requires a greater federal role, and that it was the dead hand of the federal Canadian constitution that prevented Canada responding to the crisis of the great depression. In the postwar period, the same groups took it as axiomatic that a modern Canadian welfare state would be one in which provinces played a distinctly subordinate role. Through unemployment insurance, family allowances, old age pensions and the Canada Pension Plan, the Guaranteed Income Supplement, and various provisions in the tax system, the federal government did take on responsibility for basic income security and redistributive policies.

It is important to note that these were not arguments against federalism per se. They are as much arguments about how powers and responsibilities should be distributed within federations. Nevertheless, these are powerful negative arguments about the consequences of federalism for social justice.

In fact, the evidence for the rush-to-the-bottom thesis is not strong. There appears to be little evidence of 'fiscally induced migration' or of a competitive erosion of standards in areas related to social justice such as education and the environment. As Boychuck shows, despite the fact that Canadian social policy is relatively highly decentralized, 'genuine differences between provinces persist, and there is no trend towards convergence, downward or upward.'[21] This seems to be true both within and between countries. Summarizing the most thorough empirical study of the rush-to-the-bottom thesis in a number of policy areas, Kathryn Harrison concludes that there is

> reassurance that competition for investment and to avoid benefits claimants has not decimated the provinces' capacity to govern ... Canadian provinces have continued to increase their taxes on capital, have maintained and on occasion increased their environmental standards, have restrained their reliance on subsidies to attract investment, and have successfully increased welfare benefits and excise taxes in at least some periods, though not others.[22]

A third and closely related argument for the conservative effect of federalism is that typically in federal systems, central governments have stronger and more elastic access to tax revenues than do states or provinces. Thus if spending responsibilities lie primarily at the provincial level, then national standards will be threatened. Moreover, where there are large regional disparities in wealth and incomes, some units will be able to provide more generous benefits than others. Policy differences based on genuine differences in public preferences may be justified, but differences based simply on the ability to pay are much less so.

Here again, however, federations have found a rich array of devices to adapt. In virtually all of them, including Canada, the central government is responsible for providing the costly basic income security programs such as pensions and employment insurance. In all of them, while modes of service delivery vary, the basic parameters of health care are determined by national norms, as with the Canada Health Act. Even in the extremely decentralized Belgian case, Banting notes, social policy remains one of the few policy areas still highly centralized.[23] With the important exception of the United States, all welfare state federations have broad interregional redistribution programs aimed at alleviating disparities and permitting reasonably comparable levels of service at comparable levels of taxation, as our Constitution Act, 1982 (section 36) puts it. Thus Banting argues that the evidence supports the view that federalism does not constrain and limit the welfare state. Indeed, the causal arrow runs the other way: the adoption of the welfare state fundamentally transformed federalism. In the seven federations he studied, the conclusion is that the logic of country-wide social citizenship has trumped the logic of federalism.

A fourth explanation suggests that somehow, provincial or state politics is likely to be less participatory, more elitist, more dominated by conservative interests, than are national governments. If social policy is left in provincial hands it is likely to be more mean spirited.

The classic statement of this view is William Riker's assertion of a few years ago that if you are a racist you are for federalism; if you are not a racist you must be against it.[24] He was, of course, reflecting the fact of white dominance in the American South, and in the U.S. Senate. In Canada, 'progressive' social movements have traditionally looked to Ottawa as the source of more progressive policies; hence their defence of the federal spending power, and the like. John Porter famously gave federalism as the basic reason why creative 'class politics' had failed to emerge in Canada; feminists and others have echoed his views more recently.[25]

This too needs to be qualified. The evidence from at least some federations suggests that it has often been sub-national units that have been the innovators in progressive social policy, and that it is central governments that have played catch-up. We Canadians are perhaps overly fond of citing the case of small, poor, rural Saskatchewan, which developed a universal medical care program and then sold it to the rest of the country. But there are more modern examples too, such as the highly progressive social policies in a number of areas in the province of Quebec.

Recent welfare state retrenchment in Canada, the United States, and the United Kingdom was not led by narrow-minded sub-national governments rushing to the bottom; it was led by central governments facing intense budget pressures and international competition. In such a situation, it may well be that sub-national communities become the leaders, responding to the values of their own communities. Thus Nicola McEwan argues that one factor driving towards the articulation of Scottish nationalism and home rule was the sense that Whitehall was eroding the welfare state, and that a Scottish parliament would 'nurture a better and distinctively Scottish welfare state.' In this vein, Rachel Simeon shows that with respect to home care for the elderly recommended by a royal commission, Scotland, using the limited discretion available to it, took a much more progressive position than did London.[26] These observations suggest that the commonly asserted tension between local autonomy and progressive social policy may be misplaced. National governments have no monopoly on social justice.

This discussion points to the need to qualify Banting's assertion of the deep tension between federalism and social citizenship, and by extension, between strong regional communities and national standards. It may not be necessary to equate social citizenship with the national government or the national community. First, federalism permits divergence and difference; it does not require it. Even if policy-making and delivery are highly decentralized to provincial governments, if their citizens all embrace similar conceptions of social citizenship, the results will also be similar. On fundamental issues of social policy, as distinct from, say, energy policy, regional differences in Canada do appear to be small, both at the level of public opinion and of government policies.

Second, it is possible that some communities within a country may have stronger or more robust conceptions of social citizenship than the majority at the national level or in other provinces. Not only might this mean some provinces will have a higher level of social provision, but also that their example will create pressures on the other provinces and the central government to match them. We should not rule out the possibility of a 'rush to the top,' as with certain elements of Quebec social policy.[27] Those concerned with equality might wish to place a floor below which no province should fall, but surely they would not wish, in the name of national standards, to impose a cap above which no province should rise.

To return to the quotation from Banting about the sick child: is social justice or social citizenship harmed – or enhanced – if a province chooses to improve upon the national standard? Variations in service levels that are the product of differing resources or capacities are indeed likely to offend our sense of social justice. But variations based on different choices are not so easily challenged, because no single standard can be absolute. Variations in the modes of service delivery, within common standards, are surely to be applauded, as are policies in more social democratically oriented jurisdictions that raise the bar above the national average.

To conclude, it does appear that there is a slight negative relation between federalism and distributive justice. But I would emphasize the word 'slight.' The macro-data obscures many variations; and other political, ideological, and contextual factors are likely to be far more important in explaining outcomes than whether or not a country is federal. In a careful review of the arguments, Alain Noël concludes that 'the progressive case against decentralization is much weaker, theoretically and empirically, than is usually thought. Centralization is not necessarily progressive, and neither is decentralization a monopoly of the right.'[28] Variation within the category of federations is as important as variation between federal and non-federal systems.

It is clear that whether federal regimes will be weak welfare performers depends on things other than federalism itself. For example, section 106 of the German constitution, which requires equality for all persons wherever they live, is a powerful contradiction to the potential tendency of federalism to foster regional inequalities. The Canadian system of fiscal equalization among provinces, while not perfect, allows Canada to combine a very high degree of provincial autonomy with a high degree of provincial capacity to provide 'comparable levels of public services at comparable levels of taxation.' This contrasts with the lack of equalization provisions in the United States, but it is not a function of federalism itself. Social and economic rights built into a constitutional Bill of Rights, as in South Africa, may have a similar effect.

This is not to argue for profound decentralization. It is to argue that 'national standards' is a slippery concept, and that to equate national standards and national government is wrong. The continuing intergovernmental debate about national standards and provincial variation is healthy and desirable. Messy as the process often is, the resulting Canadian pattern seems close to an appropriate balancing of competing conceptions both of social justice, and of community. Nor do I argue that federalism does not matter at all: it does. It is likely to have major impacts on the timing, financing, and design of the welfare state, if not on its basic values. The design of federal institutions varies widely, and these variations can have important effects. The debate about welfare state policies in Canada has indeed been deeply affected by federalism; the welfare state, in turn has deeply affected the dynamics of the federal system.

To return to my original question: Does federalism promote and enhance social justice? There is no evidence that federal systems have higher commitments to overall social justice defined in terms of distributive justice than other systems. With respect to social justice as the recognition and accommodation of distinct communities, I believe that federalism is an essential part of the answer, but that is a topic for another day. Does federalism inhibit, constrain, and undermine distributive justice? I have tried to show that the evidence for this proposition is weak and contradictory. Is federalism neutral with respect to social justice? This is probably my strongest, if not very robust, conclusion: the commitment to social citizenship and equality, I believe, is driven by more fundamental cultural, economic and political forces. None of this, of course, is to deny the very real and important debates about the future of social policy in Canada and its provinces, or the role of the institutions and dynamics of intergovernmental relations in shaping how those debates are expressed and played out.

This chapter has not addressed the fiscal imbalance debate that many of the other authors in this volume examine. However, my argument does suggest some broad implications for that debate. First, it does not support those who argue that the federal government will spend its revenues in ways that are more egalitarian or socially 'progressive' than provinces would if the same revenues were in their hands. Second, it suggests that 'conditionality' in federal transfers is a blunt instrument for ensuring that the provinces follow a progressive path; more promising is a collaborative intergovernmental discussion of goals, values, and broad objectives, together with broad flexibility in program design and implementation for the provinces, along with maximum sharing of information and experience. Third, this approach depends fundamentally on two other dimensions. Nothing in my argument suggests that the broad federal responsibility for sharing and redistribution should be diminished. And in a decentralized approach to social justice, a great deal depends on equal provincial capacity to meet citizens' aspirations in this area; and that requires a deep, continuing commitment to equalization.

'Social citizenship' in T. H. Marshall's sense cannot be seen as the responsibility of any single order of government; it is not a head of power under sections 91 or 92. In a federal system such as ours it is a value that must underpin programs and policies in all governments, from the design of over-arching legislation such as employment insurance or pensions to the behaviour of nurses, social workers, and police officers on the ground. Social citizenship in a federal system is inherently complex and multi-layered; moreover, federalism means that social citizenship will always be infused with a sense of place and provincial and local communities, in addition to its focus on inter-personal equity.

NOTES

This chapter draws extensively on my article 'Federalism and Social Justice: Thinking Through the Tangle,' in Scott L. Greer, ed., *Territory, Democracy and Justice* (London: Palgrave, forthcoming).

1 Thomas H. Marshall, *Citizenship and Social Class and Other Essays* (1950) (reprinted London: Pluto Press, 1991).
2 Keith Banting, 'Social Citizenship and Canadian Federalism: The Old and New Politics of Health Care,' paper presented to a conference on Welfare States and Federalism at the University of Bremen, June 2002. See also Keith G. Banting and Stan Corbett, *Health Policy and Federalism: A Comparative Perspective on Multi-Level Governance* (Montreal and Kingston: McGill-Queen's University Press for the Institute of Intergovernmental Relations, Queen's University 2002), 18–19.
3 Banting, 'Social Citizenship,' 9.
4 Sujit Choudhry, 'Citizenship and Federations,' in Nicolaidis Kalypso and Robert Howse, eds., *The Federal Vision: Legitimacy and Levels of Government in the US and the EU* (New York: Oxford University Press, 2001), 377–402.
5 James Tully, 'Introduction,' in Alain-G. Gagnon and James Tully, eds., *Multinational Democracies* (Cambridge: Cambridge University Press, 2001), 12.
6 David Cameron, 'The Growth of the State,' *American Political Science Review* 72 (1978): 1243–61.
7 Duane Swank, 'Impact of Institutions on Policy Change in Developed Democracies,' in Paul Pierson, ed., *The New Political Economy of the Welfare State* (New York: Oxford University Press, 2001).
8 Paul Peterson, *The Price of Federalism* (Washington: Brookings Institution, 1995), 14, 128.

9　Graham Maddox, 'Federalism and Democracy,' paper prepared for the Democratic Audit of Australia, 2003, 5.

10　Keith Banting, *The Welfare State and Canadian Federalism*, 2nd ed. (Montreal and Kingston: McGill-Queen's University Press, 1987).

11　Herbert Obinger, 'Federalism, Direct Democracy, and Welfare State Development in Switzerland,' *Journal of Public Policy* 18, no. 3 (1988): 241–63.

12　Alain Noël, 'Introduction: Varieties of Capitalism, Varieties of Federalism,' in Alain Noël, ed., *Federalism and Labour Market Policy: Comparing Different Governance and Employment Strategies* (Montreal and Kingston: McGill-Queen's University Press for the Institute of Intergovernmental Relations, 2004), 5.

13　Juan Linz and Alfred Stepan, 'Inequality Inducing and Inequality Reducing Federalism: With Special Reference to the "Classic Outlier – the U.S.A.,"' paper prepared for the 17th World Congress, International Political Science Association at Quebec City, 2000. See also Alfred Stepan, *Arguing Comparative Politics* (Oxford: Oxford University Press, 2001), ch. 15.

14　Barry Weingast, 'The Economic Role of Political Institutions: Market Preserving Federalism and Economic Growth,' *Journal of Law, Economics and Organization* 11 (1995): 1–31.

15　Quoted in Maddox, 'Federalism and Democracy,' 6.

16　Anthony H. Birch, *Federalism, Finance and Social Legislation* (Oxford: Clarendon Press, 1955).

17　For an analysis of this period, see Richard Simeon, *Federal-Provincial Diplomacy: The Making of Recent Policy in Canada* (Toronto: University of Toronto Press, 1972), and Richard Simeon and Ian Robinson, *State, Society and the Development of Canadian Federalism* (Toronto: University of Toronto Press, 1990), ch. 9.

18　Peterson, *Price of Federation*, 28.

19　Harold Laski, 'On the Obsolescence of Federalism,' in Asher N. Christensen and Evron M. Kirkpatrick, eds., *The People, Politics and the Politician* (New York: Holt Rinehart and Winston, 1939), 53–76.

20　Samuel Beer, 'The Modernization of Federalism,' *Publius: The Journal of Federalism* 3 (1973): 49–96.

21　Alain Noël, 'Is Decentralization Conservative? Federalism and the Contemporary Debate on the Canadian Welfare State,' in Robert Young, ed., *Stretching the Federation: The Art of the State in Canada* (Kingston: Institute of Intergovernmental Relations, 1999), 195–218. Boychuck is quoted on page 200.

22　Kathryn Harrison, 'Race to the Bottom? Provincial Interdependence in the Canadian Federation,' paper presented to the Canadian Political Science Association, Winnipeg. 3–5 June 2004.

23 Banting, 'Social Citizenship and Canadian Federalism.'
24 William H. Riker, *Federalism: Origin, Operation, Significance* (Boston: Little, Brown, 1964).
25 John Porter, *The Vertical Mosaic: An Analysis of Social Class and Power in Canada* (Toronto: University of Toronto Press, 1965).
26 Nicola McEwan, 'State Welfare Nationalism: The Territorial Impact of Welfare State Development in Scotland,' *Regional and Federal Studies* 12, no. 1 (2002): 66, 79; Rachel Simeon, 'Free Personal Care: Policy Divergence and Social Citizenship,' in Robert Hazell, ed., *The State of the Nations, 2003: The Third Year of Devolution in the United Kingdom,* Constitution Unit, University College London (London: Imprint Academic, 2003), 215–35.
27 In a related area, environmental policy, Mark Winfield notes that when the issue is high on the public's agenda, both orders of government tend to engage in a rush to the top. See 'Environmental Policy and Federalism,' in Herman Bakvis and Grace Skogstad, eds., *Canadian Federalism: Performance, Effectiveness and Legitimacy* (Don Mills, ON: Oxford University Press, 2002), 124–37.
28 Noël, 'Is Decentralization Conservative?,' 215. See also Paul Pierson, 'Fragmented Welfare States: Federal Institutions and the Development of Social Policy,' *Governance* 8 (1995): 449–78.
29 Indeed, our traditional emphasis on the role of federalism and intergovernmental relations in the development and funding of policies related to social justice has paid far too little attention to policy and delivery at the local level. The behaviour of police forces in relation to visible minorities; of many civic agencies in relation to integration and services for immigrants; of other agencies in relation to provision of social housing; and other policy areas all suggest that a full analysis of social justice in Canadian public policy must include not only federal, provincial, and territorial governments, but also municipal and aboriginal governments.

Redistribution in the Canadian Federation: The Impact of the Cities Agenda and the New Canada

SUJIT CHOUDHRY

Richard Simeon asks the question of whether federalism promotes social justice, understood in T.H. Marshall's sense of 'social citizenship.' The promotion of social citizenship in federations such as Canada requires interpersonal redistribution, either directly between individuals through direct transfers from the federal government, the federal income tax system or the design of federal social programs (e.g., the regional differences built into Employment Insurance), and/or indirectly between the residents of different regions or provinces through federal transfer payments to provinces. Canada employs both types of policy instrument. Simeon concludes that redistribution is surprisingly resilient in federations, and that the relationship between federalism and distributive justice is at best moderately negative.

I want to explore the implications of Simeon's observation in the context of the growing debate over vertical fiscal imbalance and interprovincial redistribution, which invites Canada to address basic questions regarding the design of the federal-provincial transfer system in the near future. My question is whether the existing system of federal-provincial transfer payments, which involves large-scale interprovincial transfers of wealth, is politically sustainable. Against the backdrop of Ontario's new call for a dramatic restructuring of fiscal federalism, I want to speculate that in the medium term, it may not be sustainable, because of changing conceptions of citizenship and identity in Canada's urban centres.

My starting point is the report of the Commission on Vertical Fiscal Imbalance (the Séguin Commission), which has been skilfully deployed by the government of Quebec to set the provincial agenda in fiscal federalism.[1] The commission's argument is relatively straightforward. Because of demographic pressures, the provinces face growing expenditures in areas of provincial jurisdiction such as health care and education, but they lack access to sufficient sources of revenue to meet these needs. The federal government, by contrast, reaping the benefits of deficit reduction, will enjoy surpluses that the Séguin Commission predicts will balloon in the years to come. A situation of symmetric disjunction between revenue-raising capacity and expenditures involving different orders of government – vertical fiscal imbalance – poses a number of serious problems for the healthy functioning of the federation. Echoing arguments first advanced by the Rowell-Sirois Report and the Tremblay Commission, provincial political communities require adequate financial means to effectively exercise jurisdiction in areas assigned to them by the constitution.[2] Without ensuring that provinces have adequate fiscal means to match their areas of policy responsibility, a basic objective of Confederation – provincial autonomy – would be severely undermined. And federal transfers that close the fiscal gap nonetheless undermine provincial autonomy if they impose conditions, are changed arbitrarily, or do not take into account actual levels of demand for public services. Such a situation exists in Canada, where the cash component of the Canada Health and Social Transfer (CHST) is subject to provincial compliance with the conditions spelled out in the Canada Health Act, where the CHST was introduced without either notice to or consultation with the provinces or provincial consent, and where the levels of CHST transfers are not tied to actual provincial expenditures in health and education. The solution proposed by the Séguin Commission is to eliminate the CHST, to permit provinces to occupy the GST field to make up for the lost revenues, and to enhance the existing equalization program.

Quebec has been able to convince the other provincial and territorial governments to place vertical fiscal balance at the top of the agenda of the newly created Council of the Federation.[3] It is therefore important to understand how the Séguin Commission conceptualizes vertical fiscal imbalance. The commission devotes considerable attention to quantifying the size of federal surpluses, as well as future demands on federal expenditures. But it does not indicate where the bulk of federal revenue, including monies that are redistributed to the provinces through the CHST and equalization, comes from. The answer to this question can be found in a Department of Finance working paper by Marie-Anne Deussing published in October 2003. The paper responds to Finn Poschmann's provocative argument that federal taxes and transfers have the effect of redistributing monies from lower-income Canadians in higher-income provinces to individuals with higher-incomes in other provinces. In the course of challenging this position, Deussing calculates the federal fiscal balance for each province – that is, the difference between federal expenditures made and federal revenues raised in each province. Deussing's analysis therefore helps us to track the extent of interprovincial redistribution through federal programs, and provides a financial balance sheet for the federation.[4]

For 2000, seven provinces (Saskatchewan, Manitoba, Quebec, New Brunswick, Nova Scotia, Prince Edward Island, and Newfoundland) experienced net inflows, whereas three provinces (British Columbia, Alberta, and Ontario) experienced net outflows. For Ontario, the net outflow was $26.4 billion. Let me put this figure in context. For 2000, the cash component of the CHST was $15.5 billion, and equalization payments totalled $10.9 billion.[5] The sum of these transfers was $26.4 billion, exactly the amount of the net outflow from Ontario in that year. Now I am not making the mistake of asserting that only Ontario taxes funded the CHST cash and equalization programs, because there were two other net contributing provinces, and Ontario also received significant amounts of CHST cash ($4.7 billion in 2000). But on a net basis, Ontario tax revenue accounted for a significant proportion of these transfer payments. We can also contextualize these figures in another way. In 2000, $26.4 billion was the equivalent of 42.6 per cent of Ontario's budget of $61.9 billion, exceeding the province's health care budget of $22 billion.[6]

The level of net outflows from Ontario is an astonishing and potentially politically explosive figure. What is remarkable is that in the war of numbers that characterizes the politics of fiscal federalism, this figure had only recently been mentioned in public. When Premiers Rae and Harris raised the cry of 'Fair Shares Federalism' in the 1990s, they did not deploy the province's level of federal fiscal balance to exert political leverage on the federal government. Even as late as January 2005, the new Liberal government, facing an $8 billion deficit inherited from the previous administration, did not immediately identify the net outflow of funds as a reason for the province's current financial predicament. Indeed, Ontario remained silent as the equalization program was enriched by $33 billion over ten years by the federal government in October 2004, by establishing a floor for equalization payments and an automatic escalator. It also welcomed the September 2004 Health Accord, which will distribute $41 billion in additional funds over ten years on a per capita basis, and will therefore further increase net outflows from Ontario.[7] Finally, the Séguin Commission's 150-page report, which is devoted entirely to fiscal federalism and is otherwise comprehensive and detailed, does not even mention the notion of federal fiscal balance, let alone quantify it. This is all the more striking, given that the commission proposes a radical redesign of fiscal federalism that would not reduce, and could perhaps even increase, the net outflows from Ontario. It is even more surprising, given the commission's strong call for increased transparency in fiscal federalism. Aside from Deussing's study, this figure of net outflows from Ontario until recently lay buried in the financial statements of the government of Canada.

However, in the last few months, the political scene has changed dramatically. Ontario now trumpets the '$23 billion gap' as a major public policy issue which requires immediate redress. The turning event seems to have been the agreement reached between the federal government, Nova Scotia, and Newfoundland over the treatment of royalties from offshore oil and gas projects by the equalization program in February 2005.[8] Strictly speaking, equalization payments should be reduced by one dollar for each dollar of such royalties earned. Arguing that this would have the effect of converting equalization into a welfare trap, the federal government had taxed back royalties at 70 cents on the dollar. The new agreement excludes these royalties from the calculation of equalization payments entirely.

Although the value of these agreements is relatively small (approximately $3.5 billion), it was the straw that broke the camel's back. Ontario went on the attack, noting publicly that the entire equalization program, as well as enhancements to it, is largely funded on a net basis by taxpayers in Ontario. And the provincial government has gone beyond equalization, brandishing the figure of $23 billion, which is calculated on the basis of all federal programs. Ontario's position has been supported by a recent study from the CIBC, which suggests that this gap has risen dramatically over the past decade, from $2 billion in 1995.[9] Ontario's argument is that this gap must be reduced, because a prosperous Ontario is key to a prosperous Canada, and as a starting point has asked for an immediate transfer of $5 billion. But one gets the sense that Ontario would welcome a more wide-ranging discussion on the scope of interprovincial redistribution. The depth of the Ontario government's commitment to this dramatic new agenda is illustrated by Premier McGuinty's apparent willingness to make it an issue in federal election campaigns. Thus far, Ontario's calls have met with no success in Ottawa.

The question which naturally arises is why federal fiscal balance had not become a central term in the debate over fiscal federalism until very recently in the manner that vertical fiscal imbalance has quickly become. The durability of the existing architecture of fiscal federalism, I think, can be attributed to a widely shared understanding of the nature of the Canadian political community, a conception that I have described as the 'community of fate.'[10] As a community of fate, our federation is imagined not merely as a network of political communities bound together by convenience and self-interest, which cooperate together only for mutual advantage on matters of common interest, but as a community that arises through concrete, historical experiences of interdependence. These experiences support a sense that future well-being is dependent on ongoing cooperation. Moreover, questions of fairness enter into the calculus, since cooperation will only proceed if its benefits and burdens are perceived as being distributed justly. In Canada, the move is to imagine our community of fate as a sharing community that partakes in the extensive interprovincial redistribution of wealth through programs such as the CHST and equalization.

I think that the community of fate is a description of Canada that is embedded in many of our political institutions and practices, and indeed, in the very grammar of Canadian federalism itself. For example, the national standards spelled out in the Canada Health Act tap into the community of fate, by spelling out some elements of national social citizenship. Rather than being conceptualized solely as constraints on provincial policy autonomy, these standards must be understood as the political reasons that justify to Ontarians the redistribution of resources from their province to other parts of Canada through federal-provincial transfers. In the absence of such standards – for example, if the CHST were phased out and replaced with unconditional, equalized tax points – I think the political case for interprovincial redistribution would be considerably more difficult to make in the 'have' provinces.

The question for Canada is whether the community of fate will come unstuck. The new Ontario agenda suggests that this process may have already begun. The taboo against making arguments that rely on Ontario's level of federal fiscal balance in order to challenge the existing federal-provincial transfer system has been broken. Now that this door is open, it cannot be shut. And it is not only provincial politicians who are making these arguments; the recipients of provincial funding – universities, hospitals, and municipalities – have all lined up with the province to pressure the federal government. And I want to suggest that two emerging trends could put the community of fate under further strain, especially in the medium term.

The first trend is the cities agenda. As everyone now knows, Canada's cities, principally its major urban centres, want a 'New Deal' from the federal and provincial governments. The impetus for this demand is the fact that, despite our self-description as a country spread thinly across the vast Canadian expanse, Canada is increasingly becoming a country of city dwellers. Cities are the engines of economic growth, and their health is essential to Canada's competitiveness in the global economy. Just as provinces argue that they lack sufficient resources to deliver programs within their jurisdiction, cities also argue that they require both the finances and the legal powers to deal with their particular needs, ranging from social housing and public transportation and urban sprawl, to immigrant settlement and labour market integration, to investment in universities and cultural institutions. Thus far, the New Deal has not amounted to very much; the federal government recently introduced a GST rebate for municipalities, and has announced limited funds for public transport in Toronto.

The cities agenda is gathering steam in Toronto. David Miller, who was elected Toronto's mayor in 2003, placed a New Deal for cities at the heart of his election platform. It has attracted support from an unusually broad coalition of groups from the left and right, because on the surface it marries a social agenda with the drive to economic prosperity by focusing on urban quality of life. The public campaign has been led by the Toronto Board of Trade, which has been running the following advertisement on the Toronto subway with great effect:

> Every year Toronto pays $9 billion more in taxes than it receives in services. Yet, our roads are packed, our transit system is stalled, people are searching further from the city to access affordable housing and our waterfront remains an untapped opportunity. If Toronto is to continue to generate funds that are critical to the strength and vitality of our province and nation – then Toronto needs support.

A Toronto Board of Trade study breaks down this figure, and values Toronto's federal fiscal balance at $7.6 billion (with the remaining $1.4 billion representing the gap between provincial taxes collected and provincial expenditures in the city).[11] Whether this figure is precise or not is largely beside the point, because most commentators would agree that, whatever its exact level, Toronto's federal fiscal balance is large and negative. Far more important is how the Board of Trade's argument is framed. The advertisement does not call for increased funding from Ottawa or somewhere else in Canada to solve Toronto's problems. Rather, it says that the funds to fix Toronto's problems are generated by the city's own businesses and residents, and the public policy challenge is not to bring new monies to Toronto, but to keep those funds from leaving the city in the first place.

This way of reframing the question of municipal finances is quickly catching on in Toronto. But what has not been fully appreciated is the dramatic implication it may have for Torontonians' sense of their selves as citizens of a federal political community, especially one where a strong sense of national social solidarity is necessary for maintaining political support for significant levels of interprovincial redistribution. The not-so-implicit message in the Board of Trade's campaign is that Toronto, and perhaps by extension Ontario, should no longer fund federal transfers at the level that it has in the past. And underlying this message is an even more challenging one that strikes at the very heart of Canada's self-understanding. Since Confederation, the nation-building project has been understood to include the building of strong regional communities, including in rural Canada. The message now being sent is that this interpretation should be replaced with one which holds that in the twenty-first century, Canada's prospects depend largely on the growth and vibrancy of its principal urban centres.

I do not think the potential implications for Canadian federalism of the emergence of cities as sites of political identification is yet fully understood. To the extent that there has been any thinking at all, the focus has been on the juridical and financial empowerment of local government and the relative decline in provincial power. But the demand on the part of some urban centres, such as Toronto, to keep significant resources at home could have more wide-ranging implications for interprovincial redistribution. Rural Canada seems to have realized quite quickly that the cities agenda cuts against interprovincial redistribution and that an emphasis on major urban centres implies the lack of comparable expenditures on smaller municipalities. Pressure from these municipalities resulted in the morphing of the cities agenda into the 'communities agenda.' This defensive manoeuvre on the part of smaller rural centres – made possible by the over-representation of rural Canada in the House of Commons – suggests that the old politics of interprovincial and inter-regional redistribution enjoys considerable resilience.

The second trend that could put the community of fate under strain is the increasing ethnic diversity of Canada, flowing almost entirely from extraordinarily high rates of immigration. This demographic shift shows up clearly in the 2001 census. There are two sets of statistics that I want to emphasize. First, at present, 18 per cent of Canadians are foreign-born, a rate second only to Australia's. Assuming current levels of immigration and Canada's relatively low birth rate continue, the percentage of foreign-born Canadians will only increase. Second, ethnic immigrants tend to concentrate in Montreal, Toronto, and Vancouver. Between 1996 and 2001, of the 1.2 million immigrants to Canada, 75.3 per cent went to those cities.

The impact on Canadian federalism of Canada's increasing ethnic diversity and the concentration of that diversity in Canada's urban centres is a question that has until recently been largely unexplored. Yet political arrangements, no matter how well designed by constitutional lawyers, will only function properly if they are animated by a sense that they are valuable and worthwhile. The institutions of Canadian federalism accordingly require the existence of a political culture of federalism. My sense is that federalism is in for a bit of a shock, because many recent immigrants do not identify with Canada's self-description as a federal political community; they have not taken to federalism in the same way that they have embraced other aspects of our constitutional identity, such as rights and the rule of law. Moreover, this asymmetric pattern of political identification will only intensify, because Canada has no option but to rely on extremely high rates of immigration to sustain our economic base.[12]

I suggest that ethnic immigrants have four stances on federalism: ignorance, indifference, anger, and frustration. First, ignorance means that many ethnic immigrants are only dimly aware of the constitutional arrangements that distribute governmental power in Canada. The ignorance, in extreme cases, is of the very existence of federalism. But probably more widespread is a lack of understanding about the relative powers and status of the different orders of government. Second, indifference towards federalism is part of a larger story regarding the character of democratic citizenship in twenty-first-century Canada. Many Canadians liken citizenship to consumerism, and view governments largely as sources of public services. Consumer citizens care much less about who gets the job done than about the job being done well. To the extent that policy delivery straddles jurisdictional divisions, the attitude of indifference demands that governments cooperate and sort matters out in a constructive manner, providing seamless service to the citizen.

Third, for some immigrants, federalism is a source of anger or resentment. The difficulty here is that accounts of federalism offer up a conception of the Canadian political community with which immigrants find it difficult to identify, such as those conceptions which imagine the country as the union of two or three founding nations to which immigrants cannot trace their ancestry. Deploying the language of equality, ethnic immigrants have sought to challenge these historically oriented accounts of Canada and their reflection in public policy. The mobilization against the distinct society clause in the Meech Lake Accord is a well-known example. Finally, for many recent arrivals, federalism is a source of frustration if it impedes their economic and social integration because of a lack of policy coordination. The leading example is the difficulty faced by immigrants in securing the recognition of professional or trade credentials obtained abroad. Since Canada's immigration system rewards such credentials through the point system, immigrants are surprised to find when they settle in provinces that these same credentials are difficult to convert into a locally recognized qualification. To the extent that federalism prevents policy integration in this area, ethnic immigrants feel no loyalty toward it.

A failure of New Canadians to buy into and embrace the federal project, combined with the rise of cities as sites of political identification, could potentially be deployed to threaten the political viability of the existing federal-provincial transfer system. Let me explain the point this way. The federal-provincial transfer system is sustained by narratives of solidarity of the 'other Canada' – the idea that our fellow citizens in other parts of the country are deserving of a basic level of services, no matter where they are born, and no matter where they live. For two generations of Ontarians, the other Canada has been in other provinces – in Corner Brook, Prince George, Rimouski, and Yellowknife. But for many residents of Canada's major urban centres, especially the New Canadians and even many 'Old Canadians,' the other Canada is not in a distant part of our vast country to which they may have never travelled, and to which they have no family connections, but much closer to home. In Toronto, the other Canada is now in Thorncliffe Park, Malvern, and St James Town – namely, the growing enclaves of poverty in our major urban centres that are taking on an increasingly racialized character, and which are at least in part a function of the well-documented difficulties that recent immigrants are facing in labour market integration.[13] This new urban reality is very hard for residents of Canada's largest city to ignore, and is attracting increasing media attention.

If narratives of social citizenship undergird the federal-provincial transfer system, then changes to those notions of social citizenship that emphasize local bonds of solidarity could have dramatic implications for the financial structure of the Canadian federation. Instead of redistributing their income away to provinces, Torontonians may demand that it remain in the city, not for tax reductions, but to be redirected to a new target population. In effect, they may demand that the kind of energy and resources we have long invested in regional development projects in Northern and Atlantic Canada now be thrown at our deprived inner cities and immigrant populations. In concrete terms, these demands could manifest themselves in different sorts of policy prescriptions, all of them controversial, to change Ontario's federal fiscal imbalance. It may mean that the balance of federal-provincial transfers and direct transfers to individuals be shifted toward the latter. Alternatively, building on the demand of major urban centres for direct dealings between the federal government and municipalities, it may mean that the federal government introduce new federal-municipal or federal-provincial-municipal shared-cost programs that are focused on urban populations, directing more federal funds on a net basis into Ontario. Or most dramatically of all, it could mean a large tax point transfer to Ontario. Under any scenario, fiscal federalism would undergo a major upheaval, but of a far different kind than that envisioned by the Séguin Commission.

NOTES

Thanks to Jean-François Gaudreault-DesBiens for his excellent comments.

1 Quebec Commission on Fiscal Imbalance, *A New Division of Canada's Financial Resources* (Quebec: Quebec Commission on Fiscal Imbalance, 2002), available on-line at http://www.desequilibrefiscal.gouv.qc.ca/en/pdf/rapport_final_en.pdf (accessed 18 May 2004).
2 Royal Commission on Dominion-Provincial Relations, *The Rowell-Sirois*

Report (Ottawa: Queen's Printer, 1937); Province of Quebec, *Report of the Royal Commission of Inquiry on Constitutional Problems* (Quebec: Royal Commission of Inquiry on Constitutional Problems, 1956) (chair: T. Tremblay).

3 Council of the Federation, 'Press Release: A New Study Confirms the Existence of Fiscal Imbalance,' 8 March 2004. The study referred to is Conference Board of Canada, *Fiscal Prospects for the Federal and Provincial/Territorial Governments* (Ottawa: Conference Board of Canada, 2004). This study updates and expands upon an earlier Conference Board of Canada study, *Fiscal Prospects for the Federal and Québec Governments* (Ottawa: Conference Board of Canada, 2002), available on-line at http://www.desequilibrefiscal.gouv.qc.ca/en/pdf/board_en.pdf (accessed 18 May 2004), which provided the empirical support for the Séguin Commission's analysis.

4 Marie-Anne Deussing, 'Federal Taxes and Transfers Across Canada: Impact on Families,' Department of Finance Working Paper 2003-21 (Ottawa: Department of Finance, 2003), available on-line at http://www.fin.gc.ca/wp/2003-21e.html (accessed 18 May 2004). Finn Poschmann, 'Where the Money Goes: The Distribution of Taxes and Benefits in Canada' (Toronto: C.D. Howe Institute, 1998).

5 Finance Canada, 'A Brief History of the Health and Social Transfers,' available on-line at http://www.fin.gc.ca/FEDPROV/hise.html (accessed 18 May 2004); Finance Canada, 'Equalization Program,' available on-line at http://www.fin.gc.ca/fedprov/eqpe.html) (accessed 18 May 2004).

6 Ontario, Ministry of Finance, *Public Accounts of Ontario, 2000–1* (Toronto: Queen's Printer for Ontario, 2001), 10.

7 Prime Ministers' Office, 'Prime Minister Announces New Equalization and Territorial Funding Formula Framework,' 26 October 2004, available on-line at http://pm.gc.ca/eng/news.asp?category=1&id=300 (accessed 28 April 2005); Prime Ministers' Office, 'New Federal Investments on Health: Commitments on 10–year Action Plan on Health,' 15 September 2004, available on-line at: http://www.pm.gc.ca/grfx/docs/FundingENG.pdf (accessed 28 April 2005).

8 Arrangement between the Government of Canada and the Government of Nova Scotia on Offshore Revenues, 14 February 2005, available on-line at http://www.fin.gc.ca/FEDPROV/NovaScotiaArr-e.html (accessed 29 April 2005); and Arrangement between the Government of Canada and the Government of Newfoundland and Labrador on Offshore Revenues (14 February 2005), available on-line at http://www.fin.gc.ca/FEDPROV/NfldArr-e.html (accessed 29 April 2005).

9 Warren Lovely, 'Killing the Gold Goose?' *Canadian Financing Quarterly* (15 April 2005), available on-line at http://research.cibcwm.com/

economic_public/download/cfqapr05.pdf (accessed 29 April 2005).

10 Sujit Choudhry, 'Citizenship and Federations: Some Preliminary Reflections,' in Kalypso Nicolaidis and Robert Howse, eds., *The Federal Vision: Legitimacy and Levels of Governance in the US and the EU* (Oxford: Oxford University Press, 2001), 377–402.

11 Toronto Board of Trade, *Strong City, Strong Nation: Securing Toronto's Contribution to Canada* (Toronto: Toronto Board of Trade, 2002), available on-line at http://www.bot.com/assets/StaticAssets/Documents/PDF/ StrongCityRpt.pdf (accessed 18 May 2004).

12 As Jean-François Gaudreault-DesBiens has suggested, the situation in Montreal may be different. He is of the opinion that ethnic immigrants' attitudes towards federalism and towards Canadian citizenship in Montreal are less homogeneous than in Toronto or Vancouver. The linguistic variable plays a significant role, as some ethnic groups such as South Americans, North Africans, and Haitians more easily integrate into the French-speaking mainstream society and are more likely to adopt some of its dominant narratives.

13 United Way of Greater Toronto and Canadian Council on Social Development, *Poverty by Postal Code: The Geography of Neighbourhood Poverty, 1981– 2001* (Toronto: United Way of Greater Toronto, 2004), available on-line at http://www.unitedwaytoronto.com/who_we_help/pdfs/PovertybyPo stalCodeFinal.zip (accessed 18 May 2004). Abdurrahman Aydemir and Mikal Skuterud, *Explaining the Deteriorating Entry Earnings of Canada's Immigrant Cohorts, 1966–2000* (Ottawa: Minister of Industry, 2004), available on-line at http://www.statcan.ca/english/research/11F0019MIE/ 11F0019MIE2004225.pdf (accessed 18 May 2004).

Social Justice in Overlapping Sharing Communities

ALAIN NOËL

The purpose of this volume is to reflect upon social justice in Canada, in the context of ongoing discussions on the distribution of resources and powers in the federation. In the beginning of 2002, Quebec's Commission on Fiscal Imbalance presented a report documenting the causes and consequences of fiscal imbalance in the federation and proposing a new distribution of financial resources in the country. The same year, in November, the Commission on the Future of Health Care in Canada recommended major changes in the sharing of powers and resources associated with health care. In the fall of 2004, a new federal government led by Paul Martin responded to these demands with commitments to improve the health transfer and to redesign the equalization program. It is still difficult to assess the significance of these new federal commitments. We know, however, that the stakes are high. With ever-increasing federal budgetary surpluses, the division of financial resources among orders of government is changing rapidly and this will have a profound impact on the Canadian federation and, more broadly, on Canadian society.

Is the federal government going to return to its early postwar role as the dominant player in social policy? Or are new arrangements gradually emerging that will allow the different governments to collaborate effectively, perhaps with some form of asymmetric relationship with Quebec? Can social justice be maintained through this process, in the different communities and in the country as a whole? Are some institutional arrangements more sustainable than others?

It is probably a sign of the times that these issues were raised at a law school colloquium, usually a forum more concerned with questions associated with constitutional law, individual and collective rights, or conflicting identity claims. The sharing and use of financial resources has indeed moved to the centre stage of Canadian politics. In a recent study, Keith Banting and Robin Boadway aptly captured this evolution, from a politics dominated by questions of identity and recognition to one where distribution and redistribution became more pre-eminent, by describing this country as 'a set of overlapping sharing communities.'[1]

It is in this context that Richard Simeon was asked to present and discuss the relationship between federalism and social justice. Characteristically, he does so in a very effective and clear way. I agree with most of his conclusions. This allows me, in this comment, to build upon rather than thoroughly discuss his analysis. I will therefore start more or less from where Simeon ends, to discuss further the implications of his conclusions in the current Canadian context. In doing so, I will also consider the usefulness of thinking of Canada as one or as many sharing communities, arguing that this notion is indeed appealing, but also fraught with difficulties. But first, let us consider Simeon's argument.

Federalism and Social Justice

Simeon starts his review and evaluation of the literature on the relationship between federalism and social justice by noting the overwhelming dominance, on both the left and the right, of the view according to which federalism is inimical to redistribution. This would be the case, goes the argument, because: 1) there are more obstacles to change, or veto points, in situations of divided government; 2) intergovernmental competition tends to drive down taxes and public expenditures; 3) federalism gives power over social policy to sub-unit governments that have less redistributive capacities than the federal government; and 4) local or sub-unit politics is more conservative than politics on a broader scale.

Simeon finds these arguments unconvincing. To start with, it is not even obvious that the presumed negative relationship between federalism and redistribution holds. He points to Canada, Germany, Belgium, and Spain as cases of federations or quasi-federations that do not differ markedly from comparable unitary countries. Going further, a comparative study of a number of less-developed countries suggests that political and administrative decentralization (or a small country size) actually helps the poor, by making governments more sensitive to basic needs and more responsive to popular demands.[2] Whatever the case, one should keep in mind that the evidence on these relationships remains limited and fragile. Empirical studies tend to be either anecdotal or based on regression analyses that capture federalism, or even divided government in general, with simple dichotomous variables. Significant quantitative results may appear convincing, but they must be considered with scepticism when based on crude measurements that do not represent the phenomenon under study very well.[3] Moreover, as Simeon notes, even when significant, the federalism dummy variable may explain very little of the empirical variance in the dependent variable.[4]

The theory behind the standard argument also poses problems. Federations are seen as less favourable to social justice because they would make reforms more difficult, would foster a 'race to the bottom' between governments that have less elastic revenues, and would give additional power to conservative local elites. As Simeon points out, institutional stickiness may work both ways, and contribute, for instance, to preserve social justice in a period of retrenchment. The same is true for competition, which does not always, if ever, lead to the bottom. In federations, as among countries of a same region, competition may take different forms and give rise to learning, emulation, and the diffusion of programs as much as to a drive to reduce services and lower costs. There are numerous examples of emulation and diffusion in the history of the Canadian federation, with or without the support of the federal government. Labour laws and workers' compensation, for instance, were rapidly generalized without federal intervention, as the different provincial governments rapidly followed the leaders.[5] Likewise, North American integration has not forced Canada to adjust its social policies downward, but it may have brought the country to raise its environmental standards, in line with the stricter American standards, which are themselves a product of federal emulation, as many states adjust upward to the more demanding California standards.[6] As for arguments about size and local elites, they rest on very thin ground. For one thing, states, provinces, or *Länder* are often quite large in geographical size and population, larger in fact than many countries. Second, one could just as easily argue that small units are more conducive than large ones to the type of solidarity relationships that facilitate the development of social and redistributive policies.[7] More fundamentally, what is at stake here is neither the size of the decision-making units nor their number, but who is in power.[8] The conventional view is that conservatives have a better hold on small, decentralized units. The least that can be said, in looking at today's world, is that they do not badly either in large units, starting with the United States!

Simeon, then, is right to conclude that federalism is neutral with respect to redistributive justice, and probably helpful in enhancing justice understood as the recognition and accommodation of distinct communities. Like him, I would argue that other forces account for the development of social protection and redistribution. I would go further, in fact, and contend that the best way to understand the development of social justice is to look at the politics of social justice as such. Institutions do play a role, but the key factor remains the political conflict that opposes social and political actors of the left and the right.

Consider, for instance, Germany and Austria. Here are two neighbouring federations that share many cultural, economic, and institutional features, but still diverge significantly in their political life and in their orientations towards social justice. For a long period, the two countries did appear to have developed similar welfare states, which German sociologist Jens Alber described as 'birds of a feather.'[9] In terms of income inequality or relative poverty, they evolved in parallel, with similar results.[10] Still, behind these similarities in institutions and policies, clear differences remained between the attitudes of Germans and Austrians toward domestic and international justice, the latter being more reluctant to redistribute, especially on a global scale.[11] These differences became more apparent as the two federations took opposite directions. Austria reinforced the most conservative features of its traditional model, a model premised on insurance benefits tied to employment and labour market status and on the maintenance of the traditional one-earner family.[12] Meanwhile, under the leadership of Gerhard Schröder, Germany undertook bold reforms, intended to transform significantly the German welfare state in a more liberal direction.[13] It is still too early to tell whether these diverging shifts will end up differentiating the two federations significantly, and make each country more or less egalitarian. The German reforms, for instance, could have negative impacts for the long-term unemployed, but positive ones for single-parent households. What is certain, however, is that the unfolding story will have little to do with the type of federalism existing in each country – the more conservative Austria being in many ways close to a unitary state[14] – and much more to do with conflicts over the proper role of the state in sustaining and promoting economic growth, employment, and social justice. Likewise, Canada has a more developed welfare state than the United States and it has been more successful in preventing the rise of inequality in the last two decades primarily because its partisan politics is less conservative, and only incidentally because – again contrary to the conventional view – it has a more decentralized federation.

Consider another, revealing, aspect of redistribution. In liberal democracies, social justice is usually seen as justice among individuals, whether it concerns rights, income, or access to services. In large countries, however, it can also be understood as implying a minimum of equality between the different regions of the country, so as to give every citizen more or less the same possibilities. This objective, however, can be implemented in very different ways. The Germans, for instance, seek to make *Länder* as equal as possible in wealth, services, and benefits.[15] In the United States, on the other hand, labour and capital market mobility are deemed sufficient, and in fact more efficient, in achieving equal opportunities for individuals; unlike most federations, the country has no equalization mechanisms. Federations vary significantly in this respect, from the more egalitarian Germans and Australians to the more market-oriented Swiss and Americans, with Canada somewhere in the middle, and, as Ron Watts notes, these variations are not associated with centralization or decentralization. They rather reflect the political context and the value given to equality in the different countries.[16] Indeed, federations may actually do more than many unitary countries in the promotion of inter-regional equity. Portugal, for instance, a unitary country with important regional disparities, until recently did not even acknowledge the existence of distinct regions, let alone of disparities between them. Regional development policies only emerged in the 1990s, in response to the opportunity provided by the European Union structural funds. More than ten years later, the perception of regional boundaries and of disparities remains 'fuzzy.'[17] Again, social justice is not necessarily easier to achieve in a unitary or centralized context. What matters most is the politics of justice itself, the enduring conflict between social and political actors of the left and of the right over the meaning of equality in a liberal society.

Canadian Solidarity

The contemporary Canadian context is one of gradual but significant change. As in other OECD countries, the welfare state is progressively redesigned to meet the challenges of a post-industrial, global economy. Common trends include a greater reliance on market or market-friendly mechanisms, income-support policies more favourable to labour market activity, a preference for benefits over services and for tax expenditures over transfers, and policies that are becoming less universal and more targeted. Reforms also tend to enhance gender equality and to promote, in one way or another, individual empower-ment and civic networks.[18] It is still early to foresee the full outcome of this global reform process. New social policies could become simply more market-oriented and less redistributive, but they could also pro-mote social justice more effectively by creating a better situation for women, young families, and children.[19] Most probably, as in the past, different national versions of the general model will emerge, each ver-sion embodying specific principles of justice affirmed and institution-alized in the political process.

So far, in Canada, the most significant changes have taken place in federal transfers, to persons and to the provinces. Federal transfers to persons have evolved in the expected direction, with contributory and targeted programs growing at the expense of universal measures. In some cases, with child benefits for instance, this transition has actually improved the income support provided to low-income households. In others, most notably with employment insurance, social protection has deteriorated markedly, with fewer and fewer unemployed workers being protected. Overall, the distributive impact has been detrimental to households below the median income, and even more so to those in the lowest income quintile and to persons without children.[20] Even though they improved in the last years, transfers to provinces have also been sharply curtailed, with important repercussions on the capacity of provincial governments to maintain existing social pro-grams and services.

In the provinces, changes have been less dramatic, to a large extent because provincial social expenditures are less flexible, being used largely to pay for services with important systemic costs rather than for transfers to persons.[21] The two programs that take up most of the social budget – health care services and education – have not been the object of major reforms, and they have remained defined by a univer-sal logic.[22] Reduced federal transfers and rising costs have put strains on the quality of health services and created much public dissatisfac-tion, but they have not challenged the basic structure of the system.[23] In social assistance and social services, where they are less constrained, provincial governments have innovated in various ways, advancing in the same direction as in other countries, with policies ranging from compulsory work for welfare to improved income-support measures.[24]

Overall, the recent evolution of Canadian social policies can be characterized as a gradual shift, or perhaps drift, toward policies that are less universal, more market-friendly, and probably less redistributive. There is no doubt that the reduction of federal transfers to persons and to provinces has been the key factor in this gradual transformation. Federal income-support programs became less redistributive, and provinces were not able to face adequately the rising costs of health care services. Provincial policies, however, also played a role in defining specific reform paths, which ranged from a focus on private delivery (in child care for instance), lower taxes and workfare in Alberta, to one favouring universal public services (in child care), public drugs insurance, and the promotion of the social economy in Quebec. As is the case with other OECD countries, the process is still in its beginning, and many directions remain possible, especially in a context where the federal government has important budgetary surplus and appears willing to improve transfers. For now, social programs remain largely defined by continuity, with some retrenchment and innovations at the margins.

In his contribution to this volume, Sujit Choudhry wonders whether this relatively stable situation is sustainable in the context of a new Canadian identity, less defined as a territorial community of fate than as a community of urban dwellers of various origins, who would care more about poverty in their city than, say, about the hardships of rural people on the Atlantic coast. This is an old worry, wearing new clothes. For many years, analysts have predicted the demise of social transfers in Canada, on the ground that inter-regional distribution would prove difficult to sustain in the wealthiest provinces. Among those who favoured redistribution, many believed that the best chances of the status quo rested with the relative ignorance of Canadians regarding social transfers in general and equalization in particular.

The fact is that inter-provincial redistribution has been and remains strongly supported by Canadians. Indeed, few public policies benefit from such strong and widespread support in public opinion. In 2004, 85 per cent of Canadians approved the transfer of money from richer to poorer provinces through the federal equalization program, up two percentage points from 2001. In Ontario, the province at the core of Sujit Choudhry's argument, public support was even higher than the national average, at 87 per cent.[25] The urban agenda did not prevent Canadians from seeing a tie with rural areas either. A 2001 poll indicates that 85 per cent of the population agrees to provide support for small family farms in difficult times, and nowhere is this support higher than in Toronto, at 89 per cent.[26] As for Canadians of recent origins, they do not seem to differ markedly from other citizens, or at least not for very long. Opinion surveys suggest that 'within a generation, children of immigrants have virtually identical values as other young Canadians.'[27] Finally, Canadians probably do not see any opposition between reducing poverty in their city's neighbourhoods and sharing among provinces. Usually, in Canada as elsewhere, such preoccupations go hand-in-hand: those most supportive of redistribution tend to approve it locally, nationally, and internationally, and vice versa.[28]

The urban agenda and the changing composition of the population do not seem to have affected the social foundations of redistributive politics in Canada. In a similar vein, Tom Courchene, who has long argued that the increasing importance of north-south trade relationships could erode the will of Canadians to maintain their east-west patterns of accommodation, now recognizes that this has not happened. Programs and policies have been modified and adjusted, but the basic social features of the federation have remained in place.[29]

Canada, then, still looks like what Sujit Choudhry calls a 'community of fate.' Is this community sustainable, however, given the evolution of public revenues and expenditures? This is the question at the origin of this book, the one first raised in this comment. Two issues are at stake. One concerns the evolution of public policies, and the other the normative foundations of these policies.

Communities of Sharing

Canadians basically support the status quo with respect to social transfers and equalization. This observation takes care of Sujit Choudhry's worries about the social sustainability of the current fiscal framework, but it does not guarantee that this policy framework will remain unchallenged. Indeed, important trends and forces are at work that are gradually undermining and transforming the status quo. These evolutions should be, in fact, the main elements for concern.

First and foremost, there is a significant and growing vertical fiscal imbalance in the federation. Federal revenues are high compared to those of the provinces, given the costs associated with each order of government's jurisdictions (in other words, the vertical fiscal gap is important) and transfers to provincial governments are not adequate and sufficient to compensate for this gap in resources (hence, there is vertical fiscal imbalance).[30] In this context, provincial governments have difficulties maintaining existing social programs, and demands are rising for a better sharing of resources in the country. Provincial situations also vary widely, Alberta being in a particularly favoured position. At the same time, the federal government is tempted to use its growing leverage to redefine unilaterally the country's fiscal arrangements and to redesign social policy from the centre. Without a transparent and articulate pan-Canadian debate about values and objectives, the fiscal framework of the federation is gradually changing, and so are the underlying conceptions of social justice governments implicitly define.

In an effort to clarify the issues at stake, Keith Banting and Robin Boadway present the situation as involving a normative choice between different and overlapping communities of sharing. Canadians, they explain, could privilege a predominantly countrywide community of sharing, predominantly provincial communities, or a dual sharing community, embodying both dimensions in a balanced way. History, public opinion surveys, and policy trends suggest, they argue, that Canadians prefer the idea of a dual sharing community, which combines a commitment to countrywide solidarity with a desire to maintain provincial autonomy. Public policies should therefore reflect these preferences, and create a situation where governments can collaborate to define national standards that would allow provincial innovations and variations.[31]

This representation of the choices facing Canadians is appealing because it seems fair and open to all possible choices, connected to public preferences, and reasonably balanced. The model, however, may not be as clear and helpful as it seems. First, one should note that the example Banting and Boadway give to illustrate the notion of a dual community is practically the same as the one they give to capture the idea of a predominantly countrywide one: 'the bedrock of this approach,' they write, 'is the conviction that a sick baby in British Columbia should be entitled to health services on broadly comparable terms as a sick baby in Atlantic Canada.'[32] The authors' idea of a dual sharing community looks strikingly similar to their view of a predominantly Canada-wide community. More generally, the idea of sharing communities may be slightly more specific than that of a 'community of fate,' but it is still largely undetermined. As Richard Simeon demands, would a province's improvements above the common standard be unjust and detract from community standards? What are we to make of differences in services between large cities and remote rural areas, undoubtedly a more important problem in Canada than that of putative differences between British Columbia and the Atlantic provinces? And what about federal policies that would increase inequalities in a more or less uniform way, everywhere in the country, as was the case with employment insurance?

Differences in services between British Columbia and Atlantic Canada appear more problematic in the communities of sharing argument, not so much because they are an affront to social justice, but rather because they are incompatible with symbols and views at the heart of English-Canadian nationalism.[33] Banting and Boadway are right to observe that Canadians value sharing within the federation, but this in itself does not tell us how exactly the imperatives of solidarity and autonomy should be balanced. One could argue, for instance, that the equalization principle enshrined in section 36(2) of the Constitution Act, 1982, which calls for 'reasonably comparable levels of public services at reasonably comparable levels of taxation,' is a more appropriate standard – precisely because it is reasonably vague – to balance solidarity and autonomy than the image of the sick child. Then again, this is a rather open commitment, which can be fulfilled in a number of ways.

The contrast between predominantly countrywide and predominantly provincial communities of sharing also eludes the issues raised by the multinational character of the federation, and the contending conceptions of justice that these issues entail. Debates about the social union framework agreement, health care financing, or fiscal imbalance are not only, and perhaps not primarily, about sharing. They are also manifestations of a broader ongoing conflict about national recognition and autonomy in the Canadian federation.[34] This question does not fit easily in the categories proposed by Banting and Boadway.

Starting from a more specific, empirical characterization may be less elegant but more helpful. We have seen that Canadians are strongly favourable to the equalization of provincial revenues and to some form of basic standard in rights and services. The current problem with the federation is elsewhere, in a growing fiscal imbalance that undermines the capacity of the provincial governments to maintain and develop the social programs for which they are responsible. In this context, sick children may be treated alike in all provinces, but they are likely to face waiting lists or deteriorated services and their parents may be tempted to seek private alternatives, if they can.

The issue, then, is not federalism as such, or even our contending conceptions of the sharing community, but rather an imbalance that is primarily an imbalance of power in the Canadian federation. Transfers have improved in the last years, but these improvements are not enshrined in clear and consensual rules. On the contrary, even equalization, the last program that was governed by a formula, has been redefined as a budgetary envelope to be determined every year by the House of Commons.[35] More and more decisions are taken in Ottawa, and Canada is likely to become more uniform in its policies and less multinational in its orientations. Only time will tell whether social justice, understood both as the search for equality and as the recognition of multiplicity in the federation, will be well served in the process. The outcome, in any case, will have less to do with shifting views on the nature of the sharing communities than with the ups and downs of federal and provincial politics.

Conclusion

Among OECD countries with a unitary regime, France is by all accounts one of the most centralized. The country has a broad array of social programs, and it ranks near or just below the average in terms of poverty reduction and income redistribution.[36] Geographically, however, it is also divided, with different income groups largely living apart, in their own income ghettos, with unequal life chances for their children, a point driven home by the suburban riots in 2005.[37] However uniform, national laws, rights, and intentions do not necessarily translate into similar and just living conditions for all. In North America, it is the most decentralized of the three federations that has the best – albeit imperfect – record in terms of poverty alleviation, income redistribution, and social rights.

For all practical purposes, the relationship between federalism, or even centralization, and redistribution appears insignificant. Federalism does matter, however. First, in a diverse society it makes it possible to recognize and institutionalize the existence of different national or regional identities. Second, as with any other institutional arrangement, federalism structures possibilities, choices, and democratic debates. Third, with respect to social justice, it makes it possible to balance broader solidarities with the maintenance of closer ties, or sharing on a large scale and the pursuit of differentiated ways of achieving social justice.

In the current context, the last imperative appears particularly significant. Europeans, write Daniel Béhar and Philippe Estèbe, face the difficult and paradoxical task of drawing increasingly broad and encompassing frameworks of exchange, deliberation, and solidarity while, at the same time, reinforcing social ties, local networks, and democratic responsiveness.[38] The contemporary Canadian federation has been defined by the tensions generated by this paradoxical imperative, and it has not done badly in this respect, to a large extent because it has developed diverse and decentralized arrangements.

The main risk for the time being is not in federalism as such, in a declining support for wider forms of solidarities, or in inadequate attention to our dual or predominantly Canada-wide sharing communities, but rather in losing an always difficult-to-maintain institutional and political balance between these contradictory objectives and the two orders of government that can achieve them. With a growing fiscal imbalance, the federal government is becoming less committed to the federal principle and more ambitious in its search for influence, control, and visibility.[39] As a result, over time Canada could become more uniform but not necessarily more just.

Very often, in Canada as in Europe, diversity works as an anchor, and not as a stumbling block, for social solidarity and the welfare state.[40] Specific policy outcomes usually depend more on the politics of social justice, the conflict between actors and parties of the left and of the right, than on the intricacies of intergovernmental relations. Still, multi-scale governance arrangements always matter. In multinational societies, in particular, they embody and express fundamental social values, and they contribute in their own way to the achievement of social justice.

NOTES

1 Keith Banting and Robin Boadway, 'Defining the Sharing Community: The Federal Role in Health Care,' in Harvey Lazar and France St-Hilaire, eds., *Money, Politics and Health Care: Reconstructing the Federal-Provincial Relationship* (Montreal and Kingston: Institute for Research on Public Policy and Institute of Intergovernmental Relations, 2004), 40.

2 Joachim von Braun and Ulrike Grote, 'Does Decentralization Serve the Poor?' in Ehtisham Ahmad and Vito Tanzi, eds., *Managing Fiscal Decentralization* (London: Routledge, 2002), 68–96.

3 On this question, see Jonathan Rodden, 'Comparative Federalism and Decentralization: On Meaning and Measurement,' *Comparative Politics* 36, no. 4 (July 2004): 492, 496; Alain Noël, 'Introduction: Varieties of Capitalism, Varieties of Federalism,' in Alain Noël, ed., *Federalism and Labour Market Policy: Comparing Different Governance and Employment Strategies* (Montreal and Kingston: McGill-Queen's University Press, 2004), 4–6.

4 Fritz W. Scharpf and Vivien A. Schmidt, eds., *Welfare and Work in the Open Economy*, volume 1, *From Vulnerabilities to Competitiveness* (Oxford: Oxford University Press, 2000), 17.

5 Alain Noël, 'Is Decentralization Conservative? Federalism and the Contemporary Debate on the Canadian Welfare State,' in Robert Young, ed., *Stretching the Federation: The Art of the State in Canada* (Kingston: Queen's University Institute of Intergovernmental Relations, 1999), 199.

6 George Hobert, Keith G. Banting, and Richard Simeon, 'The Scope for Domestic Choice: Policy Autonomy in a Globalizing World,' in George Hoberg, ed., *Capacity for Choice: Canada in a New North America* (Toronto: University of Toronto Press, 2002), 252–98. Looking more broadly at the OECD, Bea Cantillon finds 'an upward convergence rather than a "race to the bottom."' Bea Cantillon, 'European Subsidiarity versus American Social Federalism: Is Europe in Need of a Common Social Policy?' paper presented at the second annual conference of the Network for European Social Policy Analysis (ESPAnet) (Oxford, 9–11 September 2004), 4 (www.espanet.org).

7 Neil Gilbert, *Transformation of the Welfare State: The Silent Surrender of Public Responsibility* (Oxford: Oxford University Press, 2004), 161–2.

8 This critical but often neglected distinction is nicely presented in Deborah Stone, *Policy Paradox: The Art of Political Decision Making*, rev. ed. (New York: W.W. Norton, 2002), 363–75. Serge Terribilini's study of Swiss territorial policies shows how decentralization is often, but not always, associated with spatial inequality; in each case the outcome depends on the configuration and role of political forces. Serge Terribilini, *Fédéralisme, territoires et inégalités sociales* (Paris: L'Harmattan, 2001), 172–4.

9 Jens Alber, quoted in Philip Manow, 'The Good, the Bad, and the Ugly: Esping-Andersen's Regime Typology and the Religious Roots of the Western Welfare State,' *MPIfG Working Paper 04/3* (Cologne: Max Planck Institute for the Study of Societies, September 2004), 5 (www.mpi-fg-koeln.mpg.de).

10 See the Luxembourg Income Study key figures (http://www.lisproject .org/keyfigures.htm).

11 Alain Noël and Jean-Philippe Thérien, 'Public Opinion and Global Justice,' *Comparative Political Studies* 35, no. 6 (2002): 642.
12 Brigitte Unger and Karin Heitzmann, 'The Adjustment Path of the Australian Welfare State: Back to Bismarck?' *Journal of European Social Policy* 13, no. 4 (2003): 371–87.
13 Georges Marion, 'En réformant le chômage, l'Allemagne démantèle l'État-providence,' *Le Monde*, 25 December 2004, 2. See also Adam S. Posen, 'Who's the Comeback Kid? Germany,' *International Economy* (Fall 2003), 15–17; Irwin Collier, 'Can Gerhard Schröder Do It? Prospects for Fundamental Reform of the German Economy and a Return to High Employment,' *IZA Discussion Paper no. 1059* (Bonn: Institute for the Study of Labor, March 2004).
14 Maurice Croisat and Jean-Louis Quermonne, *L'Europe et le fédéralisme*, 2nd ed. (Paris: Montchrestien, 1999), 33.
15 Steffen G. Schneider, 'Labour Market Policy and the Unemployment Crisis in the Federal Republic of Germany: Institutional Sclerosis or Corporatist Revival?' in Noël, *Federalism and Labour Market Policy*, 83–142.
16 Ronald L. Watts, 'Comparing Equalization in Federations,' paper presented at the Forum of Federations Conference on Fiscal Equalization and Economic Development Policy Within Federations, Charlottetown, Prince Edward Island, 28–9 October 2002, 14 (www.forumfed.org).
17 Croisat and Quermonne, *L'Europe et le fédéralisme*, 51; Antonio Manuel Figueiredo, 'The Learning by Evaluating Process of Regional Policy in Portugal: A Special Case of Strong Municipalities and Weak Planning Regions,' paper presented at the Regional Studies Association Conference on 'Europe at the Margins: EU Regional Policy, Peripherality and Rurality,' Angers, France, 15–16 April 2004, 6 (www.regional-studies-assoc.ac.uk).
18 Gilbert, *Transformation of the Welfare State*, 44; Christelle Mandin and Bruno Palier, 'L'Europe et les politiques sociales: vers une harmonisation cognitive des réponses nationales,' in Christian Lequesne and Yves Surel, eds., *L'intégration européenne: entre émergence institutionnelle et recomposition de l'État*' (Paris: Presses de la Fondation nationale des sciences politiques, 2004), 263–4.
19 Contrast Neil Gilbert, who sees a shift primarily to the right, and Gøsta Esping-Andersen and his co-authors who think that a more just social welfare architecture could also emerge in the process. Gilbert, *Transformation of the Welfare State*, 182; Gøsta Esping-Andersen, Duncan Gallie, Anton Hemerijck, and John Myles, *Why We Need a New Welfare State* (Oxford: Oxford University Press, 2002).
20 Gerard Boychuk, 'The Canadian Social Model: The Logic of Policy Devel-

opment,' *CPRN Social Architecture Papers, Research Report F | 36*, Family Network (January 2004), 18.

21 Commission on Fiscal Imbalance, *Report: A New Division of Canada's Financial Resources* (Quebec: Commission sur le déséquilibre fiscal, 2002), 31.

22 Boychuk, 'The Canadian Social Model,' 11.

23 Jacob S. Hacker, 'Dismantling the Health Care State? Political Institutions, Public Policies and the Comparative Politics of Health Reform,' *British Journal of Political Science* 34, no. 4 (2004): 693–724.

24 Pascale Dufour, Gérard Boismenu, and Alain Noël, *L'aide au conditionnel: la contrepartie dans les mesures envers les sans-emploi en Europe et en Amérique du Nord* (Montreal and Brussels: Presses de l'Université de Montréal and P.I.E.-Peter Lang, 2003).

25 Centre for Research and Information on Canada, 'Portrait of Canada 2004: Fiscal Issues,' Ottawa, CRIC, 4 November 2004.

26 Centre for Research and Information on Canada, 'Press release: Urban Canadians Express Support for Rural Communities,' Regina, CRIC, 22 November 2001.

27 Matthew Mendelsohn, 'Birth of a New Ethnicity: The Canadian Identity Has Undergone a Remarkable Transformation in the Past Half Century,' *Globe and Mail*, 9 June 2003.

28 Alain Noël, Jean-Philippe Thérien, and Sébastien Dallaire, 'Divided over Internationalism: The Canadian Public and Development Assistance,' *Canadian Public Policy* 30, no. 1 (March 2004): 29–46.

29 Thomas J. Courchene, 'FTA at 15, NAFTA at 10: A Canadian Perspective on North American Integration,' in Thomas J. Courchene, Donald J. Savoie, and Daniel Schwanen, eds., *The Art of the State II: Thinking North America* (Montreal: Institute for Research on Public Policy, 2004), 14.

30 A good and dispassionate summary of the issues and debates is presented in Robin Boadway, 'Should the Canadian Federation Be Rebalanced?,' *Working Paper 2004(1)* (Kingston: Queen's University, Institute of Intergovernmental Relations, 2004).

31 Banting and Boadway, 'Defining the Sharing Community,' 75.

32 Ibid., 75, 36.

33 Will Kymlicka, 'Multinational Federalism in Canada: Rethinking the Partnership,' in Roger Gibbins and Guy Laforest, eds., *Beyond the Impasse: Toward Reconciliation* (Montreal: Institute for Research on Public Policy, 1998), 30.

34 Alain Noël, 'Without Quebec: Collaborative Federalism with a Footnote?' in Tom McIntosh, ed., *Building the Social Union: Perspectives, Directions and*

Challenges (Regina: Canadian Plains Research Center and Saskatchewan Institute of Public Policy, 2002), 13–30.

35 Alain Noël, 'Ici et ailleurs : de la formule à l'enveloppe,' *Policy Options* 25, no. 11 (2004): 67–8.

36 Christina Behrendt, 'Holes in the Safety Net? Social Security and the Alleviation of Poverty in a Comparative Perspective,' paper presented at the 2000 International Research Conference on Social Security of the International Social Security Association, Helsinki, 25–7 September 2000.

37 Éric Maurin, *Le ghetto français: enquête sur le séparatisme social* (Paris: Seuil, 2004).

38 Daniel Béhar and Philippe Estèbe, 'De l'Europe au local: vers un partage de la souveraineté territoriale?' in *L'État des régions françaises 2003* (Paris: La Découverte, 2003), 11.

39 Alain Noël, 'Power and Purpose in Intergovernmental Relations,' in Sarah Fortin, Alain Noël and France St-Hilaire, eds., *Forging the Canadian Social Union: SUFA and Beyond* (Montreal: Institute for Research on Public Policy, 2003), 47–68.

40 On Europe, see: Paul Magnette, *Le régime politique de l'Union européenne* (Paris: Presses de la Fondation nationale des sciences politiques, 2003), 272–74; Cantillon, 'European Subsidiarity versus American Social Federalism,' 11.

PART TWO

Taxation and the Search for Redistribution

Personal Income Tax and Redistribution in the Canadian Federation

PAUL BOOTHE AND KATHERINE BOOTHE

It is well known that the personal income tax (PIT) is the primary vehicle for income redistribution on the revenue side of the government budget. Government transfers to individuals and the distributional impact of government spending on programs such as health and education are important elements in government's array of redistribution tools as well, but for many citizens, the main thrust of income redistribution comes through the PIT.

Since at least the 1980s, Canadian governments have periodically focused their attention on reforming the PIT to achieve a number of objectives. In part, the impetus for reform has come from international tax competition, emanating particularly from personal tax reductions in the United States. However, international tax competition has not been the only driver of tax reform. Governments have also been motivated by a desire to target scarce resources for redistribution more precisely on specific groups, to improve the incentives the PIT creates for work effort and thus economic growth, and to simplify the tax system.

Canada's federal structure is a complicating factor in any examination of personal tax reform. Indeed, provinces have been motivated by many of the same factors underpinning federal changes. In some cases, provincial reforms have differed substantially between provinces and the federal government.

The purpose of this paper is to look at the implications of federal and provincial PIT reforms for the redistribution of income. By construction, this will be a partial analysis of the redistribution issue, since transfers to individuals and other expenditure programs will be ignored in the interest limiting the scope of the project.[1] More specifically, in this study we will try to answer the following questions: How have the amount and characteristics of PIT redistribution changed over time and, in particular, since 1995? How do provinces differ in the amount and characteristics of the redistribution in their PIT systems?

The remainder of the paper is organized as follows. In the next section we review some conceptual issues before describing the PIT and the rationale for its various features. The next section comprises a description of features of the PIT and their rationale. We briefly review the recent history of tax reform before turning to the empirical section of the study focusing on the impact of reform on redistribution. A short summary concludes the paper.

Conceptual Issues

Economic theory suggests that the design of any tax system should be governed by a number of principles including equity, efficiency, and minimization of compliance and administrative costs (Boadway and Kitchen, 1999, ch. 2). Because the focus of this paper is redistribution we will concentrate on the equity aspects of the PIT, recognizing that efficiency issues (raising revenue in such a way as to minimize distortions in the economy) are a powerful determinant of the structure of income tax systems.

Economists generally consider tax equity issues under two headings: horizontal and vertical. Horizontal equity requires that individuals in similar circumstances be treated in a similar manner by the tax system. Reforms aimed at achieving horizontal equity generally try to ensure that all types of income are subject to taxation, and at equivalent rates, although governments do make exceptions to this principle in order to create incentives for some kinds of economic activity (for example, investment).

While issues related to horizontal equity are relatively straightforward, at least at a conceptual level, issues related to vertical equity pose a unique set of problems. Vertical equity is founded on the 'ability-to-pay' principle which argues that an individual's contributions towards the cost of providing public goods (or government goods and services more generally) should be related to his ability to pay. The difficulty arises because economic theory gives little guidance regarding the interpersonal welfare comparisons inherent in judgments regarding ability to pay. Thus, arbitrary judgments regarding trade-offs between the welfare of individuals are required.

Complicating the issue further is the fact that economic theory suggests there is an inherent trade-off between equity and efficiency in optimal tax systems. In other words, at some point tax measures designed to improve the distribution of income (based on a given value judgment regarding the optimal distribution among individuals) will result in a reduction in efficiency – in other words, a reduction in the amount of income available to distribute. Even if one is only concerned with the welfare of low-income individuals, at some point their welfare will be reduced as equity-enhancing but efficiency-reducing measures shrink the overall production of the economy.

Indeed, a literature built on the work of Mirrlees (1971) shows that even when society puts a very high weight on the welfare of the poor, the optimal tax system is very close to a linear progressive tax system – that is, a single-rate income tax with a fixed exemption level (Boadway and Kitchen, 1999, 58). An important feature of such an optimal tax system is that individuals with no income receive transfers rather than pay taxes in what has come to be known as a 'negative income tax' (NIT).

Although the work of Mirrlees and others suggests that there are limits to the amount of progressivity (and therefore the redistribution of income) that should characterize the optimal tax system, it does not provide specific guidance regarding the optimal amount of progressivity. Such determinations are usually the result of the political process. As Boadway and Kitchen (1999) remark:

> Although the rationale for progressive personal income taxation is the achievement of vertical equity, there remains the thorny issue of how progressive the personal tax system should be. Clearly, there is not scientific basis for establishing the appropriate degree of progressivity and no magic formula for the 'right' rate structure. (169)

Another issue related to the progressivity of a given tax system has to do with measurement. A progressive tax system is one where 'the ratio of an individual's tax burden to his or her income increases as the individual's income rises' (Rosen et al., 1998, 84). In other words, average tax rates rise with income. However, given that the rate at which average tax rates change can only be defined relative to some range of income, measures of progressivity will, in general, depend on the range of income over which they are measured.

PIT Systems in Canada

The starting point in the design of a personal income tax system is the definition of taxable income. In keeping with the principle of horizontal equity, ideally one would want to include income of all kinds so that no tax preference was accorded simply because income was derived from one source rather than another. This was the basis of the Carter Commission dictum that, for tax purposes, a dollar is a dollar, regardless of its source.

In practice, however, the Canadian tax system gives special treatment to some kinds of income. For example, gifts, inheritances, and lottery winnings are not subject to tax. Some forms of social assistance and other social transfers, such as the child tax benefit, are not taxed. Only one-half of income derived from capital gains is taxable. Taxation is deferred on the investment income of registered pension plans (RPP), registered retirement savings plans (RRSP), and registered educational savings plans (RESP).

In addition, deductions are permitted to reduce income subject to tax. Some are related to the cost of earning income, such as union and professional dues and employment expenses. Non-refundable credits (credits that cannot be used to reduce tax payable below zero) are used for basic living costs and family-related expenses. Credits are available for dependent spouses, infirm or disabled adults being cared for at home, seniors, post-secondary education expenses, and charitable donations. Credits are also available for certain kinds of investment and for dividends as part of the mechanism to integrate personal and corporate taxation.

It is usually argued that deductions and credits are vehicles to achieve a number of different of objectives. Deductions are used to encourage savings for retirement and to remove from current income expenses required to earn current and future income. Credits are primarily used to redistribute income. Non-refundable credits differ from deductions in that they reduce tax at the lowest rather than the highest marginal rate and thus provide the same absolute benefits, but larger relative benefits to lower- than higher-income taxpayers.

Two refundable credits (credits that result in payments when income tax payable is zero) are, strictly speaking, outside the income tax system but are important vehicles for redistribution. The Goods and Services Tax (GST) credit is used to provide relief from the federal GST for low-income families and the value of the credit declines and ultimately vanishes as family income rises. The Canadian Child Tax Benefit (CCTB) provides benefits for low-income families with children and the value of this credit also declines and ultimately vanishes as family income rises. It has been argued that use of refundable credits has had the effect of moving the income tax system towards a NIT model (Boadway and Kitchen, 1999, 460). While this is probably true for the GST credit, the CCTB differs in one crucial respect: it is targeted whereas a NIT is, in principle, available to all.

Once taxable income is defined, a series of marginal tax rates is applied to a set of taxable income brackets. In 2002, federal tax was levied at 16 per cent on taxable income up to $31,677, at 22 per cent on income between $31,678 and $63,354, at 26 per cent on income between $63,355 and $103,000, and at 29 per cent on income over $103,000. The details of federal and provincial thresholds, brackets, and rates for 1995 and 2002 are provided in appendix 1.

Provincial income tax systems differ from the federal system in credits and tax rates and brackets. All except Quebec share the federal definition of taxable income and Quebec's definition is very similar. Provincial governments augment the federal credits as well as providing special credits of their own. The details of federal and provincial exemptions and credits are provided in appendix 2.

Recent PIT Reform Efforts

The personal income tax at the federal level was first imposed in 1917 as a temporary measure to finance the war effort. A major round of reforms was undertaken by the Mulroney government in 1987. The stated aims were to make the PIT simpler, fairer, and more efficient. Horizontal equity was addressed by broadening tax bases and reducing tax preferences. For example, the $1,000 interest income deduction was eliminated and sheltering of capital gains was reduced from one-half to one-quarter. Vertical equity was addressed by converting deductions to credits which gave the same dollar benefit regardless of income. To simplify the tax system, the number of brackets was reduced from ten to three, but the extensive use of surtaxes by federal and provincial governments and corresponding high marginal tax rates remained.

The 1987 PIT reforms were part of a larger tax reform package that saw the replacement of the manufacturers' sales tax with the GST in 1990. With the GST came the refundable GST credit for low-income individuals and families. Although not strictly part of the income tax system, this measure had the effect of increasing the progressivity of overall taxes on individuals.

In 1996 another round of PIT reform began, led by the newly elected Harris government in Ontario. Following the plan laid out in its 'Common Sense Revolution,' personal income taxes were cut by an average of 30 per cent (Hale, 2002, 332). Tax cuts were concentrated on low- and middle-income individuals and surtaxes, ostensibly to fund health care, were added on higher-income levels.

In 1997, in cooperation with the provinces, the federal government introduced the National Child Benefit Supplement (NCBS), a refundable tax credit targeted at lower-income families with children. Like the refundable GST credit, this income-tested measure is outside the PIT system. Indeed, it is probably better characterized as an expenditure program. In any case, it has the effect of further increasing incomes of low-income families with children. In some cases, the NCBS was augmented by complementary provincial measures.

The next major development in PIT reform occurred in 1998 in Alberta when the Klein government announced its intention to move to an 11 per cent (subsequently lowered to 10 per cent) single-rate tax with a substantially enlarged basic personal exemption. The move to a single-rate tax came as a result of the decision by the federal government to allow provinces participating in the tax collection agreements (which includes all provinces except Quebec) to levy taxes directly on federally defined taxable income rather than on federal tax.

Saskatchewan's Romanow government responded to the Alberta changes by substantially lowering, flattening, and simplifying its income tax rates over a four-year period beginning in 2000. Like Alberta, this was accompanied by a substantial increase in the basic personal exemption. Although the gap between Saskatchewan and Alberta taxation levels was not eliminated, it was reduced substantially, especially in the low- and middle-income ranges.

Unlike Ontario, which cut income taxes while running a deficit, tax reform in Alberta and Saskatchewan was portrayed to the public as part of the 'reward' for the sacrifices needed to eliminate provincial deficits. With the achievement of budget balance in Ottawa, in 2000 the federal government announced its own reward to taxpayers. Motivated, in part, by the growing gap between tax levels in Canada and the United States, especially at higher-income levels, the federal government reduced marginal rates and eliminated surtaxes over four years. Brackets were also broadened to increase the number of taxpayers subject to lower rates and to go some way to deal with the 'bracket creep' that had resulted from partial indexation for inflation. Full indexation for inflation was introduced to prevent future bracket creep. In the interest of preserving the progressivity of the PIT system, the basic personal exemption was increased substantially and CCTB was enhanced.

The Impact of PIT Reform on Redistribution

As discussed above, measurement of the progressivity of the PIT system is accomplished by comparing average tax rates at different income levels. All measures of progressivity are arbitrary to the extent that choices must be made regarding which income levels to compare. In this paper, such decisions are largely guided by the availability of data. Almost all data are taken from various editions of the Finances of the Nation published annually by the Canadian Tax Foundation and taxes on $10,000, $20,000, $50,000 and $100,000 of income are compared. Although some data are presented for the years 1980 and 1990 to show the impact of the 1987 reforms discussed above, our main focus is on the round of provincial and federal reforms that began in 1996, and for this reason we compare average tax rates in 1995 and 2002. To the extent possible, marginal rates reflect the clawback of credits as income rises.[2]

Federal PIT Changes

In table 1 we present average and marginal federal tax rates for a single taxpayer without dependants for selected years between 1980 and 2002 at four income levels. Over the period, both average and marginal rates at all income levels declined substantially. Focusing first on average rates we see that at the $10,000 income level, rates declined by about two-thirds from 8.2 to 2.9 per cent, while rates at the $100,000 income level declined by about one-third from 30.6 to 19.9 per cent. Turning to marginal tax rates, the decline at the $10,000 income level is slightly less a third from 21 to 14.9 per cent, while the decline at the $100,000 income level is exactly one third from 39 to 26 per cent.

The fact that the decline in marginal tax rates has been roughly proportional across income levels, while the decline in average rates has been proportionally larger at lower than higher incomes illustrates an important feature of the tax system. Specifically, it shows that progressivity is affected by rates, brackets, and the size of the low-income threshold – that is, the income level at which an individual begins to pay tax. Other things being equal, progressivity is increased (decreased) when marginal rates rise (fall), brackets are narrowed (expanded), or the low-income threshold rises (falls). In the PIT reforms since 1987 we have typically seen marginal rates fall, brackets expand, and low-income thresholds increase.

The impact of federal PIT reforms on progressivity is analysed in tables 2 and 3. Table 2 presents the change in average tax rates over three income ranges. The first column is lower-income range from $10,000 to $50,000, the second is upper-income range from $50,000 to $100,000 and the third is for the whole income range from $10,000 to $100,000. We see that the average tax schedule is more progressive over the lower-income range than the upper-income range, reflecting the tendency for average tax rates to flatten as income rises. A decline in progressivity over time is evident for both income ranges. Focusing on the post-1995 reforms we see that slope of the average tax schedule declined from 13.6 to 12 per cent over the $10,000–$50,000 range and from 6 to 5 per cent over the $50,000–$100,000 range. Over the lower-income range, this is offset, in part, by the federal government's move to targeted refundable credits outside the PIT system. Over the upper-income range, the flatting of the average tax schedule reflects the government's efforts to reduce top marginal rates.

Table 3 provides two measures of the dollar amount of redistribution. The first compares the federal tax paid at each income level to the average federal tax paid to measure the absolute amount of redistribution. The second compares the federal tax paid at each income level to the tax that would be paid if a simple proportional income tax was levied to measure the relative amount of redistribution. Because the amounts are unadjusted for inflation, caution should be used when comparing across time.

Looking first at the absolute measure of redistribution, we see that in 1980 taxpayers with income of $10,000 paid $1,252 or about 12.5 per cent of their income *less* in tax than the average amount paid. Taxpayers with income of $100,000 paid $29,065 or about 29 per cent of their income *more* in tax than the average amount. In 2002, the $10,000 income taxpayers paid about 51 per cent of their income *less* than the average amount while the $100,000 income taxpayers paid about 14.5 per cent of their income *more* than the average amount. The rise in

Table 1 Average and marginal tax rates (single taxpayer, no dependants)

Average federal tax rates, 1980–2002*

Year	$10,000 (%)	$20,000 (%)	$50,000 (%)	$100,000 (%)
1980	8.2	14.0	23.6	30.6
1990	6.2	12.1	19.3	24.9
1995	4.7	10.4	18.3	24.3
2002	2.9	8.9	14.9	19.9

*Actual Quebec figures differ by federal abatement
Figures exclude refundable credits.

Marginal federal tax rates, 1980–2002*

Year	$10,000 (%)	$20,000 (%)	$50,000 (%)	$100,000 (%)
1980	21.00	25.48	36.00	39.00
1990	17.85	17.85	27.30	31.32
1995	14.50	16.50	26.80	31.30
2002	14.90	14.90	22.00	26.00

*Actual Quebec figures differ by federal abatement
Source: Canadian Tax Foundation, *Finances of the Nation* (various)

Table 2 Change in federal average tax rates (single taxpayer, no dependants)

	$10,000–$50,000 (%)	$50,000–$100,000 (%)	$10,000–$100,000 (%)
1980	15.4	7.0	22.4
1990	13.1	5.6	18.8
1995	13.6	6.0	19.7
2002	12.0	5.0	17.0

Source: Authors' calculation

average incomes over time together with the rise in the average tax rate permitted individuals at both ends of income range to be relatively better off in 2002 than in 1980 or 1995.

Turning to the relative measure, we see the amount of redistribution that took place based on a different benchmark. If the counterfactual in the absolute measure is that all taxpayers pay the same tax, the counterfactual in the relative measure is that all taxpayers pay a proportional tax where the proportional rate is set at the average tax rate.

Table 3 Federal PIT redistribution relative to average and proportional tax
(single taxpayer, no dependants)

Federal PIT redistribution relative to average tax (current dollars)

Income	1980	1990	1995	2002
10,000	1,252	3,702	4,153	5,092
20,000	(791)	1,896	2,536	3,602
50,000	(10,114)	(5,324)	(4,526)	(2,087)
100,000	(29,065)	(20,597)	(19,708)	(14,553)
Average income	20,441	31,430	34,688	42,488
Average federal tax	2,134	4,317	4,619	5,386

Federal PIT redistribution relative to proportional tax (current dollars)

Income	1980	1990	1995	2002
10,000	162	759	866	974
20,000	(837)	326	580	751
50,000	(7,028)	(2,773)	(2,487)	(1,135)
100,000	(20,759)	(11,177)	(11,011)	(7,262)
Proportional tax rate	10.4%	13.7%	13.3%	12.7%

Source: Authors' calculations

In 1980 the $10,000 income taxpayers paid $162 or 1.6 per cent of their income less than the proportional tax, while the $100K income taxpayers paid $20,759 or about 20.8 per cent of their income more than proportional tax. In 2002, the $10,000 taxpayers paid about 9.7 per cent of their income less than the proportional tax, while the $100,000 taxpayers paid about 7.3 per cent of their income more than the proportional tax. Once again, the relative improvement at both low and high incomes reflects both rises in incomes and average tax rates over time.

Provincial PIT Changes

Average and marginal provincial tax rates at different income levels for a single taxpayer without dependants in 1995 and 2002 are presented in table 4. Looking first at average rates for 1995, we see substantial variation (as measured by the range) across provinces at all four income levels. On average, rates are progressive and the absolute amount of variation increases with income. Comparing 1995 with 2002 average rates, we see that variation (as measured by the range) across provinces has declined at all four income levels. Thus, one result of the post-1995 PIT reforms is the convergence of average tax rates across provinces.

The pattern is repeated with marginal rates. The average of provincial marginal rates declined substantially from 1995 to 2002 at all income levels and the proportional decline at the lowest income levels was the greatest. As with average rates, provincial marginal rates also tended towards convergence over the reform period. Interestingly however, the absolute amount of variation of marginal rates is greatest at lower-income levels, the reverse of the situation for average rates.

Our measure of progressivity, the change in average tax rates over selected ranges, is presented in table 5. On average across provinces the overall progressivity of tax rates (i.e., from $10,000 to $100,000) is slightly higher post-reform. Broken down into lower- and higher-income ranges, we see that, on average across provinces, rates over $10,000–$50,000 become more progressive, while rates over the $50,000–$100,000 range became slightly less progressive as a result of reform. This is in contrast to the federal pattern which shows a decline in progressivity over both income ranges.

Provinces exhibited wide variations in the degree of progressivity both before and after the reform period, although, overall, the degree of progressivity across provinces has tended towards convergence. Focusing on 2002, Quebec is the province with the highest degree of overall PIT progressivity, followed by the Atlantic provinces and Manitoba, while Ontario and the three most western provinces generally have lower progressivity. The differences in progressivity are largely the result of differences in average rates at the top end of the income range, so that low-income taxpayers are treated in a roughly equivalent fashion across the provinces.

Table 5 reveals an interesting divergence among provinces regarding the direction of reform. Over the reform period, the Atlantic provinces, and to a lesser extent Ontario and Manitoba, actually increased the overall progressivity of their PIT. In contrast, Quebec, and to a lesser extent the four most western provinces, reduced the overall progressivity of their PIT.

As with our analysis of federal PIT reforms, table 6 provides two measures of the dollar amount of PIT redistribution taking place across provinces. Because of complications arising from the federal abate-

Table 4 Average and marginal provincial tax rates, 1995, 2002 (single taxpayer, no dependants)

Average provincial tax rates, 1995 (%)

Income	NF	NS	NB	PEI	QC	ON	MB	SK	AB	BC	Average	Range
10,000	5.1	3.1	5.3	5.1	3.4	5.7	4.9	4.6	2.0	4.7	4.4	3.7
20,000	8.3	7.3	7.8	8.3	11.5	7.6	9.1	8.7	6.3	6.8	8.2	5.2
50,000	12.3	10.6	11.4	12.3	17.8	10.3	12.0	12.2	8.7	9.3	11.7	9.1
100,000	15.9	14.1	14.9	15.9	22.1	15.5	15.4	16.3	11.6	14.8	15.7	10.5

*Excludes federal refundable credits for consistency with 2002
Source: *Finances of the Nation 1995*, Table 3:16

Average provincial tax rates, 2002 (%)

Income	NF	NS	NB	PEI	QC	ON	MB	SK	AB	BC	Average	Range
10,000	2.2	0.0	0.0	0.0	0.2	0.0	0.8	1.7	0.0	0.8	0.6	2.2
20,000	6.0	5.4	5.4	5.6	6.2	3.3	6.0	6.1	2.7	3.2	5.0	3.5
50,000	10.8	10.0	9.6	9.4	12.0	5.9	10.4	9.7	6.8	5.9	9.0	6.1
100,000	14.9	13.5	12.8	13.5	15.8	10.5	13.6	12.4	8.4	9.2	12.4	7.4

*Excludes refundable credits for consistency with 2002
Source: *Finances of the Nation 1995*, Table 3:16

Marginal provincial tax rates, 1995 (%)

Income	NF	NS	NB	PEI	QC	ON	MB	SK	AB	BC	Average	Range
10,000	11.1	9.6	10.3	9.6	21.0	27.9	13.3	15.0	11.7	8.4	13.8	19.5
20,000	11.1	9.6	10.3	9.6	20.2	9.3	12.3	11.0	7.8	8.4	11.0	12.4
50,000	17.9	15.4	16.6	15.4	25.7	15.1	17.5	18.7	13.3	13.6	16.9	12.4
100,000	20.0	19.0	20.1	19.0	26.4	21.9	19.1	20.6	14.8	22.9	20.4	11.6

Source: *Finances of the Nation 1995*, Table 3:12

Marginal provincial tax rates, 2002 (%)

Income	NF	NS	NB	PEI	QC	ON	MB	SK	AB	BC	Average	Range
10,000	9.8	–	–	–	12.2	–	11.1	10.5	–	5.6	4.9	12.2
20,000	9.8	14.1	9.0	9.1	12.2	5.6	11.1	10.5	9.3	5.6	9.6	8.5
50,000	16.2	15.0	14.8	13.8	16.4	9.2	15.4	13.3	10.0	9.2	13.3	7.2
100,000	19.6	16.7	16.5	18.4	19.7	17.4	17.4	15.5	10.0	13.7	16.5	9.7

Source: *Finances of the Nation 1995*, Table 3:12

Table 5 Changes in provincial ATRs (single taxpayer, no dependants)

Change in provincial ATRs: $10,000–$50,000 (%)

Income	NF	NS	NB	PEI	QC	ON	MB	SK	AB	BC	Average	Range
1995	7.2	7.5	6.0	7.2	14.4	4.6	7.1	7.6	6.7	4.6	7.3	9.8
2002	8.6	10.0	9.6	9.4	11.8	5.9	9.7	8.0	6.8	5.1	8.5	6.6
Change	1.4	2.5	3.6	2.2	-2.6	1.3	2.5	0.4	0.2	0.5	1.2	-3.1

Change in provincial ATRs: $50,000–$100,000 (%)

Income	NF	NS	NB	PEI	QC	ON	MB	SK	AB	BC	Average	Range
1995	3.7	3.6	3.5	3.7	4.3	5.2	3.4	4.0	2.9	5.5	4.0	2.6
2002	4.1	3.5	3.2	4.1	3.8	4.6	3.2	2.7	1.6	3.3	3.4	3.0
Change	0.4	-0.1	-0.3	0.4	-0.4	-0.7	-0.2	-1.3	-1.3	-2.2	-0.6	0.4

Change in provincial ATRs: $10,000–$100,000 (%)

Income	NF	NS	NB	PEI	QC	ON	MB	SK	AB	BC	Average	Range
1995	10.9	11.0	9.6	10.9	18.6	9.8	10.5	11.7	9.6	10.1	11.3	9.1
2002	12.7	13.5	12.8	13.5	15.6	10.5	12.9	10.7	8.4	8.4	11.9	7.2
Change	1.8	2.5	3.3	2.6	-3.0	0.7	2.3	-1.0	-1.2	-1.7	0.6	-1.9

ment and the fact that it collects its own income tax, we omit Quebec figures from this table due to a lack of comparability. Caution in interpreting comparisons across provinces and across time is warranted for three reasons. First, data are unadjusted for inflation. Second, each province has a different average income. Third, each province has a different average tax rate.

Looking first at the absolute measure of redistribution, we see that in 1995 provincial taxpayers with $10,000 income paid between 13 (PEI) and 24 (Ontario) per cent of their income *less* than the average amount paid in their province. Taxpayers with $100,000 income paid between 12 (Alberta) and 16 (Saskatchewan) per cent *more* than the average amount paid in their province. In 2002, with average incomes higher and average provincial tax rates lower, provincial taxpayers with $10,000 income paid between 21 (PEI) and 27 (Nova Scotia) per cent of their income *less* than the average amount paid in their province. Taxpayers with $100,000 income paid between 8 (Alberta) and 15 (Newfoundland) per cent *more* than the average amount paid in their province. It is important to note that the differences between the provinces are a result of three factors: different degrees of progressivity, different average incomes, and different average levels of taxation.

Turning to our measure of relative redistribution (with the counterfactual again being a proportional tax), we see that in 1995, provincial taxpayers with $10,000 income paid between roughly 1.5 (PEI) and 4.5 (Alberta) per cent *less* of their income in tax than would be the case under a proportional tax in their province. Taxpayers with $100,000 income paid between roughly 5 (Alberta) and 9.4 (PEI) per cent of their income *more* than under a proportional tax in their province.

Looking at 2002, we see that provincial taxpayers with $10,000 income paid between roughly 4.4 (Saskatchewan) and 7.5 (Nova Scotia) per cent *less* of their income in tax than would be the case under a proportional tax in their province. Taxpayers with $100,000 income paid between roughly 3.1 (Alberta) and 7.2 (Newfoundland) per cent *more* than under a proportional tax in their province. Again, it is important to remember that the differences between the provinces are a result of three factors: different degrees of progressivity, different average incomes, and different average levels of taxation.

Table 6 Provincial redistribution relative to average and proportional tax, 1995 and 2002 (single taxpayer, no dependants)

Provincial redistribution relative to average tax, 1995 (current dollars)

Income	NF	NS	NB	PEI	QC*	ON	MB	SK	AB	BC
10,000	1,810	1,801	1,698	1,272	–	2,443	1,917	2,060	2,142	2,183
20,000	(1,665)	(1,463)	(1,559)	(1,665)	–	(1,511)	(1,814)	(1,732)	(1,266)	(1,364)
50,000	(6,126)	(5,283)	(5,682)	(6,126)	–	(5,150)	(6,017)	(6,124)	(4,333)	(4,661)
100,000	(15,942)	(14,122)	(14,889)	(15,942)	–	(15,520)	(15,414)	(16,265)	(11,573)	(14,804)
Average income	28,713	30,360	29,401	27,247	–	37,184	30,937	30,943	36,135	36,028
Average provincial tax	2,319	2,110	2,231	1,781	–	3,014	2,407	2,520	2,342	2,656

Provincial redistribution relative to average tax, 2002 (current dollars)

Income	NF	NS	NB	PEI	QC	ON	MB	SK	AB	BC
10,000	2,349	2,748	2,409	2,092	–	2,899	2,729	2,489	2,533	2,373
20,000	(1,202)	(1,079)	(1,079)	(1,115)	–	(658)	(1,190)	(1,213)	(545)	(642)
50,000	(5,375)	(4,988)	(4,798)	(4,695)	–	(2,953)	(5,217)	(4,840)	(3,413)	(2,963)
100,000	(14,861)	(13,482)	(12,831)	(13,463)	–	(10,468)	(13,617)	(12,365)	(8,413)	(9,203)
Average income	33,418	36,771	34,499	32,058	–	46,469	36,927	43,611	47,796	41,428
Average provincial tax	2,568	2,748	2,409	2,092	–	2,899	2,805	2,655	2,533	2,453

Provincial redistribution relative to proportional tax, 1995 (current dollars)

Income	NF	NS	NB	PEI	QC	ON	MB	SK	AB	BC
10,000	299	386	226	145	—	240	288	354	448	264
20,000	(49)	(73)	(41)	(357)	—	110	(258)	(103)	30	110
50,000	(2,087)	(1,807)	(1,888)	(2,857)	—	(1,097)	(2,127)	(2,052)	(1,092)	(975)
100,000	(7,864)	(7,170)	(7,300)	(9,404)	—	(7,413)	(7,633)	(8,120)	(5,092)	(7,432)
Proportional tax rate	8.1%	7.0%	7.6%	6.5%	—	8.1%	7.8%	8.1%	6.5%	7.4%

Provincial redistribution relative to proportional tax, 2002 (current dollars)

Income	NF	NS	NB	PEI	QC	ON	MB	SK	AB	BC
10,000	549	747	698	652	—	624	684	443	530	512
20,000	335	415	317	190	—	590	329	5	515	542
50,000	(1,533)	(1,252)	(1,307)	(1,433)	—	166	(1,418)	(1,796)	(763)	(2)
100,000	(7,178)	(6,010)	(5,849)	(6,938)	—	(4,230)	(6,020)	(6,277)	(3,114)	(3,282)
Proportional tax rate	7.7%	7.5%	7.0%	6.5%	—	6.2%	7.6%	6.1%	5.3%	5.9%

*Quebec data not comparable as a result of Quebec abatement and separate tax collection.
Source: Authors' calculations

Federal and Provincial Taxation of Families

Unlike the United States, Canada does not have joint filing of tax returns (sometimes called 'income splitting') by spouses. In a progressive tax system, the impact of joint filing is to 'average' incomes across spouses and thereby reduce the total amount of tax payable by the family (Boadway and Kitchen, 1999, 170). Despite the absence of joint filing, both the federal and provincial income tax systems do include a number of measures aimed specifically at families. Further, some of the income-tested measures outside the PIT system rely on family income to determine eligibility.

From appendix 2, we see that at the federal level, families are provided with non-refundable, income-tested credits for spouses and infirm adult dependants. Outside the PIT system, the income-tested GST credit takes into account family composition, as does the income-tested CCTB and NCBS (National Child Benefit Supplement). Provinces augment the federal credits with a number of refundable and non-refundable credits of their own. Post-1995 the federal government and some provinces enhanced selected income-tested refundable and non-refundable credits to increase progressivity, especially at lower incomes.

We analyse the impact of 2002 federal GST credits and the income-tested child benefits on two family types in table 7. For comparison purposes, in the first panel we show first the impact of the GST credit on a single individual. We see that the impact of the GST credit is felt at the $10,000 and $20,000 annual income levels but not at incomes of $50,000 or $100,000. Comparing the average rates (including the credits) with the average rates found in table 1, we see that the rate on $10,000 annual income is essentially zero and the rate on $20,000 annual income has fallen from 8.9 to 7.3 per cent. Progressivity at the low end of the income spectrum and overall likewise increases.

In the second panel of table 7 we examine a single-earner family with spouse and two dependent children. The impact of the CCTB is substantial – essentially creating a negative income tax for families. At the $10,000 annual income level, net taxes are substantially negative, with an average rate of about 55 per cent. At the $20,000 annual income level, the average rate is again negative at about 24 per cent. Even at the $50,000 annual income level, the net average tax rate is 9.5 per cent compared with 14.9 per cent for the single taxpayer. Consequently, progressivity is increased sharply when the CCTB is included in the measure.

Table 7 Tax rates, 2002

A. Single taxpayer – no dependants

Average Federal Tax Rates, 2002 (per cent)

Income	Quebec	Other Provinces		GST credits	
10,000	–0.3	0.2		10,000	275
20,000	5.8	7.3		20,000	325
50,000	12.5	14.9		50,000	–
100,000	16.6	19.9		100,000	–

Source: *Finances of the Nation 2002* and SaskFinar

Change in Federal Average Tax Rate (per cent)

Income	Quebec	Other Provinces
$10K–$50K	12.8	14.8
$50K–$100K	4.2	5.0
$10K–$100K	16.9	19.7

Source: Authors' calculation

B. Married taxpayers – one income, spouse and two dependants

Average Federal Tax Rates, 2002 (per cent)

Income	Quebec	Other Provinces		GST/CCTB credits	
10,000	–55.6	–55.6		10,000	5,560
20,000	–24.7	–24.1		20,000	5,560
50,000	7.4	9.5		50,000	1,678
100,000	15.8	18.9		100,000	–

Source: *Finances of the Nation 2002* and SaskFinar

Change in Federal Average Tax Rate (per cent)

Income	Quebec	Other Provinces
$10K–$50K	63.0	65.1
$50K–$100K	8.4	9.4
$10K–$100K	71.4	74.5

Source: Authors' calculation

C. Married taxpayers – two incomes (60/40), two dependants

Average Federal Tax Rates, 2002 (per cent)

Income	Quebec	Other Provinces		GST/CTB credits
10,000	–55.6	–55.6	10,000	5,560
20,000	–25.3	–24.8	20,000	5,560
50,000	5.1	6.8	50,000	1,678
100,000	12.5	14.9	100,000	–

Source: *Finances of the Nation 2002* and SaskFinance

Change in Federal Average Tax Rate (per cent)

Income	Quebec	Other Provinces
$10K–$50K	60.7	62.4
$50K–$100K	7.4	8.2
$10K–$100K	68.1	70.5

Source: Authors' calculation

In the final panel, we examine a dual-earner family with two dependent children. The results essentially mirror the results for the single-earner family at the $10,000 and $20,000 annual income levels. Average rates are lower for the dual-income family at the higher levels, reflecting the progressive nature of the personal tax system itself.

Summary

The findings of this study are easily summarized. Post-1995 reforms have rendered the federal PIT system less progressive, but increased the amount of income being redistributed through the tax system to lower-income Canadians. This result holds even without including enhanced refundable GST and child benefit credits. Redistribution, especially to families, is further augmented through these refundable credits. Lower marginal and average rates at middle- and upper-income levels have improved work incentives for taxpayers in those income ranges. These changes are consistent with normative prescriptions of optimal income tax theory when a high weight is placed on the welfare of low-income individuals. The use of non-refundable credits has focused the benefits of such measures on lower-income taxpayers and targeted redistribution towards lower-income families with children.

Post-1995 changes in provincial PIT systems have led to some convergence across provinces. However, substantial variation remains, especially among marginal rates at lower income levels. Six of ten provincial PIT systems have become more progressive overall, but an examination of the two sub-ranges shows that, in general, provincial systems have become more progressive over the $10,000–$50,000 range and less progressive over the $50,000–$100,000 range. This change in overall progressivity is in contrast to the direction of federal reforms, but may simply reflect Ottawa's greater reliance on refundable credits outside the PIT system to redistribute income post-1995.

Quebec's PIT system is most progressive, followed by the systems of the Atlantic provinces, Manitoba, and Ontario. Differences in progressivity across provinces are largely a result of differences in average rates at higher income levels. Average tax rates for low-income taxpayers are roughly equivalent across provinces. While they redistribute less than other provinces, Saskatchewan, Alberta, and British Columbia impose the smallest tax burden on low-income taxpayers.

APPENDIX 1

PIT Thresholds – 1995

Gov't	Income, $	Significance
Fed	6,749	Basic federal tax is greater than zero from $6,749 and above.
	63,438	5% surtax on basic federal tax in excess of $12,500
PEI	92,777	10% surtax on provincial tax above $12,500 starts at this amount.
NS	8,846	No provincial tax charges below this level.
	78,288	10% surtax on provincial tax above $10,000 starts at this amount.
NB	93,701	8% surtax on provincial tax above $13,500 starts at this amount.
QC	10,069	No provincial tax charges below this level.
	33,942	5% surtax on provincial tax in the range of $5000 and $10,000 starts at this amount.
	55,269	10% surtax on provincial tax above $10,000 starts at this amount.
ON	8,957	No provincial tax charges below this level.
	52,324	20% surtax on provincial tax in the range of $5,000 and $8,000 starts at this amount.
	67,897	30% surtax on provincial tax above $8,000 starts at this amount.
MB	8,868	No provincial tax charges below this amount.
	30,001	2% surtax on net income above $30,000 starts at this amount.
SK	7,399	No tax charges below this level.
	12,891	10% surtax on the sum of provincial basic tax and flat tax below $4,000 starts at this amount.
	40,371	25% surtax on the sum of provincial tax and flat tax above $4,000 starts at this amount.
AB	9,994	No provincial tax charges below this level.
	45,438	8% surtax on provincial tax above $3,500 starts at this amount.
BC	7,344	No provincial tax charges below this level.
	54,680	30% surtax on provincial tax in the range of $5,300 and $9,000 starts at this amount.
	79,447	50% surtax on provincial tax above $9,000 starts at this amount.
	67,188	5% surtax on provincial tax above $6,000 starts at this amount.

Source: *Finances of the Nation 1995* – Table 3.13

PIT Thresholds, 2002

Government	Income, $	Significance
Fed	8,030	Federal tax is greater than zero at this amount
NF	7,790	Provincial tax is greater than zero.
	60,175	9% surtax on provincial tax above $7,032 starts at this amount.
PEI	10,535	No provincial tax charges below this level.
	53,695	10% surtax on provincial tax above $5,200 begins at this amount.
NS	10,895	No provincial tax charges below this level.
	81,045	10% surtax on provincial tax above $10,000 starts at this amount.
NB	11,005	No provincial tax charges below this level.
QC	9,545	No provincial tax charges below this level.
ON	11,165	No provincial tax charges below this level.
	58,030	20% surtax on provincial tax above $3,685 starts at this amount.
	67,685	Additional 36% surtax on provincial tax above $4,648 starts at this amount.
MB	9,330	No provincial tax charges below this level.
SK	8,425	Provincial tax is greater than zero.
AB	14,160	Provincial tax is greater than zero.
BC	8,610	Provincial tax is greater than zero.

Source: *Finances of the Nation 2002* – Table 3.13

Federal taxable income brackets, 1995

Rate %	Brackets
17	From $0 to $29,590
26	From $29,591 to $59,180
29	From $59,181 and above

Source: *Finances of the Nation 1995* – Table 3.4

Quebec taxable income brackets, 1995

Rate %	Brackets
16	From $0 to $7,000
19	From $7,000 to $14,000
21	From $14,000 to $23,000
23	From $23,000 to $50,000
24	Over $50,000

5% surtax on provincial tax payable between $5,000 and $10,000
10% surtax on provincial tax payable over $10,000

Source: *Finances of the Nation 1995*

Provincial PIT as a percentage of basic federal tax, 1995

Province	Basic PIT, % of basic federal tax	Flat tax, % of net income	Surtaxes, % of provincial tax payable
NF	69.0	–	–
PEI	59.5	–	10% on the amount payable over $12,500
NS	59.5	–	10% on the amount payable over $10,000
NB	64.0	–	8% on amount payable above $13,500
ON	58.0	–	– 20% on the amount payable in the range of $5,500 and $8,000; – 30% on the amount payable above $8,000
MB	52.0	2.0	2% on the net income above $30,000
SK	50.0	2.0	– 10% on sum of basic provincial tax and flat tax below $4,000 – 25% on sum of basic provincial tax and flat tax above $4,000
AB	45.5	0.5	8% on amount payable over $3,500
BC	52.5	–	– 30% on amount in the range of $5,300 and $9,000 – 50% on amount payable above $9,000

Source: *Finances of the Nation 1995* – Table 3.9

Federal taxable income brackets, 2002

Rate %	Brackets
16	From $0 to $31,677
22	From $31,678 to $63,354
26	From $63,355 to $103,000
29	Above $103,000

Source: *Finances of the Nation 2002* – Table 3.4

Provincial PIT Brackets, 2002

Province	Tax Brackets	Rate %	Surtax, % of provincial tax payable
NF	From $0 to $29,590	10.57	9% on amount over $7,032
	From $29,591 to $59,180	16.16	
	Above $59,180	18.02	
PEI	From $0 to $30,754	9.80	10% on amount over $5,200
	From $30,755 to $61,509	13.80	
	Above $61,509	16.70	
NS	From $0 to $29,590	9.77	10% on amount over $10,000
	From $29,591 to $59,180	14.95	
	Above $59,180	16.67	
NB	From $0 to $31,677	9.68	na
	From $31,678 to $63,354	14.82	
	From $63,355 to $103,000	16.52	
	Above $103,000	17.84	
QC	From $0 to $ 26,700	16.00	na
	From $26,701 to $53,405	20.00	
	Above $53,405	24.00	
ON	From $0 to $30,892	6.05	20% on amount over $3,685 36% on amount over $4,648
	From $30,983 to $63,786	9.15	
	Above $63,786	11.16	
MB	From $0 to $30,544	10.90	na
	From $30,545 to $65,000	15.40	
	Above $65,000	17.40	
SK	From $0 to $30,000	11.25	na
	From $30,001 to $60,000	13.25	

Provincial PIT Brackets, 200

Province	Tax Brackets	Rate %	Surtax, % of provincial tax payable
	Above $60,000	15.50	
AB	10% tax on taxable income		na
BC	From $0 to $31,124	6.05	na
	From $31,125 to $62,249	9.15	
	From $62,250 to $71,470	11.70	
	From $71,471 to $86,785	13.70	
	Above $86,785	14.70	
	From $31,678 to $63,354	9.68	
	From $63,355 to $103,000	11.44	
	Above $103,000	12.76	

Source: *Finances of the Nation 2002* – Table 3.9 For Quebec, information is taken from Table 3.10 of the same edition

APPENDIX 2

Selected Federal Credits and Deductions, 1995
Non-refundable
Basic ($1,098)
Spousal ($915 – income tested on spousal income)
Infirm dependants over 17 ($269)
Senior ($592)
Disability ($720)
Refundable
GST credit (income tested – for single individual: $270 @ $10,000, $304 @ $20,000, $0 @ $50,000)
Child tax benefit (income tested – for family of four with children 6 and 12: $2,753 @ $10,000, $2,753 @ $20,000, $1,049@ 50,000, $0 @ $100,000)

Selected Provincial Credits and Deductions, 1995
Nova Scotia
Low-income tax reduction (maximum $200 for single individuals)
Seniors (refundable – maximum $300)

Quebec (separate tax collection)
Basic ($1,180)
Person living alone ($210)
Married person ($1,180)
Single-parent family ($260)
Dependent children ($520 for first and $480 for subsequent
Other dependants ($480)
Infirm dependants ($700)
Direct ascendant over 70 yrs living with family ($550, refundable)
Physical or mental handicap ($440)
Over 65 yrs ($440)
Families (income tested – maximum of $1,500)
Low-income (income tested, complex formulae)
Sales tax (income tested – maximum of $104 for single individual)

Ontario
Low-income tax reduction (no tax payable for tax liability up to $205, more with dependants)
Refundable sales tax credits for individuals, families and seniors (income tested, complex formula)

Manitoba
Low-income tax reduction (income tested – maximum $430 for single
    individual)
Cost-of-living tax credit (refundable, income tested – maximum $190 for single
    individual plus $110 for seniors, $110 for disabled, $25 for dependants and
    $60 for disabled dependants)

Saskatchewan
Low-income deduction (income tested, maximum $200 for single individual
plus $300 for dependent spouse, $250 for dependent child under 18 and $200
for seniors)

Alberta
Low-income tax reduction (income tested)

British Columbia
Refundable sales tax credit (income tested – maximum of $50 per family
    member)

Selected Federal Credits and Deductions, 2002
Non-refundable
Basic ($1,221)
Spousal ($1,037 – income tested on spousal income)
Infirm dependents over 17 ($577)
Senior ($596)
Disability ($989)
Refundable
GST credit (income tested – for single individual: $274 @ $10,000, $321 @
    $20,000, $0 @ $50,000)
Child tax benefit (income tested – enhanced over 1995, complex formula)

Selected Provincial Credits and Deductions, 2002
Quebec (separate tax collection)
Basic ($1,212)
Person living alone ($216)
Married person ($1,212)
Single-parent family ($267)
Dependent children ($534 for first and $493 for subsequent)
Other dependants ($493)
Direct ascendant over 70 yrs living with family ($550, refundable)
Physical or mental handicap ($440)

Over 65 yrs ($440)
Families (income tested – maximum of $1,500)
Low-income (income tested, complex formulae)
Sales tax (income tested – maximum of $106 for single individual)

Ontario
Refundable sales tax credits for individuals, families and seniors
(income tested, complex formula)

Manitoba
Cost-of-living tax credit (refundable, income tested – maximum $190 for single
individual plus $110 for seniors, $110 for disabled, $25 for dependants and $60
for disabled dependants)

Saskatchewan
Refundable sales tax credit (income tested)

Alberta
Family employment tax credit (income tested)

British Columbia
Sales tax credit

NOTES

The views expressed in this paper are our own and should not be attributed to
any other individual or organization. We are grateful to Thomas Courchene,
David Duff, and David Perry for their comments and to EnCana for financial
support of this research.

1 Examples of broader examination of tax redistribution include Vermaeten et
   al. (1994) and Ruggeri et al. (1994).
2 It is important to note that the average PIT rates presented in tables 1–5 do
   not include the impact of the refundable GST credit and provincial sales tax
   credits which provide income-tested relief from sales taxes, or the CCTB or
   NCBS which are income-tested expenditure programs targeted at low-
   income families with children. These programs are examined separately at
   the end of the section.

REFERENCES

Boothe, Paul. 2003. 'Income Tax Competition in a Federation: Evidence from a Natural Experiment.' Paper presented at the Banca d'Italia Fiscal Policy Workshop, Perugia, April.
Boadway, Robin and Harry Kitchen. 1999. *Canadian Tax Policy*, 3rd ed. Canadian Tax Paper #103, Toronto: Canadian Tax Foundation.
Hale, Geoffrey. 2002. *The Politics of Taxation in Canada*. Toronto: Broadview Press.
Mirrlees, James. 1971. 'An Exploration in the Theory of Optimum Income Taxation,' *Review of Economic Studies* 38: 175–208.
Rosen, Harvey, Paul Boothe, Bev Dahlby, and Roger Smith. 1998. *Public Finance in Canada*. Toronto: McGraw-Hill Ryerson.
Ruggeri, Giuseppe, Donald Van Wart, and Robert Howard. 1994. 'The Redistributional Impact of Taxation in Canada.' *Canadian Tax Journal* 42: 417–41.
Treff, Karin and David Perry. 1995. *Finances of the Nation 1995*. Toronto: Canadian Tax Foundation.
– 2002. *Finances of the Nation 2002*. Toronto: Canadian Tax Foundation.
Vermaeten, Frank, W. Irwin Gillespie, and Arndt Vermaeten. 1994. 'Tax Incidence in Canada.' *Canadian Tax Journal* 42: 348–16.

Taxation, Redistribution, and Fiscal Federalism

DAVID G. DUFF

In this comment, I wish to discuss broader issues related to taxation and redistribution in the Canadian federation arising from Paul Boothe and Katherine Boothe's paper. In order to do so, I intend to address the following three questions:

1. Should the tax system generally and the personal income tax in particular redistribute economic resources, and if so how?
2. If we think that economic resources should be redistributed among individuals and/or among regions, can we say anything about the level of government that should be responsible for this task?
3. What implications do different methods of redistribution have for Canadian constitutional law and what implications does Canadian constitutional law have for different methods of redistribution?

Taxation and Redistribution

Beginning with the subject of taxation and redistribution, it is important to emphasize at the outset that it is somewhat artificial to talk about the tax system redistributing economic resources without considering the kinds of expenditures to which tax revenues are devoted. Indeed, by means of direct transfers as well as program spending, modern governments tend to affect the distribution of economic resources through expenditure decisions much more than tax policy.

Nonetheless, it is useful to consider the redistributive role of taxation for two reasons. First, in theory and in practice, taxes may be integrated with redistributive transfers, which may themselves be delivered through the tax system. Second, and more importantly, the choice of different taxes and the design of these taxes can have a significant impact on the distribution of economic resources, regardless of the manner in which the resulting revenues are spent.

On this basis, at least two arguments are commonly made in favour of redistributive taxation: first, that redistributive taxation is necessary in order to implement a particular conception of distributive justice;[1] second, irrespective of more substantive conceptions of distributive justice, taxes are allocated fairly where they apply more heavily to those with greater economic resources or ability to pay than to those with fewer resources and a lesser taxable capacity.[2] As a general rule, moreover, income is viewed as the most appropriate measure for redistribution through taxation, though tax scholars continue to debate the relative merits of income and consumption for this purpose, as they have at least since the time of Thomas Hobbes,[3] and much consideration is also devoted to the taxation of wealth and/or the transfer of wealth particularly from one generation to the next.[4]

With respect to income, redistributive taxation is often assumed to require progressive rates, which impose proportionately higher taxes on those with higher annual incomes.[5] Nonetheless income taxes can be redistributive even if they are levied at flat or declining rates, since those with more income may still pay more tax than those with less income.[6] With respect to progressivity, moreover, it is important to distinguish between *marginal* rates which apply to the last dollar received at different income levels, and *average* rates which apply to taxpayers' aggregate incomes at different income levels. While marginal tax rates are generally assumed to affect taxpayers' behavioural responses to taxation, average tax rates determine the overall distribution of the income tax at different income levels. In order to appreciate the significance of marginal and average tax rates, it is useful to consider Figure 1.

The first line in the legend shows a 'progressive marginal rate structure' with a basic personal exemption of $10,000, and rates of 10 per cent on taxable income up to $30,000, 20 per cent on taxable income between $30,000 and $60,000, 30 per cent on taxable income between $60,000 and $100,000, and 40 per cent on taxable income exceeding $100,000. From these marginal rates, it is possible to define average tax rates (total tax divided by total taxable income) at different levels of taxable income, which are represented by the second line in the legend. Unlike marginal rates that increase in discrete steps, average rates increase gradually as taxable income increases – approaching the top

Figure 1. Marginal and average rates for different rate structures

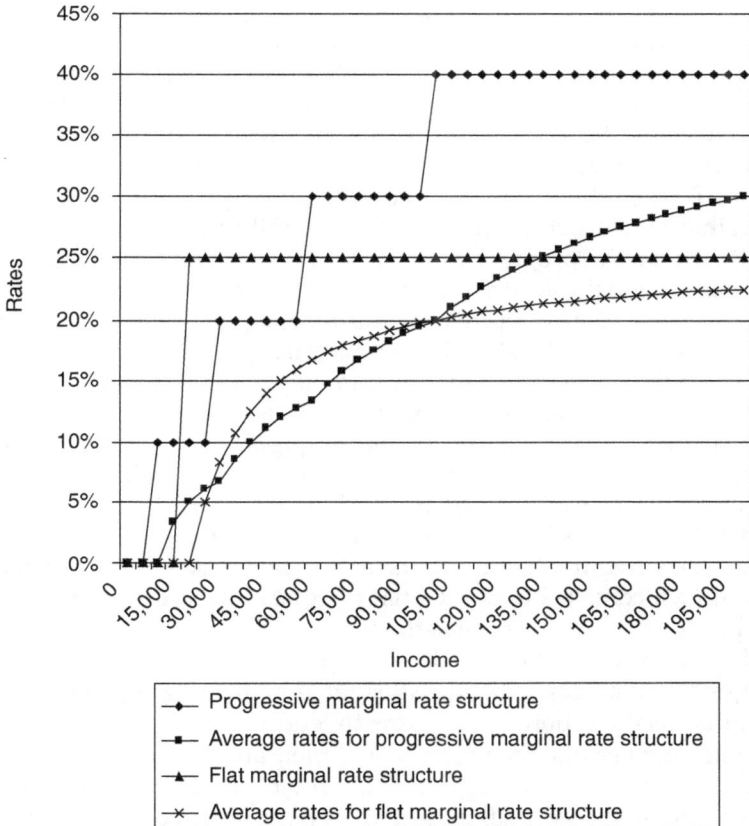

marginal rate at very high income levels, but always less than this rate on account of the basic personal exemption and the lower marginal rates that apply to lower 'slices' of taxable income.

In contrast to this progressive marginal rate structure, the third line in the legend portrays a 'flat marginal rate structure' with a basic personal exemption of $20,000 and a single marginal rate of 25 per cent on taxable income exceeding this amount. Although purely illustrative, the choice of these figures is intended to isolate the effect of different rate structures (as opposed to the level of tax rates) by defining an alternative rate structure that might be expected to raise revenues roughly comparable to the progressive marginal rate structure. The fourth line in the legend demonstrates the average tax rates associated with this alternative rate structure.

Comparing the two sets of average tax rates defined by these different rate structures, there are four points worth noting. First, despite the fact that the flat rate marginal rate structure has a single marginal rate, the effect of the exemption creates progressive average rates that increase as taxable income increases. Second, for taxable incomes between $20,000 and $60,000, the average rates produced by the flat marginal rate structure increase more rapidly than the average rates produced by the progressive marginal rate structure, suggesting that the flat marginal rate structure is more progressive than the progressive marginal rate structure over this income range. Third, for taxable incomes exceeding $60,000, the average rates produced by the flat marginal rate structure increase more gradually than the average rates produced by the progressive marginal rate structure, suggesting that the flat marginal rate structure is less progressive than the progressive marginal rate structure at higher incomes. Finally, while those with taxable incomes less than $26,667 and more than $100,000 pay less tax under the flat marginal rate structure than under the progressive marginal rate structure, those with taxable incomes between these ranges pay more income tax under the flat marginal rate structure than under the progressive marginal rate structure.

Returning to Boothe and Boothe's paper, the relationship between marginal and average tax rates illustrated in the diagram makes it easier to understand both the reforms to federal and provincial personal income tax rates that they recount and their impact on overall progressivity. Beginning with federal and provincial reforms, Boothe and Boothe rightly note that these have generally involved fewer (and wider) rate brackets, lower top marginal rates, and increased personal exemptions.[7] These reforms, they also explain, are generally consistent with the normative prescriptions of optimal income tax theory, which supports reductions in high marginal tax rates on efficiency grounds and the pursuit of distributional objectives through increased exemptions and/or direct transfer payments.[8] The impact on overall progressivity, as the diagram illustrates, is increased average rate progressivity at low- to middle-income levels and reduced average rate progressivity at higher-income levels – precisely the kinds of impacts that Boothe and Boothe report in their paper. The other result, which is also illustrated in the diagram, is a necessary shift in the overall distribution of federal and provincial income taxes away from very low and very high income earners toward middle income earners.[9]

Whether one considers these results desirable necessarily depends on one's conception of distributive justice and presumably whether one accepts the conclusions of optimal income tax theory. With respect to the former, those with more egalitarian inclinations might be expected to question decreases in progressivity at high income levels, while applauding increases in personal exemptions and transfers to the least well-off. With respect to the latter, critics have challenged many of the simplifying assumptions of optimal tax theory[10] – for example that high and low-income taxpayers make the same labour-leisure tradeoffs,[11] that people choose how much to work based on perfect knowledge of their wage rate,[12] and that markets are perfectly competitive with no economic rents[13] – as well as the assumption that a society will accept whatever mix of personal exemptions and transfer payments is required to achieve the desired distribution of economic resources.[14] As a result, the answer to 'how' the personal income tax should redistribute economic resources is certainly not settled, and those (myself included) who consider the progressive income tax to be an important instrument for distributive justice are likely to be somewhat less sanguine than Boothe and Boothe about the direction of personal income tax reform in Canada over the last decade.

Allocation of Taxing and Spending Responsibilities

This brings me to my second question, concerning the appropriate level of government that should be responsible for redistribution. The answer to this question is not easy, because it depends ultimately on how we define the spheres of our communities. As a general rule, theories of distributive justice, such as Rawls's, don't address this issue, but assume a defined political community within which principles of distributive justice apply. In reality, of course, we inhabit multiple communities, each of which may suggest different kinds of redistributive responsibilities. At one pole are family, friends, and colleagues, with whom we share special responsibilities unlike those we may have with strangers. At the other pole is the global community – an increasingly familiar community within which our redistributive responsibilities are too easily and too often ignored. Between these, of course, are towns, cities, and states – shaped by shared and different histories and visions that together define what we think we owe each other.

Within this broad framework, however, public finance scholars have devised various guidelines for the allocation of tax and spending responsibilities based on theory and practice.[15] As a general rule, these guidelines suggest that redistributive taxes are best allocated to higher levels of government, which are less likely to suffer erosion of the tax base from relocation, while taxes based on less mobile factors of production and specific benefits received are best levied by lower levels of government.[16] At the same time, it is often argued that many kinds of spending programs are best left to lower levels of government where program delivery is likely to be more responsive to local needs and differences in preferences are more easily accommodated.[17] To the extent that the resulting allocation of tax and expenditure responsibilities produces a vertical fiscal imbalance, the appropriate solution is generally thought to involve intergovernmental transfers.[18] While the design of these transfers involves important equity, efficiency, and constitutional considerations, these are beyond the scope of this comment.

From this perspective, it follows that central governments should have a leading role in progressive income taxes as well as other redistributive taxes such as taxes on the intergenerational transfer of wealth.[19] Sub-national governments, on the other hand, might reasonably be assigned sole or primary authority for taxes on real property or immovables, various kinds of benefit taxes and user fees, excise taxes, and more general sales or consumption taxes.[20] While sub-national governments might also levy progressive income or wealth transfer taxes, the efficiency and long-term sustainability of these taxes is likely to depend on concurrent central government taxation in these fields and considerable harmonization between the sub-national and central government taxes. When the federal government repealed its gift and estate tax in 1972, for example, provincial governments were unable to sustain their own wealth transfer taxes in the face of inter-provincial tax competition.[21]

For this reason, advocates of progressive income taxation might justifiably question reductions in federal personal income taxes over the last twenty-five years designed to enable provincial governments to increase their own personal income taxes.[22] While provincial personal income taxes increased significantly in the 1970s and 1980s, a wave of provincial tax rate reductions since the mid-1990s may suggest an emerging interprovincial tax competition that could undermine progressive provincial income taxes. Recent amendments to the Tax Collection Agreements, which permit participating provinces to impose personal income taxes as a percentage of federal taxable income rather than federal tax, may accelerate this process by liberating provincial personal income taxes from the federal rate structure – allowing Alberta, for example, to adopt a flat rate personal income tax in 2001. Not surprisingly, therefore, Boothe and Boothe's paper provides evidence of this interprovincial tax competition in the form of reduced progressivity at the upper end of the income scale and a general convergence in average tax rates among provincial personal income taxes.

At the same time as one might question a diminished federal role in personal income taxation, one might also challenge the federal government's continuing role in sales and excise taxation through the Goods and Services Tax (GST) and federal excise taxes on alcohol, tobacco and motive fuels (gasoline and diesel).[23] To the extent that these federal taxes accentuate an already existing vertical fiscal imbalance, they deprive provincial governments of necessary tax room to satisfy their own expenditure responsibilities, lessen government accountability by blurring the connection between taxes and expenditures, facilitate federal participation in areas of provincial jurisdiction through fiscal transfers, and create pressure on the federal government to devolve taxing powers to provincial governments in other less appropriate fields such as personal income taxation. Although it is often suggested that value-added taxes like the GST are best levied by central governments, experience in Quebec (where the federal GST is collected by the province and remitted to the federal government) suggests otherwise.[24] As a result, the Séguin Commission's recommendation that the federal government should relinquish the GST in favour of the provinces seems eminently reasonable. Relinquishment of federal excise taxes would further alleviate the fiscal imbalance that the commission and others have documented,[25] enabling the federal government to re-establish its dominant position in personal income taxation.

Taxation, Redistribution, and Constitutional Law

This brings me finally to constitutional law, which is a dangerous place for a tax scholar to conclude, particularly in a volume edited by constitutional scholars. The brief point that I wish to make here, however, is less about constitutional law than about the relevance of tax policy for an important issue in constitutional law, namely the characterization of federal spending as it relates to the constitutionality of the federal spending power.

In tax policy over the last thirty years, it has become commonplace to distinguish between normal tax provisions that are necessary to define the 'normative tax' and so-called 'tax expenditure' provisions that provide subsidies or transfer payments in the form of exemptions, deductions, or credits.[26] While the characterization of a tax expenditure is rarely uncontroversial,[27] designation as such does suggest that it should be viewed as government spending rather than taxation. For this reason, these provisions might rightly be subject to a constitutional challenge to the so-called federal spending power.

NOTES

1 See generally Liam Murphy and Thomas Nagel, *The Myth of Ownership: Taxes and Justice* (Oxford: Oxford University Press, 2002). Traditionally associated with utilitarian conceptions of distributive justice, redistributive taxation is also supported by different versions of liberal-egalitarianism as well as feminist and communitarian conceptions of distributive justice.

2 See, e.g., Richard A. Musgrave, Peggy B. Musgrave, and Richard M. Bird, *Public Finance in Theory and Practice* (Toronto: McGraw-Hill Ryerson, 1987), 214–26. This argument typically depends on the assumption that privately-held economic resources have a diminishing marginal utility to their owners, such that higher rates of taxation are necessary to impose a similar sacrifice (in terms of foregone utility) on more affluent taxpayers as is imposed on less affluent taxpayers by lower rates. In addition to this equity argument, progressive taxes may also be justified on the efficiency grounds that they establish an approximate relationship between the marginal costs and benefits of public expenditures to individual taxpayers.

3 Thomas Hobbes, *Leviathan*, edited by Michael Oakshott (1960), chapter 30 (favouring taxation on the basis of consumption). For useful discussions, see Alvin Warren, 'Would a Consumption Tax Be Fairer Than an Income Tax?' *Yale Law Journal* 89 (1980): 1081; Mark Kelman, 'Time Preference and Tax Equity,' *Stanford Law Review* 35 (1983): 649: and Barbara H. Fried, 'Fairness and the Consumption Tax,' *Stanford Law Review* L4 (1992): 961.

4 For recent discussions of wealth taxation, see 'Symposium on Wealth Taxes,' *Tax Law Review* 53 (2000). For recent discussions of wealth transfer taxation, see Edward J. McCaffery, 'The Uneasy Case for Wealth Transfer Taxation' *Yale Law Journal* 104 (1994): 283; Anne L. Alstott, 'The Uneasy Liberal Case Against Income and Wealth Transfer Taxation: A Response to Professor McCaffery,' *Tax Law Review* 51 (1996); 363–402; and Eric Rakowski,

'Transferring Wealth Liberally,' ibid., 419–72. For the author's views on the taxation of wealth transfers, see David G. Duff, 'Taxing Inherited Wealth: A Philosophical Argument,' *Canadian Journal of Law and Jurisprudence* 4 (1993): 3–63.

5 See, e.g., Richard A. Musgrave, 'Progressive Taxation, Equity, and Tax Design,' in Joel Slemrod, ed., *Tax Progressivity and Income Inequality* (Cambridge: Cambridge University Press, 1994), 341.

6 For this reason Boothe and Boothe's measures of redistribution relative to the average tax paid would show redistribution even with a flat rate or declining rate tax.

7 In 1980, for example, the federal income tax contained thirteen rate brackets, the top marginal rate was 43 per cent on taxable income over $60,000, and the basic personal exemption was $2,890. In 2002, the federal income tax contained four rate brackets, reached a top marginal rate of 29 per cent on taxable income over $103,000, and exempted the first $7,634 of income. Provincially, the Tax Collection Agreements in force in 1980 effectively meant that all provinces but Quebec adopted the same rate brackets and personal exemptions as those of the federal income tax for that year, while top marginal rates as a percentage of taxable income ranged from a low of approximately 16.5 per cent in Alberta to almost 25 per cent in Newfoundland. In 2002, after amendments to the Tax Collection Agreements which allowed participating provinces to levy personal income tax as a percentage of federal taxable income, the number of rate brackets varied from one in Alberta to five in British Columbia and Ontario, top marginal rates were between 10 per cent in Alberta and approximately 20 per cent in Newfoundland, and basic personal exemptions ranged from $7,231 in Nova Scotia and a high of $12,900 in Alberta. In Quebec, which had three rate brackets in 2002, the top marginal rate was the highest in Canada at 24 per cent on taxable income exceeding $53,405, while the personal exemption was the lowest at $6,060.

8 The classic statement of this approach is James A. Mirrlees, 'An Exploration in the Theory of Optimum Income Taxation,' *Review of Economic Studies* 38 (1971): 175. For a useful summary of the vast body of literature generated by this study, see Matti Tuomola, *Optimal Income Tax and Redistribution* (Oxford: Clarendon Press, 1990). For an excellent discussion of this and other views of the income tax rate structure, see Joseph Bankman and Thomas Griffith, 'Social Welfare and the Rate Structure: A New Look at Progressive Taxation,' *California Law Review* 75 (1987): 1905.

9 While tax rates have also decreased during this period, it is important to distinguish the effect of rate reduction, which lower taxes for all taxpayers,

from changes in the rate structure which affect the distribution of the income tax among taxpayers at different income levels.

10 See, e.g., Lawrence Zelenak and Kemper Moreland, 'Can the Graduated Income Tax Survive Optimal Tax Analysis?' *Tax Law Review* 53 (1999): 51.

11 Contrary to the assumptions of optimal income tax theory, it is possible that high-income taxpayers get more enjoyment out of work and are therefore less elastic in their labour supply decisions than low-income taxpayers, suggesting that higher marginal tax rates for these taxpayers may be efficient.

12 To the extent that labour supply decisions are based on prior investments in human capital (at which time future wage rates are not known), this assumption is clearly problematic.

13 Where market returns include economic rents, taxation may capture these rents without affecting economic behaviour. Recent theories of 'winner-take-all markets' suggest that progressive marginal tax rates may affect economic behaviour much less than previously thought. See, e.g., Martin J. McMahon, Jr and Alice G. Abreu, 'Winner-Take-All Markets: Easing the Case for Progressive Taxation,' *Florida Tax Review* 4 (1998).

14 In practice, public willingness to support transfer payments beyond a very low level seems to be limited to payments directed at children, the elderly, and the disabled.

15 For an excellent summary of this literature, see Robin Boadway, 'Recent Developments in the Economics of Federalism,' in Harvey Lazar, ed., *Toward a New Mission Statement for Canadian Fiscal Federalism* (Kingston: Queen's University for the Institute of Intergovernmental Relations, 2000) 41.

16 See, e.g., Richard A. Musgrave, 'Who Should Tax, Where and What?' in Charles E. McLure, Jr., ed., *Tax Assignment in Federal Countries* (Canberra: Centre for Research on Federal Financial Relations, Australian National University, 1983).

17 See, e.g., Wallace Oates, *Fiscal Federalism* (New York: Harcourt Brace Jovanovich, 1972). To the extent that individuals are mobile across subnational jurisdictions, one might also expect that decentralized decision-making would facilitate the formation of communities with similar preferences. See Charles M. Tiebout, 'A Pure Theory of Local Expenditures,' *Journal of Political Economy* 64 (1956): 416.

18 See, e.g., Richard M. Bird, 'Threading the Fiscal Labyrinth: Some Issues in Fiscal Decentralization,' *National Tax Journal* 46 (1993): 207.

19 See, e.g., Jack M. Mintz and Thomas A. Wilson, 'The Allocation of Tax Authority in the Canadian Federation,' in Robin W. Boadway, Thomas J.

Courchene, and Douglas D. Purvis, *Economic Dimensions of Constitutional Change*, vol. 1 (Kingston: John Deutsch Institute for the Study of Economic Policy, 1991), 169.

20 See, e.g., Richard M. Bird, 'Rethinking Subnational Taxes: A New Look at Tax Assignment,' *Tax Notes International* 20 (2000): 2069.

21 See Richard M. Bird, 'Canada's Vanishing Death Taxes,' *Osgoode Hall Law Journal* 16 (1978): 133. Ontario repealed its succession duty in 1978. Quebec became the last Canadian province to repeal its wealth transfer tax in 1985.

22 In personal income tax reductions that were deliberately designed to transfer tax room to provincial governments, the federal government reduced the top marginal rate from 47 to 43 per cent in 1977 and from 43 to 34 per cent in 1982. The federal government reduced the top marginal rate again in 1987 to 29 per cent, where it has remained (ignoring the effect of a federal surtax that was subsequently introduced and then repealed).

23 See, e.g., Irene K. Ip and Jack M. Mintz, *Dividing the Spoils: The Federal-Provincial Allocation of Taxing Powers* (Toronto: C.D. Howe Institute, 1992).

24 On the experience with and prospects for value-added taxation at the subnational level, see Richard M. Bird and Pierre-Pascal Gendron, 'VATs in Federal Countries: International Experience and Emerging Possibilities,' *Bulletin for International Fiscal Documentation* 55 (2001): 293.

25 See, e.g., Giuseppe C. Ruggeri, Robert Howard, and Donald Van Wart, 'Structural Imbalances in the Canadian Fiscal System,' *Canadian Tax Journal* 41 (1993): 454 (recommending, contrary to the argument in this comment, that the federal government should relinquish personal income taxation to the provinces).

26 See, e.g., Stanley S. Surrey, *Pathways to Tax Reform: The Concept of Tax Expenditures* (Cambridge, MA: Harvard University Press, 1973); and Stanley S. Surrey and Paul R. McDaniel, *Tax Expenditures* (Cambridge, MA: Harvard University Press, 1985).

27 Consider, for example, a tax deduction or credit for the costs of higher education (tuition and interest expenses on student loans), which might be viewed as a tax expenditure designed to subsidize the costs of higher education or an element of the normative income tax designed to recognize costs that must be incurred in order to earn income.

Is Vertical Equity a Virtuous End?

LORNE SOSSIN

Equity is one of the central planks of Canadian federalism. It is represented most graphically through equalization transfers between 'have' and 'have-not' provinces and through constitutional provisions such as section 36 of the Constitution Act, 1982, which, inter alia, commits all Canadian governments to 'promoting equal opportunity for the well-being of all Canadians.' Equity is also one of the core values of the Canadian progressive income tax system (which includes both federal and provincial components), which seeks, at least in part, to redistribute income from those advantaged to those in need. However, paradoxically, the Canadian federation has been built on principles of asymmetry and Canadian society is characterized by significant social and economic inequality. Can these defining characteristics be reconciled? Or is this simply one further illustration of Canada's storied ambivalence?

One of the aims of this study is to analyse the place of redistributive aspirations in the Canadian federation. As I briefly explore in this comment on Paul Boothe and Katherine Boothe's analysis of the progressive income tax (PIT), redistribution lies at the heart of the nexus between politics and markets in Canada. Boothe and Boothe's contribution to our knowledge about the extent and effect of redistribution through the progressive income tax system is noteworthy in at least two respects. First, they confirm that progressivity is not always what it seems in terms of redistributing income: in other words, steeper and steeper progressivity does not necessarily equal greater redistribution. Second, they highlight provincial disparities in vertical equity in Canada. Both observations have important implications for the nature and future of federalism in Canada. I am not an economist and do not purport to take issue with any of Boothe and Boothe's conclusions with respect to the empirical data they have analysed. What I wish to do, instead, is flesh out three vital questions raised, but not resolved, by Boothe and Boothe's analysis:

1. Why is vertical equity a significant or defining characteristic of Canadian federalism?
2. Why is provincial convergence with respect to vertical equity desirable?
3. Why should the tax system be a principal vehicle for attaining vertical equity in Canada?

I discuss each of these questions in turn. I conclude that the debate surrounding levels of vertical equity, degrees of provincial convergence, and the uses to which the tax system should be deployed should yield as much space for weighing questions of political preference and legal principle as for weighing economic logic.

Vertical Equity and Canadian Federalism

Vertical equity has emerged as a central question for Canadian federalism. Horizontal equity is the principle that taxpayers with the same income should pay the same tax, while vertical equity means that taxpayers with higher incomes should pay tax at higher rates. Writing from the economic theory perspective, Boothe and Boothe assert in their paper that because judgments regarding interpersonal welfare are inherently subjective (how is one to measure one's 'ability to pay' for public goods and services?), 'arbitrary judgments regarding tradeoffs between the welfare of individuals are required.' Must trade-offs be arbitrary? Because economic answers are not available to this question, political compromises and legal principles must be explored. Because such answers rely on compromises and principles, however, they are, by definition, not arbitrary. As Donna Byrne has observed:

> Tax theorists who are willing to put considerable energy into discussion of progressivity are often unwilling to enter into debate about redistribution. Rather, they characterize the preference for progressive taxation as 'purely subjective' or as based on something other than logic. While this element of personal preference is not necessarily a bad thing, it generally is seen as beyond the scope of economics and thus not suitable for logical debate. Professor Boris Bittker once noted in a defense of progressivity

that in the end, decisions about the choice of a rate structure do not depend on logic, but on 'faith, personal preference, or fiat.' It is probably true that ultimately the choice of a rate structure rests on personal prefer-ence. But the choice does follow rationally from those preferences whether those preferences lead to a wealth maximization model of eco-nomic efficiency or to some other analytical framework. Thus, it is not so much that decisions about the rate structure cannot rest on logic, only that the logical analysis of the underpinnings of these decisions is largely ignored ...

While economics purports not to make claims on grounds of equity, assumptions about what is equitable are built into the economic model itself. To that extent, claims for efficiency are also claims about equity. For example, the choice of wealth maximization as the good to be achieved is a choice of one social goal – a large wealth pie – over other possible social goals, such as greater equality of wealth or a guaranteed minimum stan-dard of living. Economists and tax analysts often state or imply that there is no principled way to make this choice, yet political philosophers and legal theorists address exactly this question in very principled ways.[1] (notes omitted)

Boothe and Boothe themselves recognize that, with respect to judg-ments regarding vertical equity, 'such determinations are usually the result of the political process.' Politics, of course, requires deliberation – spaces where the normative infrastructure of the tax system may be worked out, and the relative burdens and benefits which flow from progressive tax rates calculated and justified.[2] Such deliberative spaces on this question are suspiciously absent from Canadian politics.

Federalism may be one explanation for why this is so. Because the income tax has both federal and provincial dimensions, the goals of distributive justice to which redistribution is aimed are more diffuse. It is one thing to argue that wealthier people should pay progressively higher taxes than low-income people, but quite another to contemplate redistribution from the standpoint of someone who is middle class by Ontario standards, but relatively well-off by Maritime standards. Redistribution becomes more nettlesome still when one factors in rural-urban divides, and regional or ethno-cultural tensions within and across provincial boundaries (for example, Aboriginal peoples).

Whether due to the multiple identities of Canadians or to the low degree of class consciousness in Canada, redistribution rarely surfaces as a subject of political debate in Canada. Indeed, 'tax competitiveness' appears far more often in campaign speeches than 'redistribution.' This is not the only reason for the remoteness of redistribution as a political force in Canada. It is often said that we have a tax system run by and for an expert community of tax lawyers, accountants and government managers, which has become increasingly unhinged from basic norms of redistribution, justice and fairness. As Neil Brooks has noted, the tax system is unintelligible virtually to all citizens affected by it:

> When first enacted in 1917, the income tax was legislated in under 11 pages; today the consolidated legislation requires more than, 1,400 very finely printed pages. The drafting is undeniably Byzantine. In some sections, single sentences roll on for almost a dozen pages as refinements are grafted on to the exceptions to the provisos. The terms used are unfamiliar: balance of annuitized voluntary contributions, butterfly transactions, capitalization of soft costs, cumulative offset account, and countless other concepts used in the *Act* are not part of everyday language ... Since the legislation is so fundamental to each citizen's responsibilities to the state, the idea that everyone should be able to read and understand the *Act* seems uncontentious.[3]

In such settings, political discourse on the fundamental preferences advanced or hindered by the tax system is all the more crucial. Politics in Canadian federalism provides a set of organizing principles which balance core values of equity on the one hand and asymmetry on the other. Politics in Canadian taxation provides a set of organizing principles which balance core values of redistribution and fairness. The tax system, on this view, allows for the articulation and exercise of social rights. As Esping-Andersen asserted, 'the outstanding criterion for social rights must be the degree to which they permit people to make their living standards independent of pure market forces. It is in this sense that social rights diminish citizen's status as commodities.'[4]

Because the tax system is either unintelligible or unhinged from norms (such as fairness and redistribution), I suggest we lack a vocabulary with which to make claims about why one degree of vertical equity is preferable over another. Unless we are clear on the purposes of vertical equity, arguments about the desired degree of vertical equity will be settled on economic grounds. Boothe and Boothe, for their part, observe that taxpayers at the bottom and at the top of the income spectrum were better off in 2002 than in 1980 or 1995. This is a product both of rises in incomes and average tax rates over time. The question raised but not resolved by Boothe and Boothe's analysis is whether improving the lot of the wealthiest and the poorest Canadians (at the expense of the middle class) is the appropriate equity balance, and if so, why? Boothe and Boothe might consider such questions 'political,' but I would question the wisdom of unhinging economics from politics when it comes to taxation.

Provincial Divergence and Convergence

Just as redistribution represents the intersection of politics and markets, it also highlights the tensions inherent in a federation. The progressive income tax system in many ways mirrors the redistributive transfers undergirding Canadian federalism. Equalization payments, as indicated above, are intended to transfer money from 'have' provinces to 'have not' provinces. But to what end? Presumably, at least one end is to achieve a degree of equity between provinces and to reduce the divergence of economic prosperity across provincial boundaries. But how is this different than equalization between 'have' and 'have not' individuals?

Is sameness desirable as between provinces when it comes to redistribution and systems of vertical equity? Boothe and Boothe detail the host of post-1995 PIT reforms which have resulted in the convergence of average tax rates across provinces and the average provincial marginal rates. They identify Quebec as the province with the highest degree of progressivity, followed by the Atlantic provinces, while Ontario and the western provinces are less progressive. These divergences are attributed to different degrees of progressivity, different average incomes, and different average levels of taxation.

Should such differences be celebrated? Certainly, they should be framed against a backdrop which has demonstrated remarkably little movement in the postwar era in terms of income and wealth distribution in the country as a whole.[5] Canadian federalism has a long and fairly well-regarded tradition of provincial experimentation and competition with tax as well as social programs.[6] This is usually characterized as creating laboratories for innovation, with universal, public health care, originating in Saskatchewan in the early 1960s, as the dominant archetype. Provincial initiative can also, of course, bring an end to national programs, such as the decision by Alberta to abolish the death tax in the 1970s. This type of provincial competition through the tax system to attract investment, job creation, and growth accelerated in the 1990s and continues to be a defining feature of federalism. Boothe and Boothe's analysis once again raises without resolving the question of the usefulness of provincial tax competition, and alludes to one approach to addressing this question – namely, that it depends on whose interests one has in mind.

Tax, Federalism, and Equity

The summary of Boothe and Boothe's finding are as straightforward as they are puzzling: post-1995 PIT reforms rendered the federal tax system less progressive but increased the amount of income being redistributed – a phenomenon even more pronounced when one factors in refundable tax credits such as the GST credit and the child benefit credit. Even assuming one is clear on the normative ends of vertical equity and the appropriate degree of provincial experimentation and divergence, there remains a question of whether the tax system is the most effective or desirable means to achieve these ends. While Boothe and Boothe discuss tax credits and other direct transfers, they do not explore the efficacy of such measures as compared with changes to the progressivity of the PIT.

The final question which is raised but not resolved by Boothe and Boothe is the consistency of their findings with the accepted wisdom regarding the impact of the neoliberalism on Canadian economic and social policy in the 1980s and 1990s.[7] In Louis Eisenstein's 1961 study entitled *The Ideologies of Taxation*, two perceptions are identified as the central tenets of a conservative approach to income tax: that the income tax be tied to one's ability to pay (and not to the redistribution of wealth); and that one's tax burden not act as a barrier or deterrent to investment. Eisenstein points out that an argument for both these claims can be found in the classical discourse of liberalism. For example, a redistributive income tax must, by definition, discriminate against the prosperous, and therefore contradicts a pure notion of equality in government interference.[8]

Contrary to the empirical implications of the New Right's critique of the income tax, there seems to be little historical or empirical correlation between tax incentives and economic performance. In other words, when progressive or high tax rates have been imposed, or capital gains from investments taxed, or tax avoidance rigorously deterred, or tax evasion vigorously prosecuted, capital investment continues and continues to be profitable.[9] When the reverse occurs, there are usually other more determinant factors influencing investment and business conduct.[10] However, the ingenuity of Eisenstein's contribution to the study of income taxation stems from the second tier of his argument – namely, that favouring equality along the classical liberal model offers clear advantages to those who happen to be wealthy already. In other words, since the market creates inequality, any government regulation of the market that treats all individuals as equal only reinforces and exacerbates that inequality. The history of income distribution in Canada bears out this assertion.[11] Equity, seen through the lens of history, often requires asymmetry. This is both an axiom of progressive taxation and an axiom of the Canadian federation.

Conclusion

While there is little in Boothe and Boothe's analysis which I believe to be misguided, their approach and assumptions reflect the limitations of an economic analysis to answer key questions surrounding the redistributive goals of the Canadian federation. As they identify in their introduction, tax reform has a number of drivers, ranging from tax competitiveness, to targeting assistance to groups in need, to improving work incentives and simplification. With this context in mind, it is difficult to say whether the changes which are chronicled, and the resulting provincial/federal divergence, reflect goals that have been attained or goals which have proven elusive. And this, in my view, is part of the problem. The search for a defensible and principled optimal degree of vertical equity should reflect a deeply political question – it is a challenge to the normative foundations of federalism.

NOTES

1 Donna Byrne, 'Progressive Taxation Revisited,' *Arizona Law Review* 37 (1995): 739.
2 See Edward J. McCaffery, 'The Holy Grail of Tax Simplification,' *Wisconsin Law Review* (1990), 1280 (noting that few tax theorists have explored the political justifications for tax equity).
3 Neil Brooks, 'Flattening the Claims of the Flat-Taxers,' *Dalhousie Law Journal* 21 (1998): 313–14.
4 Esping-Andersen, *The Three Worlds of Welfare Capitalism* (Cambridge: Polity Press, 1990), 3. See also Douglas Ashford, *The Emergence of the Welfare State* (Oxford: Basil Blackwell, 1986).

5 See François Vaillancourt, ed., *Income Distribution and Economic Society in Canada* (Toronto: University of Toronto Press, 1985).
6 Keith Banting, *The Welfare State and Canadian Federalism*, 2nd ed. (Montreal: McGill-Queen's University Press, 1987).
7 With respect to the rise of neoliberalism in Canadian tax and social policy, see Patricia Marshak, *The New Right and the Restructuring of Global Markets* (Montreal: McGill-Queen's University Press, 1991).
8 Louis Eistenstein, *The Ideologies of Taxation* (New York: Ronald Press, 1961). See generally, Michael Sandel, *The Limits of Liberalism* (Cambridge, MA: Harvard University Press, 1982).
9 See Brooks, 'Flattening the Claims.'
10 See Linda McQuaig, *Behind Closed Doors* (Toronto: Viking, 1987), 66. See also Fred Block, 'Rethinking the Political Economy of the Welfare State,' in Fred Block et al., eds., *The Mean Season: The Attack on the Welfare State* (New York: Pantheon Books, 1987), 113–18.
11 The wealthiest quintile of Canadians has accounted for between 41 and 43 per cent of total income earned annually in Canada throughout the postwar era, while the poorest quintile has accounted for between 3.6 and 5 per cent of total income earned annually. See J. Harvey Perry, *A Fiscal History of Canada: The Postwar Years*, Canadian Tax Paper No. 85 (Toronto: Canadian Tax Foundation, 1989), table 28.1, 752.

Personal Income Tax, Redistribution and Fiscal Federalism in Canada: Some Observations

FRANÇOIS VAILLANCOURT

In their paper, Paul Boothe and Katherine Boothe address one aspect of the redistributive dimension of the personal income tax (PIT) in the Canadian federation – namely, the impact on the personal distribution of income of the PIT and of the recent changes resulting from the replacement of the tax-on-tax by the tax-on-income; this allows the nine provinces that have their PIT collected by the federal government to vary the progressivity of their tax system by means of tax rates and brackets, based upon the federal definition of income. This gives them more choice than before 2000, although still not as much as what Quebec has, as it can also vary the definition of income.

This comment briefly examines the impact of the PIT on the inter-personal distribution of income, then turns to the inter-provincial distribution of the PIT, and finally addresses at some length the inter-governmental distribution of the PIT.

Personal Income Tax and Interpersonal Redistribution

Boothe and Boothe examine the progressivity of the PIT using information on marginal and average tax rates. Another way to examine this is to look at the changes in the Gini coefficient that result from the application of the PIT,[1] an approach followed by Gagné and Vaillancourt (1999).

Table 1 presents the total income and after-tax income Gini coefficients for the ten Canadian provinces for 1998 and 2002, two years before and after the 2000 changeover in provincial taxation practices. The following points are worth noting:

- The distribution of total income has become less unequal in eight

provinces, with New Brunswick and British Columbia the exceptions, from 1998 to 2002;
- New Brunswick, Saskatchewan, and British Columbia show an
increase in after tax income inequality from 1998 to 2002;
- It is in Quebec that the impact on the Gini coefficient of moving from
total income to after tax income (after federal and provincial PIT) is
greatest in both 1998 (column 6) and 2002 (column 7); and
- The difference between the impact of moving from total to after-tax
income in 1998 and 2002 is greatest for Manitoba, followed by
Saskatchewan, Alberta, and Quebec very close together. Hence one
does not see a major impact of moving to a flat tax on the distribution of after-tax income in Alberta.

PIT and Interprovincial Redistribution

While the implications of a less progressive rate for the personal redistribution of income are addressed by Boothe and Boothe, one other
interesting consequence is the possible inter-regional impact of
reduced progressivity. A priori, one would expect that a reduction in
progressivity would reduce the share of PIT collected in richer provinces since their higher mean nominal incomes imply higher PIT payments with a greater share of their personal income subject to higher
PIT rates. Such a result can be accentuated or mitigated by differences
within provinces in the distribution of income between rich and poor
provinces but is unlikely to be overturned by such differences.

Table 2 presents by province the amount and shares of federal PIT
and provincial PIT federally collected (all but Quebec PIT) for 1998 and
2002. Examining it, one notes:

- Lower shares of PIT collection in poorer provinces (lower share of
GDP than population) than their population shares and the reverse
in richer provinces;
- No obvious impact of the reduced progressivity in federal PIT.
Indeed, the shares of federal PIT in Alberta and Ontario increase
from 1998 to 2002. Improved economic activity overall appears to
trump decreased progressivity;
- Interesting changes in the provincial shares of provincial PIT from
1998 to 2002 with the two provinces (Alberta and British Columbia)
that reduced PIT rates showing lower shares of PIT revenues in 2002.

Table 1 Provincial Gini coefficients, total and after-tax income, Canada, 1998–2002 and ratios of interest

	1998	1999	2000	2001	2002	1998 total Gini/ after-tax Gini %	2002 total Gini/ after-tax Gini %	(1998 ratio – 2002 ratio)/1998 ratio %
Nfld total	.400	.402	.402	.392	.384	111.7	110.3	1.24
Nfld – after-tax	.358	.356	.360	.353	.348			
PEI total	.388	.388	.392	.375	.374	110.9	109.0	1.64
PEI – after-tax	.350	.357	.355	.344	.343			
NS total	.399	.395	.399	.394	.398	110.2	109.9	0.25
NS after-tax	.362	.359	.362	.360	.362			
NB total	.394	.384	.391	.389	.395	110.7	109.4	1.13
NB – after-tax	.356	.346	.355	.355	.361			
QC total	.415	.406	.412	.410	.403	113.4	111.3	1.82
QC – after-tax	.366	.360	.367	.369	.362			
ON total	.412	.417	.416	.409	.401	110.8	109.3	1.34
ON – after-tax	.372	.378	.378	.374	.367			
MA total	.403	.382	.386	.376	.383	111.0	107.6	3.09
MA – after-tax	.363	.348	.353	.346	.356			
SA total	.396	.390	.396	.393	.393	111.2	109.2	1.86
SA – after-tax	.356	.352	.359	.358	.360			
AL total	.415	.394	.401	.401	.389	110.1	108.1	1.84
AL – after-tax	.377	.359	.368	.371	.360			
BC total	.403	.410	.403	.415	.417	108.6	107.5	1.06
BC – after-tax	.371	.374	.371	.385	.388			–

Source: Statistics Canada, CANSIM II Table 202-0705

One possibility is that we could be missing the impact of changes in progressivity by looking at the overall PIT collections rather than at the PIT collections among higher income groups. We examined this looking at the share of PIT collected from the $250,000+ income group and from the $50,000+ group. As shown in table 3, there is a tendency for the share of PIT collection in lower-income provinces (Atlantic Canada) to have increased from 1998 to 2002 for the $50,000+ group, which may represent a more suitable higher income group than the $250,000+. The regional impact of changes to PIT progressivity may thus be worth monitoring.

Personal Income Tax and Intergovernmental Redistribution

The third part of this paper is divided into three sections. The first presents the current sharing of PIT between provinces and the federal government, the second examines recent changes in the financing of health care in Canada, and the third evaluates these changes from a PIT sharing perspective.

Existing Arrangements

PIT is the tax field that has been the most haggled over by provinces and the federal government since 1945 when the federal government occupied 100 per cent of it. Table 4 presents the sharing of that tax field since 1947 when the first postwar tax-sharing arrangements were initiated.

Since the election of the Martin government in June 2004, both expected and unexpected changes have been made to fiscal federalism in Canada; yet none have modified the sharing of the PIT or of any other tax between the federal and provincial governments.

We examine one change, health financing, assessing if the change is the desirable one or if a change in sharing of the PIT tax field would have been preferable. We do not address the financing of municipalities (fuel tax sharing) and of child care (transfers). Nor do we examine the 2004 changes to equalization, as this would take us too far away from our PIT focus. We note, however, that equalization in Canada is funded entirely out of federal general revenues and thus PIT. There are no province-to-province transfers. As a result and contrary to good economic policy, natural resource revenues and particularly oil and gas revenues, which are provincial revenues, are not available to the federal government to fund equalization. We say contrary to good policy

Table 2 Share of federal PIT and federally collected provincial PIT, 1998 and 2002, and population and GDP shares, 2001, Canada

	Federal PIT 1998 $millions	Provincial PIT federal collection 1998 $millions	Federal PIT 2002 $millions	Provincial PIT federal collection 2002 $millions	Federal PIT 1998 %	Provincial PIT federal collection 1998 %	Federal PIT 2002 %	Provincial PIT federal collection 2002 %	Population shares, 2001	GDP shares 2001
NP	825	565	914.8	663.4	1.0	2.0	1.1	2.1	1.7	1.3
PEI	226	135	236.1	151.4	0.3	0.5	0.3	0.5	0.4	0.3
NS	1,838	1,012	2,004.4	1,326.3	2.3	3.6	2.3	4.1	3.0	2.3
NB	1,324	796	1,449.4	910.4	1.7	2.9	1.7	2.8	2.4	1.9
QC	16,205	23	17,842.3	42.9	20.6	0.1	20.6	0.1	23.8	21.1
ON	34,581	12,806	38,560	17,737.7	44.0	46.1	44.5	55.0	38.2	40.6
MB	2,399	1,526	2,417.6	1,601.8	3.1	5.5	2.8	5.0	3.7	3.2
SK	1,960	1,312	2,020.9	1,248.2	2.5	4.7	2.3	3.9	3.3	3
AB	8,982	4,146	10,545.6	4,113.4	11.4	14.9	12.2	12.7	9.9	13.8
BC	9,853	5,314	10,328	4,355.8	12.5	19.1	11.9	13.5	13.2	12
Yukon	68	34	73.8	32.3	0.1	0.1	0.1	0.1	0.001	n/a
NWT	116	51	138.9	59.4	0.1	0.2	0.2	0.2	0.001	n/a
Nunavut	45	20	60	17.1	0.1	0.1	0.1	0.1	0.001	n/a
Outside Canada	166	56	121.2	5.3	0.00	0.00	0.00	0.00	n/a	n/a
Canada	78,587	27,794	86,713	32,265.4						

Sources: 2001 Population and GDP, Bird and Vaillancourt (2003)
Canada Revenue Agency Income Statistics at:
2002 http://www.cra-arc.gc.ca/agency/stats/gb02/pst/final/csv/table1.csv
1998 http://www.cra-arc.gc.ca/agency/stats/gb98/pst/final/csv/table1.csv

Table 3 Share of PIT collected within a given income group by province, 1998 and 2002, Canada

Income group	$50,000+		$250,000+	
	1998 (%)	2002 (%)	1998 (%)	2002 (%)
NF	0.77	0.87	0.43	0.49
PEI	0.19	0.19	0.18	0.10
NS	1.91	2.02	1.35	1.41
NB	1.26	1.33	0.86	0.81
QC	17.93	18.41	13.01	13.62
ON	48.16	47.54	53.52	53.30
MB	2.58	2.37	2.34	1.90
SK	2.12	2.06	1.60	1.22
AB	12.61	13.39	16.44	16.89
BC	12.46	11.82	10.26	10.25
PIT$000	47,135,757	58,123,678	10,380,994	12,678,061

Source: Canada Revenue Agency Income Statistics
   2002: http //www.cra-arc.gc.ca/agency/stats/gb02/pst/final/csv/table1.csv
   1998: http //www.cra-arc.gc.ca/agency/stats/gb98/pst/final/csv/table1.csv

since this induces more migration to revenue-rich provinces than economically appropriate since this is the only way to benefit from such wealth. Yet permanently higher oil and gas revenues will lead to larger disparities between Alberta and other provinces in terms of the capacity to self-finance public services. This will lead to more demands for federal transfers from provinces while the federal share of public revenues will have dropped. It would be appropriate to include a share (50 per cent?) of natural resource revenues, which in practice means mainly oil and gas royalties from Alberta, in the equalization pool from both an economic efficiency and from an equity (inter-temporal sharing of risk) perspective.

Health Funding, 1999–2004

Before examining recent funding arrangements for health, let us note that from 1957 until 1977, federal health funding was done through cost-shared programs, from 1977 to 1995, it was done through block funding of health and postsecondary education through Established Program Financing, and from 1995 to 1999, it was done through the CHST, block funding of health, postsecondary education, and welfare.

Table 4   Personal income tax (PIT) revenues in Canada 1947–2002

	Total PIT ($millions)	Federal % of PIT	% Federal in Quebec	% Federal R.O.C.	Total PIT % GDP
1947	660	100.0	100.0	100.0	5.4
1952	1,225	100.0	100.0	100.0	5.5
1954	1,309	98.1	n/a	100.0	5.6
1957	1,676	97.6	n/a	100.0	5.6
1962	2,378	84.9	83.5	87.0	6.2
1967	5,112	71.4	55.9	75.8	7.3
1972	11,385	69.3	50.7	75.8	10.3
1977	23,656	60.4	40.6	69.0	10.7
1982	43,932	58.6	38.1	66.8	11.6
1987	70,333	59.3	41.4	66.0	12.6
1992	101,226	58.7	43.0	64.1	14.5
1997	120,956	60.6	47.8	64.5	13.8
2002	138,906	61.8	50.8	66.2	12.7

Source: Bird and Vaillancourt (2006)

Starting in 1999, the federal funding for health entered a state of flux that seems to have been resolved in 2004. Five changes were made:

1 The 1999 federal budget made what was then a one-time commitment to health care: $11.5 billion over five years would be added to the health component of the CHST. This was the first time since 1977–8 that federal funding had been explicitly assigned to this specific policy area. This was done using both current spending in future budgets and entrusted funds from the 1998–9 Fiscal Year (FY) surplus. Ex post, it can be seen as a precursor of the CHT implemented in 2004 (see below).
2 The 2000 budget added another supplement of $2.5 billion over a four-year period for the purposes of health care and postsecondary education.
3 Then, as part of the agreement reached by the first ministers in September 2000, two provincial health funds were created. The federal Medical Equipment Fund and the Health Transition Fund were established at $1 billion and $800 million respectively. Under the agreement, the provinces were free to use the money as they wished in the general areas of new medical equipment and primary care.
4 In February 2003 the Health Care Renewal Accord was reached

between the federal government and the provinces. In terms of federal-provincial relations, the key aspects are:

- The division of the CHST into a Canada Health Transfer (CHT) and a Canada Social Transfer (CST) as of 2004–5, with the breakdown between the two determined on the basis of the share of health spending in total social spending by the provinces, the remainder of the spending being on postsecondary education and social assistance and services (including early childhood education). In the 2003 federal budget, the share of provincial health spending in total social provincial spending is estimated at 62 per cent and this was used in the breakdown in 2004–5.
- The creation of the health reform fund targeted at: first, primary health care, with the intent to increase the use of multidisciplinary teams and with the specific goal of 50 per cent coverage of the population on a 7/24 basis in 2011; second, home care, particularly acute care for mental health and end-of-life care; and, third, catastrophic drug care to be implemented by the end of 2005–6.
- An additional payment of up to $2 billion in 2003–4, conditional on the existence of a surplus above the normal Contingency Reserve ($3 billion), with this surplus established in January 2004. This was the object of much public discussion in the fall of 2003 as some feared that this would not be paid. The federal government confirmed in February 2004 that this $2 billion would be paid[2] even if the Contingency Reserve requirement was not respected, much to the relief of the provinces which in most cases had already booked these funds in their revenues. Ex post, one knows that the federal surplus at $9.1 billion was more than adequate to make the payment.[3]
5 In September 2004, a new accord, *A Ten Year Plan to Strengthen Health Care*, was reached. Its goals are the same as the 2003 Accord,[4] but one notes: an explicit recognition of the Romanow gap in 2004–05 ($1 billion) and 2005–6 ($2 billion in the CHT base funding); an additional $500 million in 2005–6 for home care and catastrophic drug coverage in the CHT base funding; and a base of $19 billion for the CHT to be escalated by 6 per cent a year. This brings back the use of an escalator that was present in the EPF transfers but suspended in 1990.[5]

Examining the 2004 accord, one also sees a reiteration of the objectives enunciated in the 2003 accord, such as improvement in access to primary care and home care. One notes, however, an explicit financial commitment to reducing waiting times for specific services. Moreover, the implementation of pharmacare is pushed back.[6] Another change is the reduction in the number of sources of health funds to two by 2006–7. As shown in table 5, funding for health was obtained from one source in 1998–9, two in 1999–2000, six in 2000–1, seven in 2001–2, five in 2002–3, eight in 2003–4 and seven in 2004–5.

Changes in Health Funding and PIT

The changes described above do not involve any change in the sharing of the PIT between provinces and the federal government. This is a departure from the historical norm since in the 1960s and 1970s, when such changes were made to fund various federal-provincial programs, including health financing. Have things changed in such a way that this is no longer appropriate? We argue not, although some others would say yes (Boadway, 2004). We will examine the issue from two perspectives: that of the alleged fiscal disequilibrium and that of fiscal federalism.

THE FISCAL DISEQUILIBRIUM PERSPECTIVE

Quebec's Séguin Commission of 2002 argues that there will be fiscal balance when: the division of tax fields allows each level of government sufficient financing to ensure accountability towards its electorate; total revenue (own and transfers) must be sufficient to cover the expenditures each level is responsible for; and transfers should be unconditional unless conditions are agreed to by all.[7]

But it then goes on to argue that 'a federation's fiscal imbalance is normally reflected in the budgetary balances of each order of government' (15). This is caused by a structural gap between revenues and expenditures of orders of governments (17). This is where the argument becomes fallacious as noted by the Economic Council of Canada (ECC), which wrote in 1982 that 'in order to say that there is a "structural" economic problem relating to fiscal imbalance, it must be argued that one of the levels of government does not have access to the revenues required to fulfill its obligations ... The mere existence of *deficits* at one level of government does not indicate the existence of such a structural imbalance nor does it mean that such *deficits* have to be rectified at the expense of another level of government.'[8]

TABLE 5 Children, health CHST, and CHT/CST federal funding commitments 1999–2008 ($billions). Shading for commitments

	1999/2000	2000/01	2001/02	2002/03	2003/04	2004/05	2005/06	2006/07	2007/08
CHST (1)	12.5	15.5	15.5	15.5	19.8	21.5	27.2	28.6	30.1
CHT (2)	n/a	n/a	n/a	n/a	12.3	13.6	19.0	20.1	21.3
CST (3)	n/a	n/a	n/a	n/a	7.5	7.9	8.2	8.5	8.8
Original CHST amount (4)		12.5	12.5	12.5	12.5				
1999 increase for health (5)		1.0	2.0	2.5	2.5				
1999 supplement from 1998–9 fiscal year in 1999–2000 B.S (6)	2.0	1.0	0.5						
2000 budget increase (7)		1.0	0.5	0.5	0.5				
September 2000 increase (8) into CHST			2.5	3.2	3.8	4.4*	5.0		
February 2003 supplement trust fund (2003–4 budget) (9)					1	1	0.5		
Early childhood development (10) into CST			0.3	0.4	0.5	0.5	0.5	0.5	0.5
Early learning and child care (11) into CST					0.025	0.15	0.225	0.3	0.35
Budget surplus grant (12)						1.0	1.0		
10-year plan to strengthen health care (13) (Romanow gap)						1.0			
Wait time reduction funding (14)						0.625	0.625	1.2	1.2
Health reform transfer (integrated in CHT in 2005–6) (15)					1.0	1.5	3.5	4.5	5.5
Medical diagnostic/equipment fund 2000 (2000–2) and 2002–3 (trust fund) (16)		0.5	0.5		0.5	0.5	0.5		
Health info technology 2000(2001–2) and		0.5			0.2	0.2	0.2		

2002–3 budget (2003–6) (17)		0.5	0.2	0.2	0.2	0.2	0.2		
Health transition (18)									
Earmarked health cash (19)	0	2.0	2.7	2.7	1.9	3.0	1.3	1.2	1.2
Earmarked social cash (20)	0	0	0.3	0.4	0.5				
Total CHST cash (21)	14.5	15.5	18.3	19.1	21.8	25.0	28.7	28.6	30.1
Total cash federal transfers however labelled (22)	16.5	16.5	19.0	19.3	22.7	26.7	30.1	29.8	31.3
For reference: CHST tax points	13.9	16.4	16.15	15.9	16.5	17.1	18.1	19.4	20.6

Sources: a) Department of Finance, Federal Financial Support for the Provinces and Territories, "The 1999 Budget and the CHST"; Canadian Intergovernmental Conference Secretariat News Release No. 800-038/007

b) Budget 2003 Investing in Canada's Health care System, tables 1 and 5

c) Budget 2004 Growing and Predictable Funding for Canada's Health Care System, Tables 4.1 and 4.2

d) Total Federal Support for Health, Post-Secondary Education, and Social Assistance and Social Services (2004–05) October: 2004 http://www.fin.gc.ca/facts/tfsh2_e.html#Annex%201

e) FFM 2004 Investments for Health and new Funding levels (10 years): http://www.pm.gc.ca/grfx/docs/tables1_e.pdf

f) http://www.pco-bcp.gc.ca/aia/default.asp?Language=E&Page=PressRoom&Sub=PressRelease&Doc=20000911_e.htm

g) Federal Support for Early Childhood Development and Early Learning and Child Care: http://www.fin.gc.ca/fedprov/ecde.html

Note the key items are CHST, CHT and CST; these items are regularly increased to include ad hoc amounts in their base

– 2000–1: CHST increased from 12.5 to 15.5 by adding items 4 to 7 together (see source f) (19) = (5) + (16) + (17); (22) = (16) + (17) + (21)

– 2001–2 (21) = (1) + (8) + (10); (19) = (5) + (16) + (18); (22) = (16) + (18) + (21)

– 2002–3 (21) = (1) + (8) + (10) ; (19) = (5) + (18); (22) = (18) + (21)

– 2003–4 here the CHST is notionally divided into CHT and CST (which only legally come into force in 2004–2005) but some funding is still labeled CHST. Hence the sum of CHT + CST is less than CHST (Compare sources d) and f)) (21) = (1) + (9) + (15); (22) = (11) + (16) + (17) + (21); (19) = (15) + (16) + (17) + (18)

– 2004–5 CHST is now gone except for past supplements. (8) is in CHT, (10) and (11) in CST, (21) = (1) + (9) + (12) + (15); (22) = (21) + (14) + (16) + (17) + (18); (19) = (14) + (15) + (16) + (17) + (18)

– 2005–6 The Romanow gap funding of 2.0 billions is in the base CHT as well as homecare and catastrophic drug coverage. 21 = (1) + (9) + (12); (19) = (14) + (16) + (17); (22) = (21) + (9) + (12)

*Underlined indicates amounts previously agreed to that have been incorporated in the CHST/CST. Shaded amounts are the amounts used to reach the CHST total for a given year. Items rounded to nearest 10 million.

We agree with the ECC. The argument that budgetary surpluses indicate fiscal room is inappropriate. Moreover, no demonstration has been made that there exists a fiscal disequilibrium in Canada, as the Séguin Commission defines this notion. Provinces are free to raise taxes to spend as they wish in their areas of responsibilities. Indeed, the existence of federal surpluses is appropriate given the accumulated federal debt. Table 6 presents four elements that support this conclusion:

1 The relative importance of provincial own revenues with respect to federal own revenues has gone from 86.5 per cent in 1990 to 90.3 per cent in 2003. The provinces can thus expand their relative take from the fiscal pie.
2 The importance of federal transfers to provinces as a percentage of federal spending has gone from 22.6 per cent in 1990 to 20.1 per cent in 2003 and the importance of federal transfers to provinces as a percentage of total revenues of provinces has gone from 20.7 per cent in 1990 to 18.2 per cent in 2003. Hence provinces are fairly autonomous in terms of revenues, although some provinces less than others.
3 The net negative worth of the federal government is ten times in absolute value that of the provinces in 2003. Calls for it to give up its annual surpluses imply that it is appropriate to bequeath this debt to future generations, a position with which we disagree.
4 The federal government and the provinces have both lowered their revenues as a share of GDP from 1990 to 2003. If the provinces had maintained their share of GDP, their revenues would be higher by $12.2 billion. If they had occupied the room vacated by the federal government, they would be higher by an additional $20 billion. Provinces could do that but choose not to.

THE FISCAL FEDERALISM PERSPECTIVE

While we do not see any Séguin fiscal disequilibrium, recent changes (2003–4) that increase anew the share of provincial revenues coming from conditional federal transfers will increase classical or Hunter fiscal disequilibrium. Hunter (1977) put forward various indicators of fiscal balance. The preferred one is: $V = 1 - (T + R + G + B)/E$, where V is the vertical fiscal balance indicator, ranging from 0 to 1 with 1 indicating fiscal equilibrium, and

Table 6 Financial position of Canadian federal and provincial governments, 1990–2003

Year	Federal budgetary revenues	Provincial own source revenues	Transfers to provinces from federal government	Total revenues provinces	Net worth federal government	Net worth provincial government	Federal budgetary revenues as % of GDP	Provincial own source revenue as % of GDP
1990	116,326	100,619	26,299	126,918	–327,210	+53,518	17.1	14.8
1995	131,397	119,397	29,752	149,148	–518,903	–47,407	16.2	14.7
2000	182,748	169,333	29,588	198,921	–484,397	–61,886	17.0	15.7
2003	186,207	168,328	37,404	205,732	–446,955	–43,549	15.3	13.8

Source: Fiscal Reference Tables 2004, Department of Finance, http://www.fin.gc.ca/frt/2004/frt04_6e.html Revenues (tables 3–4 and 30–31)
Net worth is from CANSIM Table 378-0004, Net Total Worth.

T = federal tax revenues shared with subnational entities
R = federal non tax revenues shared with subnational entities
G = federal conditional grants to subnational entities
B = sub-national borrowing authorized by the federal government
E = total expenditures of subnational entities

In the case of Canada, the only relevant component of the numerator is G with the key point being the *conditional* nature of the grants; increases in equalization payments do not increase vertical fiscal imbalance.

But what conditions exactly? Examining the various federal programs we would argue that one should distinguish among six types of conditions (Laurent and Vaillancourt, 2004).

The first three types are *economic* conditions directly applicable to the spending by recipient governments:

- Micro-conditions specify precise items (lists of items, technical conditions, etc.) that funds can be spent on by recipient governments.
- Meso-conditions[9] specify broad policies that must be respected by recipient governments for funds to flow to them, such as the conditions of the Canada Health Act.
- Macro-conditions set the overall amount of spending in a given area by recipient governments.

The other three conditions are more *political* in nature:

- Labelling conditions occur when a transfer is given a name such as by the federal government, with or without the agreement of the provinces, but nothing is done to insure that it is spent on the labelled item, for example, the 1999 CHST increase.
- Linking conditions occur when direct spending on one item by one order of government is linked to direct spending on another item in the same policy area by another order of government.
- Reporting conditions occur when the recipient of a transfer must provide information to receive it.

The tendency since 2000 to see increases in federal transfers to provinces as the appropriate way to fund provincial spending, particularly in the health sector, has several consequences. First, it weakens provincial autonomy in fields of provincial responsibility by making it easier for the federal government to require more or less binding constraints. This may be desired by those who believe that the federal government should be more present in these areas of public policy, but would the proper route to achieve this not be to modify the constitutional division of powers? Second, it weakens the interest of provinces in ensuring proper management of public funds. One should recall that the transfer system put in place in 1997 to fund social programs, which used so-called block grants that are set in terms of a per capita amount with no links to spending, was introduced to replace the funding of health expenditures based on 50/50 sharing between the federal government and the provinces. Such a system was seen as generating fifty-cent dollars with the provinces knowing that any increase in expenses that brought them the benefits of public acclaim was financed in half by a silent partner, that is, the federal government. Why should we go down that road again, especially as it makes it more difficult for the electorate to hold accountable the proper level of government and thus may make the electorate less interested in the democratic process?

Conclusion

As Boothe and Boothe aptly show, the federal PIT can be used to modify the distribution of individual income. Changes in the PIT (progressivity, taxable income) can also modify the share of federal PIT obtained from residents of various provinces. Finally, changes in the distribution of the PIT tax base between the federal and provincial governments were from 1954 to 1977 one of the main aspects of federal-provincial financial arrangements. Since 1977 this distribution of the PIT tax base between these two levels of government has not been re-examined. We argue that this should be examined anew with a view not to address the illusory Séguin fiscal disequilibrium, but the Hunter fiscal disequilibrium that the recent emphasis on using transfers to finance health care has accentuated. Put differently, the federal government, flushed with surpluses, has abused its spending power. It should be reined in by a new distribution of the PIT field between provinces and the federal government, which, coupled with more generous equalization, will make provinces responsible for raising the highest possible share of the monies they spend.

140   François Vaillancourt

NOTES

An earlier version of this paper was presented at the tax law and policy work-shop of the Law Faculty of the University of Toronto, 24 November 2004. Thanks to the participants for useful comments and to Jean-François Gaudreault-DesBiens for the invitation to adapt it for inclusion in these conference proceedings.

1 The Gini coefficient is a measure of inequality of income. The closer to zero, the lower the inequality, the closer to 1 the greater the inequality.
2 See http://www.fin.gc.ca/news04/04–010e.html
3 Government of Canada Records Seventh Consecutive Surplus, http://www.fin.gc.ca/news04/04–065e.html
4 For the text of the 2003 and 2004 accords and the Romanow report, see http://www.hc-sc.gc.ca/english/hca2003/fmm/releases.html
5 The EPF escalator was modified throughout the 1980s; see Vaillancourt (2000) for details.
6 The proposal by provincial premiers that the federal government be responsible for a national pharmacare program plan was not accepted. This is appropriate as the provision of various substitutable health inputs such as home/hospital drugs should be integrated.
7 Commission on Fiscal Imbalance, *A New Division of Canada's Financial Resources* (2002) at http://www.desequilibrefiscal.gouv.qc.ca/en/pdf/rapport_final_en. pdf
8 From http://www.fin.gc.ca/facts/fbcfacts8_e.html
9 Meso-economics examines issues between single unit (individual, firm, etc.) and aggregate levels; thus, by analogy, we label as meso-conditions those between micro and macro.

REFERENCES

Bird, Richard and François Vaillancourt. 2006. 'Changing with the Times: Success, Failure and Inertia in Canadian Federal Arrangements, 1945–2002' (with Richard Bird) in *Federalism and Economic Reform: International Perspectives* (Jessica Wallack and T.N. Srinivasan, eds.) New York: Cambridge University Press, 189–248.
– 2003. *Reconciling Diversity with Equality: The Role of Intergovernmental Fiscal Arrangements in Maintaining An Effective State in Canada.* Mimeo, World Bank.
Boadway, Robin *Should the Canadian Federation Be Rebalanced?* Institute of

Intergovernmental Relations. Available at http://www.iigr.ca/pdf/publications/343_Should_the_Canadian_Fede. pdf

Gagné, Robert, and François Vaillancourt. 1999. 'Personal Income Taxes in Canada : Dissimilarities, Redistributive Impacts and Social Policy,' *Canadian Tax Journal* 47(4): 927–44.

Hunter, J.S.H. 1977. *Federalism and Fiscal Balance: A Comparative Study.* Canberra: ANU Press.

Laurent, Stephen, and François Vaillancourt. 'Federal-provincial transfers for social programs in Canada: their status in May 2004.' Institute for Research on Public Policy working paper 2004–7. Available at http://www.irpp.org/miscpubs/archive/wp/wp2004-07.pdf

Vaillancourt, François. 2000. 'Les transferts fédéraux-provinciaux au Canada, 1947–1998: évolution et évaluation,' in *Les défis de la gouvernance à l'aube du XXIᵉ siècle*, A. Downs and G. Paquet, eds., 191–212. Montréal: Actes du Congrès 1999, ASDEQ.

PART THREE

The Spending Power and the Constitutional Architecture of Redistribution

The Federal Spending Power and Fiscal Imbalance in Canada

ANDRÉE LAJOIE

In federations, centralization is the name of the game. Canada is both a pro and a constant winner at that game, which it plays with an array of tools, of which the spending power is but one, albeit not a new one. The spending power has been around since 1912, when the first program of conditional subsidies for the provinces was implemented by federal authorities in the field of agricultural education in the provinces. My interest in the subject, although it does not date that far back, is not new either. It springs from my work in the 1970s about the law of health and of higher education. Those of you who are familiar with the field may recognize elements of my first paper on that topic, which have been integrated, up-dated and expanded in my contribution to the Séguin Commission in 2002.[1]

Indeed, to properly determine the relationship that exists between the spending power and the fiscal imbalance, it is necessary to have a definition of these concepts, but not without having first provided, as a backdrop to this exercise and especially for non jurists, a broad sketch of the division of powers in the Canadian Constitution. It is only against this backdrop that it will be possible to determine the current scope of the spending power within the context of Canadian federalism and its historical relationship with fiscal imbalance in Canada.

Division of Powers in the Canadian Constitution

Initial Distribution

In Canada, the Constitution Act, 1867, which established the federation, provides for an initial distribution of legislative powers, the bulk of which are found in sections 91 to 95. Section 91 is entitled 'Powers of the Parliament' and comprises twenty-nine subsections ranging from the debt and public property to general residual competence. Section 91 includes unemployment insurance, the raising of money by any mode or system of taxation, as well as quarantine and the establishment of marine hospitals, to name but those subjects linked to the spending power. To these federal powers must be added old age pensions, inserted in 1951 by section 94A (which nonetheless gives precedence to provinces' legislation in this respect), as well as paramount jurisdiction over natural resources exports, inserted by section 92A in 1982.

As a counterpart, section 92 is entitled 'Exclusive Powers of Provincial Legislatures' and lists sixteen subjects, including 'direct taxation within the province in order to the raising of a revenue for provincial purposes,' the establishment, maintenance, and management of hospitals, asylums, charities, and eleemosynary institutions in and for the province, other than marine hospitals, as well as a residuary power specific to its sphere ('generally all matters of a merely local or private nature in the province'). To this list must be added education, which is covered separately in section 93, the provincial portion of the power over resources provided for in section 92A, and the joint powers stipulated in section 95 over immigration and agriculture.

By contrast, the powers of the executive are the subject of a few provisions scattered throughout the text of 1867, which incorporate the powers already granted to the executives of the colonies that would form the federation, while specifying other powers, notably those concerning certain judicial appointments and the expropriation of provincial lands for defence purposes. But the spending power of the federal executive is not mentioned therein, just as no mention is made of the spending power of the provinces. Seized with a dispute that involved the question of the division of the powers of the executive, the Judicial Committee of the Privy Council ruled that these powers were distributed along the line of division of legislative powers stipulated in the Constitution Act, 1867, in a decision whose contemporary binding character was reiterated by the Supreme Court in the *Reference Re Secession of Quebec*.[2]

But it is not so much the initial constitutional text that is responsible for the current centralization of the distribution of legislative powers under the Canadian Constitution, and consequently, of the executive powers related thereto. Rather, this centralization ensues from the judicial interpretations to which this division has given rise, and from government practices that have developed at its margin.

Interpretative Theories

By reason of its colonial origins, the Canadian Confederation had a paradoxical judicial system for a long time: a foreign authority was responsible for ruling on the conflicts of interpretation that inevitably arose as a result of the distribution of legislative powers between the federal Parliament and several provincial legislatures on our territory for many years. Indeed, it was the Judicial Committee of the Privy Council in London which decided these matters in the last resort until 1949, even after the establishment of the Supreme Court of Canada. All constitutional scholars agree that the precedents established by this colonial court were the most decentralizing that our constitution has ever known. André Tremblay considers that it is the Privy Council that best actualized the federal potential of the Canadian constitution by affirming a dualistic model of federalism capable of attenuating the centralizing elements of the Constitution Act, 1867 and guaranteeing the provinces against the erosion of their autonomy.[3]

This phenomenon is explained by the foreign status of the tribunal: London did not lose the powers that the Privy Council confirmed as being provincial, unlike Ottawa, which, incidentally, appoints the justices of the Supreme Court. Throughout this period, the Privy Council affirmed the legislative autonomy of the provinces and rejected any notion of federal tutelage over the provinces. Moreover, the Privy Council insisted on the strict compartmentalization of the division of powers; there was a broadening of the explicitly listed provincial powers and a parallel narrowing of the federal powers liable to encroach on these provincial powers, such as those dealing with peace, order, and good government and with trade.

Yet before handing over the reins to the Supreme Court of Canada, the Privy Council created the tools of centralization of which the Supreme Court would subsequently make use when defining a federalism that was successively unilateral, dialogic, and normalizing.[4] There are five main tools. The first three are linked to the constitutional text itself: namely, the ancillary power, federal paramountcy, and residuary powers. In contrast, the other two tools present themselves as exceptions to the federal division of powers: the national dimensions theory and emergency powers. Without analysing here the judgments that gave rise to these theories and which subsequently applied them, it is important to show how all these theories promote centralization.

Ancillary power. The ancillary power allows the federal Parliament to legislate in fields of 'exclusive' provincial jurisdiction if the effective exercise of its powers so requires.[5] The intrusive effect of this technique would have required a strict interpretation of the criterion of necessity, and the logic of the concept should have meant that the provincial legislatures would also benefit from this power. But such was not the case.

Federal paramountcy. In case of conflict between two pieces of legislation, one provincial, the other federal, both constitutionally valid, dealing with an identical subject matter and being incompatible in their application, the Privy Council decided that the federal legislation would prevail. Subsequently, as may be seen, the Canadian courts would extend the scope of this theory by applying it to conflicts of potential application between two standards.[6]

Residuary powers. The Privy Council also affirmed federal competence over any remaining subject, namely any subject not stipulated in the list of provincial powers, unless it involves a matter that is clearly local in nature.[7] One can easily imagine the centralizing effect of this theory, one and a half centuries after the drafting of the constitution, when unnamed subjects – either because they did not exist at the time or because they did not lend themselves to being governed by the liberal state of the nineteenth century – have since taken on such importance in contemporary legislation.

National dimensions. Only one step would be needed to go from competence over residuary powers to the theory of national dimensions. The Privy Council took this step outside the constitutional text, by stating that a law prohibiting the sale and public consumption of alcohol fell within federal jurisdiction on the grounds that this scourge had taken on 'national dimensions.'[8] Combined with emergency powers, from which it is still not clearly distinguished, this theory would be applied on several occasions thereafter. It has made a comeback recently due to its correlation with the concept of subsidiarity.[9]

Emergency powers. Subsequently, emergency powers were invoked on their own and without the support of the theory of national dimensions.[10] What is more, it served as a basis for 'special measures to deal with crisis situations, whether they originate from civil unrest, insurrections, wars or economic disruptions. In fact, Canada has been subject to some form of emergency legislation for approximately 40 per cent of the time since it was passed.'[11]

The effect of these theories must be assessed cumulatively. What remains for the constituent states of a federation when the central authorities can legislate first in their own field, then on residual subjects, and finally in the field of 'exclusive' provincial jurisdiction each time they find it 'necessary' for the exercise of their own jurisdiction, whenever there is a potential conflict of application with respect to the same subject, or if the subject involves 'national dimensions' or a state of emergency is feared?

Government Practices

As a complement to these extensive and centralizing judicial interpretations of the constitutional text, a number of government practices have developed in the constitutional field. Those to which the Canadian state limited itself up until the Second World War were at least authorized by the constitution, whereas other practices have developed since then at the margin of the constitution, even in contradiction to the principles which, according to the Supreme Court, underlie the constitution. Their pervasive character is such that certain federal powers can be described as being indefinitely extensible.

Federal political, legislative, and administrative authorities have thus used the power granted to them under the constitution to centralize control of the territory, followed by the economy as a whole. Several tools have successively been employed: the federal power to disallow provincial legislation, the federal declaratory power, and federal power over public property, as well as other unilateral interventions, including the spending power, which is the focus of our concerns here.

Disallowance. The Constitution Act, 1867 made provision in sections 56 and 90 for the governor general's power to disallow legislation, including provincial legislation. This involves the discretionary cancellation of provincial legislation in the two years following its passage by way of a message to the federal Houses or a proclamation by the governor general. Used mainly in relation to the legislation of the western provinces in the early days of Confederation, the disallowance power fell into disuse because the principle of federalism rapidly prevailed after 1867, according to the recent opinion of the Supreme Court.[12]

Declarations to the general advantage of Canada. Provided for in the constitutions of several federal countries, the 'declaratory power' involves the power of the federal parliament to modify, on its own initiative, to the detriment of the constituent members of the federation and without their consent, the sphere of its legislative power by extending it to the 'works' that the federal Parliament declares to be to the general advantage of the federation.

In Canada, wording of the federal declaratory power in section 92(10)(c) of the Constitution Act, 1867 authorizes discretionary declarations. Up until 1961 when, until recently, we thought this power went into disuse, Parliament has proclaimed 470 such declarations concerning not only railroads, roads, and other means of intra-provincial transportation, but also the tramways of Montreal, Quebec City, and Ottawa, local bus networks, hotels, restaurants, and theatres, businesses active in the wood trade, stock-rearing, construction, factories manufacturing liquid air, chemicals, metal refineries, aqueducts, parks, not to mention the Montmorency Falls.[13] But we were wrong: it has not gone into disuse, it is alive and kicking, as Parliament recently introduced, though it did not pass, a bill where such a declaration could be found.[14] Is there any need to emphasize further the effects of this mechanism, to which the courts have been willing accomplices, by refusing to exert control over Parliament's discretion?

Acquisition of public properties. Because Parliament has legislative power over public property, the government simply needs to acquire lands or buildings to subject them to such power. Later, federal governments would use expropriation for these purposes, but before the Second World War the federal authorities generally limited themselves to purchases, notably in the downtown areas of the country's largest cities. Officially planned to permit the construction of federal public buildings, these acquisitions in fact sought to control urban development – a local matter if ever there was one, which by reason of this fact was originally vested in provincial jurisdiction. This jurisdiction was sidestepped by the combined interplay of public property and the theory of federal paramountcy. These practices, combined with the granting of public lands to crown corporations (in particular in the transportation field), along with established federal jurisdiction over ports and national airports, gave federal authorities mastery over the development of the urban territory of the provinces at a crucial time when states had not yet privatized their land planning powers.

Other unilateral interventions. Several unilateral federal interventions also strengthened the centralized character of the Canadian federation: the unilateral patriation of the constitution and the adoption of the 'Canadian Social Union without Quebec' (known outside Quebec as the Social Union Framework Agreement) are examples, set against the backdrop of the successive failures of the Meech Lake and Charlottetown accords. But the most persistent of these unilateral interventions is undoubtedly the spending power.

Present Scope of the Spending Power within the Context of Canadian Federalism

Having established the general framework of the tools of centralization that have been incorporated in the Canadian constitution, the definition and scope of the spending power may now be addressed in their true context, before we look at its relationship with fiscal imbalance.[15]

Definition

The very label of this federal tool of centralization leads to confusion, giving rise to one of the most spectacular effects of the ideological legitimization of the constitutional vocabulary. Indeed, what could be more normal than for a government to spend? Can a government act in any way without spending? It is possible to imagine that federalism may imply that the governments of a federation have no spending power? Of course not, such that by presenting its spending power as the basis for an intervention, a federal government seems to confer on its action irrefutable validity.

To make matters worse, this is partly justifiable. It is clear that both the federal and provincial authorities can spend within the sphere of their respective legislative powers, as this is an essential method for implementing the legislative measures that they adopt. For example, the federal authorities could pay the expenses of the army, foreign relations, or the post office, whereas the provincial authorities can pay those of the public service, the courts, prisons, and hospitals without violating the constitution. Moreover, federal expenditures in areas of provincial jurisdiction are also justifiable when the constitution makes express provision, as with equalization payments introduced in section 36(2) of the Constitution Act, 1867 by the Constitution Act, 1982:

> Parliament and the government of Canada are committed to the principle of making equalization payments to ensure that provincial governments have sufficient revenues to provide reasonably comparable levels of public services at reasonably comparable levels of taxation.[16]

But far from designating these valid practices, the expression 'spending power,' as consecrated by Canadian constitutional jargon, refers to the ideological affirmation of a non-existent power invoked by Canadian federal authorities, in particular within the framework of Established Programs Financing (EPF) and later the CHST.

Scope

Legal scholarship is divided on the federal spending power in fields of provincial jurisdiction, and it is important to dwell on this point before showing that this power is not part of our constitutional law as it currently reads, even though the question of its constitutionality is still open for want of a binding Supreme Court decision, and the direction the Court would take if confronted with the problem is quite uncertain as the law now stands.

A DIVIDED LEGAL SCHOLARSHIP

Since when Pierre Trudeau was still alive, the spending power has drawn the attention of leading constitutional scholars, both jurists and political scientists, and even economists. Some of them (Pierre Blache, Pierre Fortin, Stephan Dupré, and André Tremblay, in particular) have not expressed an opinion on its constitutional validity, contenting themselves on promoting it from a normative position, one that will not be the focus of our attention here.[17]

Others have considered that the spending power of the federal state in fields of provincial jurisdiction is not part of our constitutional law. They are Pierre Trudeau, Jean Beetz, Jacques Dupont and, more recently, Andrew Petter.[18] As their arguments largely confirm arguments developed further on in support of the non-constitutionality of the spending power, there is no need to dwell on these arguments here before proceeding to make an initial analysis of the constitutional bases suggested by those authors who believe that the spending power is already validly entrenched in our constitution.

The predominant current among the advocates of the constitutionality of the spending power ground it in the 'gift' theory: federal authorities, once they are owners of tax revenues, would be allowed to distribute such revenues as they see fit, as a gift to the provinces or to legal or natural persons who are under no obligation to accept these revenues – and hence who are not involuntarily subject to the normative conditions that the authorities may establish – either by virtue of the royal prerogative and common law, according to the oldest position held by Frank Scott[19] or, more often, by virtue of federal legislative power over public property, provided for in section 91(1A) of the Constitution Act, 1867 (a position held by, among others, Hogg, Smiley and Burns, Haussen, and Schwartz[20]). In summary, the advocates of these theories claim that the ownership of public funds gives the government the right to spend these funds as it sees fit, including by imposing normative conditions.

Other authors add other sources of revenues that would permit conditional spending. Peter Hogg – who incidentally is willing to justify the spending power based on the fact that it has been practised constantly by the federal government – also invokes in its support the grounds of an isolated decision of the Alberta Court of Appeal,[21] namely, the powers dealing respectively with the levying of taxes (s. 91(3)), and appropriations for the public service (s. 106), by virtue of which the federal authorities can levy taxes to pay the expenses of the public service and presumably, in their opinion, spend these taxes as they see fit. This latter line of argument is also invoked by Dreidger,[22] jointly with the power to create the Consolidated Revenue Fund (s. 102). Finally, François Chevrette[23] considers that the spending power is part of our constitutional law because it is necessary and because it is impossible to dissociate the expenses that a government incurs as a government from those that it would incur as a simple legal entity. Some authors have adopted an intermediate position whereby the law on the question is undecided, although the first of them, Gérard La Forest, has leaned towards the constitutionality of the spending power, whereas the second, Michel Maher, would like to see its constitutionalization to control this power.[24]

A common origin unites all these lines of argument proposed for the federal spending power in fields of provincial jurisdiction. In all cases, it involves a specific source of revenues contributing to federal public property – the Consolidated Revenue Fund (Hogg, Smiley, Haussen, Schwartz); monies other than income tax: public domain, spoils of war, profits of crown corporations (Trudeau); appropriations for the public service (Hogg, Dreidger).

The favourite source of each author would then produce revenues that could be spent by the federal government under the conditions of its choice, either by virtue of its prerogative (Scott), as the result of legislative power over public property (Hogg, Smiley, Haussen, Schwartz), or because the state has a legal personality of general juris- diction (Chevrette) and may, as such, dispose of the 'resources' of which it is 'the private holder' (Trudeau), as if public funds were not part of the public domain and could be considered as private.

The problem (or perhaps this is a solution) is that none of these theories – undoubtedly valid in a unitary state – stands up within the context of a federation. Indeed, the Privy Council confirmed that the prerogative and the powers of the executive are divided on the line applying to legislative powers;[25] the Privy Council also indicated that the fact that the federal government has legally collected the taxes in no way implies that it may dispose of them as it sees fit.[26] Nothing in the constitutional attributions of federal powers relating to the Consol- idated Revenue Fund or to appropriations for the public service autho- rizes conditional expenditures in fields of provincial jurisdiction.

As for the claim that the legal personality of the federal government is a 'person' not limited in its legal capacities by the constitution and should be seen like that of a private individual, it does not take into account, just as do not the other arguments raised thus far, the federal character of the Canadian constitution, with which they are totally incompatible. We will see that the precedents established by the higher courts do not lean in the same direction, but instead reinforce the posi- tion whereby the spending power is still not part of Canadian constitu- tional law. These precedents will be examined here in a historical perspective, by inserting the negotiations of agreements, none of which thus far has resulted in changes to the constitutional status of the spending power.

Inconclusive Judicial Discourse

Initially, in the 1930s, our Supreme Court favourably commented on the constitutionality of the spending power in the *Reference re Unem- ployment Insurance*,[27] but it was not confirmed on that point by the

Privy Council which, in the same case, held a different view, expressed in these terms: 'But assuming that the Dominion has collected by means of taxation a fund, it by no means follows that any legislation which disposes of it is necessarily within Dominion competence.'[28]

Such a statement left the question expressly open, and Professor La Forest – as he then was – acknowledged that it still remained as late as 1981, even though his personal normative position had evolved since then.[29] Since the *Reference re Unemployment Insurance*, other courts have rendered decisions without settling the question, either because they skirt it, or because the scope of their decision was not that of a precedent. The decisions rendered in *Central Mortgage* and *Porter* followed the Supreme Court decision in the *Unemployment Insurance Reference*, which, as noted, was not upheld by the Privy Council.[30] Although these two decisions and that in *Angers*[31] were on record when La Forest re-edited his work on fiscal powers in 1981, he nevertheless concluded that the question was still open, as the basis of the first decisions had not been upheld by the Privy Council and as the latter decision did not emanate from the Supreme Court. What is more, he refuted the Exchequer Court which, in *Angers*, had attempted to base the spending power upon the residual legislative competence of Parliament.

Three other decisions settle disputes in which this question, indirectly raised, was skirted. In the *Lofstrom* case, the Saskatchewan Court of Appeal decided that no individual right to social benefits derives from the federal-provincial agreements providing for the setting up of shared-cost programs in this field, because only governments are parties to these agreements. Therefore, the status of beneficiary is for the provinces to define, a position confirmed by the Supreme Court in the *Alden* case. But in that case, Mr. Justice Ritchie stopped short of any pronouncement on the constitutionality of the agreement, as did Mr Justice Le Dain in the case of *Finlay*.[32] At the same time a pronouncement was made by Mr Justice Pigeon in the *Reference re Agricultural Products Marketing Act*, where he declared unconstitutional even unconditional federal expenditures in a field of provincial jurisdiction.[33] This statement is part of the *ratio* of a majority opinion of the Court, but it has gone unnoticed in the spending power debate, undoubtedly because it was pronounced in a case that, although concerned with federal spending in a provincial sphere, did not deal with a shared-cost program.

Mention must also be made, without granting them the scope of precedents, of two pronouncements emanating, respectively, from courts of the first instance of Saskatchewan and Alberta, both issued in the context of declaratory actions. The first (*Dunbar*) deals with the provincial spending power and only throws light on the matter of concern to us by analogy.[34] Provincial grants in the international field had been contested. Although the judge had linked these grants to the federal legislative jurisdiction over external affairs, he nevertheless concluded that the appropriation bills were valid from a constitutional standpoint. The *ratio* of this decision, supported by two other decisions of the same level[35] (obviously not having the status of a precedent), seems to be that the legislature did not purport, in such an appropriation, to regulate activity under federal legislative competence.

This same line of argument was again invoked in *Lovelace*,[36] making it possible to conclude that the power of the provinces was confirmed only in their legislative competence, an interpretation that is universally accepted and has not given rise to controversy.

Without going into the question of whether the attribution of such grants falls within federal jurisdiction, it must be noted that the grants in all these cases were unconditional and therefore did not truly qualify as an exercise of legislative power. Consequently, the effect of such a decision, even though it emanated from a higher court, would not extend to conditional grants, the issue with which we are concerned in the present context.

In contrast, one decision, *Winterhaven Stables* confronts this question directly. In a declaratory action, the Alberta Court of Appeal ruled constitutional certain sections of the federal Income Tax Act. The monies the collection of which these sections authorize are subsequently transferred to the provinces under statutory provisions imposing conditions on the recipient provinces in the application of shared-cost programs in the fields of health, welfare, and post-secondary education, all matters within exclusive provincial jurisdiction. The court considered all these laws valid because they concerned, 'in pith and substance,' raising money by taxation, without reference to the provincial purposes for which such money would be earmarked. The whole issue posed by the federal spending power in fields of provincial jurisdiction being one of characterization, the relevant question in this instance is to know if Mr Justice Medhurst correctly characterized the purpose of the contested federal statute, and whether it is permissible for Parliament to do indirectly what the constitution directly prohibits. At any rate, despite its thorough treatment of the question, this isolated decision from a court of appeal from one province cannot settle the question for all of Canada. Such was the state of the law when two attempts were made to constitutionalize the spending power, included respectively in the Meech Lake Accord (1987) and the Charlottetown Agreement (1992) which, not having been ratified, did not alter the constitutionality of the spending power. Since then, four other Supreme Court decisions have addressed the subject, but only indirectly, such that they have not altered the substantive law on this question.

In the first of these decisions, *YMHA Jewish Community Center v. Brown*, Justice L'Heureux-Dubé wrote on behalf of the court that 'Parliament may be free to offer grants subject to whatever restrictions it sees fit.'[37] This statement is not part of the *ratio* of her decision but rather an *obiter*, which Justice L'Heureux-Dubé confirmed as such in the presence of several other justices of the Supreme Court and of the Court of Appeal at a session of the Association of Comparative Law at McGill University in 1990. The second opinion handed down since 1987 by the Supreme Court which implicitly concerns the spending power was rendered by Justice Sopinka in the *Reference re Canada Assistance Plan*.[38] It involved an appeal in which British Columbia alleged that the federal law reducing the grants awarded to the provinces in the health field constituted an invalid breach of contract. In this case, the court upheld the standing doctrine whereby Parliament has jurisdiction to cancel or modify past contracts of the crown.

This pronouncement can be seen as being implicitly based on the prior validity of the federal-provincial agreement dealing with these grants. But the validity of this agreement had not been called into question either by British Columbia, which seeing no other way to obtain the funds from the federal authorities, demanded the performance of the contract, or by the federal authorities, who wanted to continue governing health in the provinces. On this basis it may hardly be concluded that the Court has confirmed the validity of the federal power to spend conditionally in spheres of provincial jurisdiction without even discussing the question, which incidentally had not been raised before it. Furthermore, the contrary opinion of Justice La Forest in *Eldridge* does not change matters, given that he had made an express *obiter*, pronounced in a case which, moreover, involved not the spending power but the application of the Canadian Charter of Rights and Freedoms to provincial laws. What is more, neither the mere withdrawal of federal grants from the provinces, nor the limiting of the growth of these grants, which was addressed in the *Reference re Canada Assistance Plan*, is equivalent to passing legislation in areas of provincial jurisdiction. It goes without saying that to stop doing what is unconstitutional is not itself unconstitutional. By stating this obvious point, the Court is not necessarily giving an opinion on the constitutionality of the activity to which the federal executive is putting an end by withdrawing from shared-cost programs.

Finally, more recently, the *Lovelace* case dealt with the spending power of the provinces. Decided entirely within the context of the right to equality enshrined in the constitution under section 15 of the Charter, this judgment states that the casino project put forward by Ontario and contested by some First Nations does not affect the essence of aboriginality (which falls under federal jurisdiction) but falls within the spending power of the province and that the province in no way encroached on the jurisdiction of the federal government. In other words, this case, like the *Dunbar* case, involves the provincial spending power in the field of provincial jurisdictions, which is indeed perfectly valid from the standpoint of the constitution.

In short, as far as the Supreme Court is concerned, two *obiter dicta*, including one pronouncement on the withdrawal of a federal intervention in a field of provincial jurisdiction – moreover stated in a reference – and a decision dealing with the spending power of a province in its own field of legislative powers cannot have as their effect to dissociate the Court from earlier judgments to the contrary by the Privy Council, and even less so to amend the constitution on this subject. The federal spending power, which imposes conditions that are equivalent to the exercise of normative power in fields of provincial jurisdiction, is still not part of this constitution, unless more weight is given to a decision of the Alberta Court of Appeal than to all of the precedents of the Privy Council and of the Supreme Court. In light of the direction and scope of all these decisions, it still seems accurate to say that the law is not yet decided on the matter of the constitutionality of the federal spending power in areas falling under provincial legislative jurisdiction.

A final element, and not the least, must be kept in mind; all these decisions must be read in light of the principle of federalism that the Court has reiterated several times in its recent precedents. Admittedly, the concept of federalism is not completely unequivocal and most Canadian constitutional scholars are not very prolific, to say the least, on the subject of the theory of federalism and especially on the differences between federalism and administrative decentralization.[39] They all agree, however, on a threshold below which there may be no real federalism: that line is drawn when local authorities are subordinate to central authorities. Some authors even specify that this independence in relation to the central authorities needs to be constitutionalized.[40] Except for Rémillard,[41] who gears his discussion towards the federation/confederation dichotomy and who does not even address the question of the minimal requirements of federalism, all Canadian constitutional scholars are in agreement concerning this threshold. Some even mention that local authorities must have sufficient fiscal powers to guarantee this independence.[42]

But within this context, it is mainly the opinions of the Supreme Court that matter, where it recently restated on three occasions in landmark decisions[43] the principle of federalism, in the very words used by Lord Watson in *Re the Initiative and Referendum Act*[74] in the last century:

> The object of the Act was neither to weld the provinces into one, nor to subordinate provincial governments to a central authority, but to create a federal government in which they should all be represented, entrusted with the exclusive administration of affairs in which they had a common interest, each province retaining its independence and autonomy.[44]

At the end of this up-to-date examination of the precedents of the Privy Council, the Supreme Court, and even the lower courts of competent jurisdiction, it may be stated that the constitutionality of the federal spending power in fields of jurisdiction of the provinces has not given rise to a favourable pronouncement having the scope of a precedent.

Nor is it the recent conclusion of the Canadian Social Union 'without Quebec', to plagiarize a title that has rightly become famous,[45] that may have changed things. This agreement is expressed as an administrative agreement and not a constitutional amendment, whose formal procedures, prescribed by the Constitution Act, 1982, the agreement did not even try to follow. What is more, even if the temporary nature of this agreement were to dissolve within renewed continuity, it would not constitute, for Quebec at least, a 'constitutional convention' within the meaning that the court gave this instrument in the *Reference re the Constitution of Canada*,[46] because it does not meet the condition that the Court deems the most important to establish a convention – namely, the acceptance or the recognition of such a convention by the actors in a context where the constitutional amendments involved must receive the approval of the provinces whose legislative power is being affected.

Historical Relationship between the Spending Power and Fiscal Imbalance in Canada

The relationship between the spending power and fiscal imbalance lies in the very definition of this last concept, and can be shown to have existed in Canada throughout the history of conditional federal spending in the provinces' areas of jurisdiction.

Definition

Fiscal imbalance is not an all-inclusive concept describing any kind of public finance disequilibrium in any kind of state. By definition, it can only obtain in a federation where fiscal powers as well as legislative competence are constitutionally divided between federal and consti-tutent entities. In such states, fiscal imbalance is said to occur when – to paraphrase the Séguin Commission Report – there is too great a fiscal gap between the constituent entities' own revenue sources and their direct spending, because such a difference threatens to subordinate those entities to the federal government, which is contrary to the fed-eral principle. Specifically, the commission writes:

> fiscal imbalance exists when the federal government invokes a 'spending power' to intervene in the provinces' fields of jurisdiction [because] this power limits the decision-making and budgetary autonomy of the prov-inces, has a direct influence on their level of spending and is facilitated, on practical terms, by excess revenue of the central government in relation to its spending within the jurisdictions allocated to it by the Constitution.[47]

History

Despite the fact that the federal conditional spending power is not part of our constitution, it has been practised by the federal authorities since at least 1912. Seven programs had already been implemented before the great crisis of the 1930s, invading provincial legislative com-petences in education, local infrastructures, and social assistance.[48] With the Depression, the financial self-sufficiency of the provinces was even more compromised and the federal government intervened both with direct transfers and specific conditional programs. One of those measures, unemployment insurance, was declared unconstitutional by the Privy Council and prompted a consequent modification of the constitution in favour of the federal authorities, thus confirming the provincial competence over remaining social policies, even in the field of old age security where, despite another constitutional modification, the provinces retained their paramountcy.[49] As this particular kind of welfare state was emerging in Canada, the war opened the way for yet another expedient: tax rental agreements, by which the provinces 'rented' their fiscal space to the federal authorities in exchange for transfer payments, so that the federal government could pursue the war effort.

This situation prevailed until 1947, when Ontario and Quebec refused to extend the lease and negotiated the transfer of income tax points, indicating the renunciation by federal fiscal authorities of some percentage of the income and other taxes they were previously collecting, so as to free up that fiscal space for the provinces' taxation powers. In more simple language, a proportion of taxes that hitherto were collected by the federal treasury would now be levied by the provinces for their constitutionally valid legislative purposes.

However, such transfers were insufficient for both the provincial needs and the federal appetite for intervention in fields relevant to the daily lives of voters, and brought about the shared-cost programs, which invaded provincial jurisdiction in health, education, labour, municipal and regional development and income security, by imposing conditions on provincial programs of which the cost was to be shared between federal and provincial treasuries. Most provinces complied as they had no other way of retrieving the taxes of their constituents from the federal authorities, until the economic conditions of the early 1980s brought the federal government to curtail its contribution, without however retracting the conditions they imposed on the provinces.

To circumvent their objections, the federal government has resorted to a new transmission channel for its spending in the provinces: direct grants to individual taxpayers (for example, tax exemptions for education expenditures, or scholarships/chairs so as to intervene in the higher education field) or to cities and other municipalities, entities within provincial legislative competence.

Conclusion

It must now be apparent that conditional federal spending has taken different forms since early last century – subsidy programs, tax rental agreements, conditional transfers and shared-cost payments to provinces, and direct grants to individuals and provincial entities – but has always directly invaded provincial fields of jurisdiction: education, health, labour, income security, local economic development, and soon municipal institutions. This is a serious violation of the federal principle which is still supposed to govern our constitution.

But this practice has also indirectly violated the constitution by producing fiscal imbalance, by depriving provinces of the share of the tax revenue they need to properly exercise the legislative and executive powers bestowed on them by the constitution. It has come to the point where Canada is not a real federation any more, but rather a centralized monist state. Maybe it is not a coincidence that the only federations we know of where the conditional spending power of the central authorities is subject to little or no control are either classical federations emanating from the British Empire where colonial powers were transferred to the federal authorities (Australia, the United States) or quasi-federations of regional entities (Italy, Spain, United Kingdom).

Of course, such centralization may be the wish of the federal authorities and of some provinces in Canada, although not all, especially not Quebec. However, for such a wish to become a reality, a modification of the constitution is necessary, and until it happens, conditional federal spending in the realm of provincial jurisdiction is unconstitutional and disruptive of the federal principle and spirit, not to mention national harmony.

NOTES

1 Andrée Lajoie, 'The Federal Spending Power and the Meech Lake Accord,' in Katherine E. Swinton and Carol S. Rogerson, ed., *Competing Constitutional Visions: The Meech Lake Accord* (Toronto: Carswell, 1988), 175–85; Commission on Fiscal Imbalance, *The 'Federal Spending Power,' Report – Supporting Document 2* (Quebec: Bibliothèque nationale du Québec, 2002). Large excerpts are used in this paper with the authorization of the Quebec ministère des Finances.
2 *Liquidators of Maritime Bank v. Receiver General of New Brunswick*, [1892] A.C. 437 (P.C.); *Reference re Secession of Quebec*, [1998] 2 S.C.R. 217, para. 56.
3 André Tremblay, 'Judicial Interpretation and the Canadian Constitution,' *National Journal of Constitutional Law* 1 (1991–2): 163, 165. This section of the text draws much of its inspiration, with the author's consent, from this article, which is an excellent summary of this period.

4 On this question, see Andrée Lajoie, Michèle Gamache, and Pierette Mulazzi, 'Political Ideas in Quebec and the Evolution of Canadian Constitutional Law,' in Andrée Lajoie and Ivan Bernier, eds., *The Supreme Court of Canada as an Instrument of Political Change* (Toronto: University of Toronto Press and Supply and Services Canada, 1986), 1–110.

5 See *Cushing v. Dupuy* (1880), 5 App. Cas. 409 (P.C.).

6 *Attorney General of Ontario v. Attorney General of Canada*, [1896] A.C. 348, (P.C.); *Bank of Montreal v. Hall*, [1990] 1 S.C.R. 121.

7 *John Deere Plow Co. v. Wharton*, [1915] A.C. 330 (P.C.).

8 *Russell v. The Queen* (1882) 7 App. Cas. 829 (P.C.).

9 *R. v. Crown Zellerbach* [1988] 1 S.C.R. 401; *Friends of the Oldman River v. Canada*, [1972] 1 S.C.R. 3.

10 *Fort Frances Pulp and Power Co. v. Manitoba Free Press*, [1923] A.C. 695 (P.C.).

11 François Chevrette and Herbert Marx, *Droit constitutionnel* (Montréal: Les Presses de l'Université de Montréal, 1982), 389 (my translation).

12 *Reference re Secession of Quebec*, para. 55.

13 Andrée Lajoie, *Le pouvoir déclaratoire du Parlement, augmentation discrétionnaire de la compétence fédérale au Canada.* (Montreal: Les Presses de l'Université de Montreal 1969), 123ff and 67ff.

14 *An Act to amend the Canada Transportation Act and the Act the Railway Safety Act, to enact the VIA Rail Canada Act and to make consequential amendments to other Acts*, Bill C-44, clause 51, first reading, 24 March 2005.

15 The text of this section takes up in part, updating it, data found in Andrée Lajoie, 'L'impact des Accords du Lac Meech sur le pouvoir de dépenser,' in Réal Forest, ed., *L'adhésion du Québec à l'Accord du Lac Meech* (Montreal: Éditions Thémis, 1988), 163–80 and Lajoie, 'The Federal Spending Power.'

16 Constitution Act, 1982, Schedule B to the Canada Act, 1982 (UK) 1982, c. 11.

17 Pierre Blache, 'Le pouvoir de dépenser au cœur de la crise constitutionnelle canadienne,' *Revue générale de droit* 24 (1993): 29–64. Pierre Fortin, 'The Meech Lake Accord and the Federal Spending Power: A Good Maximin Solution,' in Swinton and Rogerson, eds., *Competing Constitutional Visions*, 213–23; Stefan Dupré, 'Section 106A and the Federal-Provincial Fiscal Relations,' in ibid., 203–11; and André Tremblay, 'Federal Spending Power,' in Alain G. Gagnon and Hugh Segal, eds., *The Canadian Social Union without Québec* (Montreal: IRPP, 2001), 155–89. It should be noted that this author's position at the time of the Meech Lake Accord implicitly approved the constitutionality of the spending power, the scope of which he sought to limit by clarifying it.

18 Pierre E. Trudeau, 'Les octrois fédéraux aux universités,' in Pierre E. Trudeau, ed., *Le Fédéralisme et la société canadienne française* (Montréal: Édi-

tions HMH, 1967), 79–103. Trudeau was reaffirming here a position that he had first adopted in *Cité Libre* in February 1957. He would implicitly disso-ciate himself from it two years later when his government published a working document entitled *Federal-Provincial Grants and the Spending Power of Parliament* (Ottawa: Queen's Printer, 1969). Initially, he already felt that his reasoning applied only to federal revenues from taxes, stating that the federal state could dispose, as it saw fit, of its 'private revenues' from the public domain, spoils of war, and profits of crown corporations; Jean Beetz, 'Les attitudes changeantes du Québec à l'endroit de la Constitution de 1867,' in Paul A. Crépeau and C.B. MacPherson, eds., *The Future of Canadian Federalism / L'avenir du fédéralisme canadien* (Toronto/Montreal; University of Toronto Press/Les Presses de l'Université de Montréal, 1965), 113ff.; Jacques Dupont, 'Le pouvoir de dépenser du gouvernement fédéral: A Dead Issue?' *University of British Columbia Law Review / Cahiers le droit* (1967); 69–165; and Andrew Petter, 'Meech Ado about Nothing? Federal-ism, Democracy and the Spending Power,' in Swinton and Rogerson, eds., *Competing Constitutional Visions*, 187–201 and 'Federalism and the Myth of the Federal Spending Power,' *Canadian Bar Review* 68 (1989); 448.

19 Frank Scott, 'The Constitutional Background of the Tax Agreement,' *McGill Law Journal* 2 (1955): 667.

20 Peter Hogg, 'Analysis of the New Spending Provision (Section 106A),' in Swinton and Rogerson, eds., *Competing Constitutional Visions*, 155–62, Donald V. Smiley and Ronald M. Burns, 'Canadian Federalism and the Spending Power: Is Constitutional Restriction Necessary?' *Canadian Tax Journal* (1969): 468; K. Hanssen, 'The Constitutionality of Conditional Grant Legislation,' *Manitoba Law Journal* 2 (1966–7): 191; and Bryan Schwartz, *Fathoming Meech Lake* (Winnipeg: Legal Research Institute of the University of Manitoba, 1987), 150–207.

21 *Winterhaven Stables Ltd. v. Attorney General of Canada* (1986), 29 D.L.R. (4th) 394 (Alta. Q.B.), aff'd (1988), 91 A.R. 114 (Alta. C.A.), leave to appeal to S.C.C. refused, [1988] S.C.C.A. (Quicklaw) 543 (S.C.C.).

22 E.A. Dreidger, 'The Spending Power,' *Queen's Law Journal* 7 (1981–2): 135.

23 François Chevrette, 'Contrôler le pouvoir de dépenser: un gain ou un piège?' in A. Costi, ed., *L'adhésion du Québec à l'Accord du Lac Meech* (Mon-tréal: Éditions Thémis, 1988), 153–61.

24 Gérard V. La Forest, 'The Allocation of Taxing Power under the Canadian Constitution,' *Canadian Tax Papers* 65 (1980–1): 50, in which the author favours the constitutionality of the spending power while admitting that it has not been decided by the courts. Subsequently, following *Reference re*

Canada Assistance Plan, [1991] 2 S.C.R. 525, he would consider in *obiter* in *Eldridge v. A.G.B.C.*, [1997] 3 S.C.R. 624, that the spending power had been constitutionalized, Michael Maher, 'Le défi du fédéralisme fiscal dans l'exercice du pouvoir de dépenser,' *Canadian Bar Review* 75 (1996): 404.

25 *Liquidators of the Maritime Bank of Canada.* See also Andrée Lajoie, *Expropriation et fédéralisme au Canada* (Montréal: Presses de l'Université de Montréal, 1972), 43 ff.

26 *Attorney General of Canada v. Attorney General for Ontario*, [1937] A.C. 355, 366 (P.C.).

27 *Reference re the Employment and Social Insurance Act*, [1936] S.C.R. 427.

28 *Attorney General of Canada v. Attorney General for Ontario.*

29 La Forest, 'Allocation of Taxing Power.'

30 *Central Mortgage and Housing v. Cooperative College Residences* (1974), 44 D.L.R. (3d) 662 (Ont. High Ct) and (1977), 71 D.L.R. (3d) 183 (Ont. C.A.); *Porter v. The Queen*, [1965] Ex. C.R. 200.

31 *Angers v. Minister of National Revenue*, [1957] Ex C.R. 83.

32 *Re Lofstrom and Murphy and al.* (1972), 22 D.L.R. (3d) 120 (Sask. C.A.)., *Alden v. Gaglardi*, [1973] S.C.R. 199; *Finlay v. Canada (Minister of Finance)*, [1986] 2 S.C.R. 607.

33 *Reference re Agricultural Products Marketing Act*, [1978] 2 S.C.R. 1198.

34 *Dunbar v. Attorney General of Saskatchewan* (1985), 11 D.L.R. (4th) 374 (Sask. QB).

35 *Dow v. Black* (1875), L.R. 6, P.C. 272, and *McMillan v. City of Winnipeg* (1919), 45 D.L.R. 351 (Man. K.B.).

36 *Lovelace v. Ontario*, [2000] 1 S.C.R. 950.

37 [1989] 1 S.C.R. 1532, 1549.

38 *Reference re Canada Assistance Plan*, [1991] 2 S.C.R. 525.

39 Except Henri Brun and Guy Tremblay, *Droit constitutionnel* (Cowansville, QC: Éditions Yvon Blais, 1982), who devote an important chapter to this question.

40 See André Tremblay, *Précis de droit constitutionnel* (Montreal: Éditions Thémis, 1982), 88; François Chevrette and Herbert Marx, *Droit constitutionnel*, 219; Neil Finkelstein, *Laskin's Canadian Constitutional Law*, 5th ed. (Toronto: Carswell, 1986), 1: 16; Gérald-A. Beaudoin, *Le partage des pouvoirs*, 2nd ed. (Ottawa: Éditions de l'Université d'Ottawa, 1982), 11; Joseph E. Magnet, *Constitutional Law of Canada* (Toronto: Carswell, 1983), 1.

41 Gilles Rémillard, *Le fédéralisme canadien*, t. 1, 'La Loi constitutionnelle de 1867' (Montreal: Éditions Québec/Amérique, 1983), 48.

42 See John Whyte and William R. Lederman, *Canadian Constitutional Law*, 2nd ed. (Toronto: Butterworths, 1977), 1–19.

43 *Reference re Secession of Quebec; Re Resolution to amend the Constitution*, [1981] 1 S.C.R. 753; *Re Manitoba language rights*, [1985] 1 S.C.R. 721.
44 *Liquidators of Maritime Bank*, 441–2.
45 Alain G. Gagnon, ed., *L'Union sociale canadienne sans le Québec: huit études sur l'entente-cadre* (Montreal: Éditions St-Martin, 2000).
46 [1982] 2 S.C.R. 793.
47 Commission on Fiscal Imbalance, *A New Division of Canada's Financial Resources – Report* (Quebec: Bibliothèque nationale du Québec, 2002), 16.
48 Commission on Fiscal Imbalance, *Fiscal Imbalance in Canada: Historical Background, Report – Supporting Document 1* (Quebec: Bibliothèque nationale du Québec, 2002), 18.
49 Constitution Act, 1940, 3–4 Geo. VI, c. 36 (UK); Constitution Act, 1964, 12–13 Eliz. II, c. 73 (UK).

Liberty and Overlapping Federalism

DANIEL M. WEINSTOCK

Professor Lajoie claims in her interesting and thought-provoking paper not to be interested in the question of whether a conditional federal spending power conforms to federalism construed as a normative theory of government. Her claim is more limited, though important if true: the Canadian federal government's practice of conditional spending in areas of provincial jurisdiction has no basis in Canadian constitutional law.

At the very end of the paper, however, Lajoie makes a slightly more ambitious claim. In her view, the federal spending power 'is unconstitutional *and disruptive of the federal principle and spirit*, not to mention national harmony' (my emphasis). My response in this brief comment will address this normative claim. Does federalism, *as such*, condemn the practice that is the object of Professor Lajoie's paper? I will argue that this is unclear, and that neither side to the dispute can claim to be exclusive holders of federalist truth.

Part of the problem lies with the state of normative federalist theory. Quite simply, political philosophers have paid little attention to federalism understood as a set of normative propositions about government. Given the proportion of the world's population that now lives in political systems that purport to be federal, this is, to say the least, a regrettable state of affairs.[1] So there is no settled body of thought that might help us to determine what the broad parameters of federalism are, no *Theory of Justice* that might serve as a common focus for normative work on federalism.

Let us begin with an uncontroversial definition. According to a recent definition, 'federalism is a constitutionally determined tier-structure,' in which the integrity of constituent units is guaranteed, and in which these units share political power with a central govern-ment. Federalism requires that there be some government functions that fall entirely within the province of the units, and some that fall entirely under the jurisdiction of the central government.[2] The relation-ship between the two levels must not be one of subordination, a point on which Professor Lajoie insists particularly.

Note that this definition is compatible with two variants, that I will term, respectively, side-by-side federalism (SSF) and overlapping fed-eralism (OF). SSF requires that all powers be distributed into discrete sets; that is, any power falls within the jurisdiction of either one level of government or the other, but not both. SSF allows that some powers be shared between levels, as long as at least one power is held exclusively by both levels, and the distribution is not decided upon unilaterally by one or the other levels.

Which, of SSF and OF, is preferable from a normative point of view? Does one or the other better capture 'the federal spirit and principle'? To begin to answer this question, we have to delve into the reasons that might motivate political entities to federate rather than opt for unitary government.

The discovery of such reasons is itself made complicated by the fact that there are different possible paths to federalism, and that the rea-sons of the political entities that follow different paths will naturally be quite different. Ideal-typically, we might say that there are two princi-pal paths to federalism.[3] First, a set of previously self-governing politi-cal entities can decide to join together within a federation. I will refer to this type of process as *federal integration*. Second, a previously unitary state can decide to create new constituent units to which it alienates some of its powers. These boundaries may, though they need not, over-lap with already existing cultural, linguistic, or religious boundaries. This type of process I shall term *federal restructuring*. The reasons that might justify integration and those that motivate restructuring will not be exactly the same.

From the point of view of citizens, however, there is something both processes share. Whereas antecedently citizens had lived under one central political authority (which is not to say that they didn't live under different overlapping *administrations*), they are now subject to coordinated but distinct political authorities, neither one of which can claim total sovereignty. This has seemed to many observers and theo-rists to be a crucial political condition for the realization of individual freedom. Where there are two orders of government that are in a sense placed in competition with one another, each one wanting to be able to present itself as the level at which 'good' government is exercised, each level will exercise vigilance in ensuring that the predations of the other level on the freedom of citizens are exposed and criticized. By distributing power and by creating a structure in which levels of government both cooperate and compete, federalism acts as a break on the untrammelled exercise of power by any one level of government.

There are other reasons that might underpin federal restructuring. First, the creation of smaller, partially self-governing units encourages active democratic citizenship. As Mill pointed out, citizens are both epistemically and practically more likely to act at the local level, where the main political issues impinge upon them directly, and where the institutions through which citizenship can be exercised are readier at hand.[4] In certain cases, where federal units overlap with cultural lines, federalism provides groups that might be natural candidates for statehood with meaningful self-determination, while avoiding the crazy quilt that would arise on the international scene if every group legitimately aspiring to self-determination were to acquire its own state. It creates a political context in which real choices are made, and in which a group that is a minority on the broader federal scene can be a majority, and thus enact legislation that furthers the interests of the group in question.

What reasons might sovereign states have to integrate into a federation? What values does the emergence of federations serve? To begin with, federations give political expression to the increasingly complex identities of modern political identities. A Catalan living in contemporary Europe, for example, can legitimately feel that his identity cannot be reduced to its Catalan, Spanish, or European dimensions. Rather, it is made up in complex ways by all of these. And, all things being equal, there are advantages to political arrangements that allow people to express the various aspects of their identities in ways that are more than simply folkloric. Unitary states require of citizens that they relegate aspects of their identities that might be important to them to the private realm, subordinating them to a political identity that is often officially claimed to be culturally neutral, but which in fact most often carries with it important aspects of the majority culture. Federations ideally do not require such a sacrifice. They allow all aspects of one's identity to bear political relevance.

Second, federations give greater scope to principles of distributive justice. It is empirically the case that much more distribution of resources between rich and poor occurs within the boundaries of states than between states. Some theorists argue that this has to do with fairly deep-seated motivational considerations. People on this view feel more disposed to make sacrifices on behalf of others with whom they are more than simply contingently related.[5] If this is the case, then one way of ensuring that principles of distributive justice hold sway over greater populations is to create institutions whereby citizens come to feel more than just contingently related to a wider range of other people. Federal institutions created out of the agreement of sovereign states increase the number of people that citizens of these states can regard as fellow citizens.

There are trade-offs, of course. A hundred and fifty years ago, Alexis de Tocqueville, surveying the American federation, was made aware of the many inefficiencies that federal political arrangements seem to create. Even an institutional design that managed in theory to seal levels of government off from one another would, Tocqueville noted, end up giving rise in practice to countless points of friction. Compromises have to be reached and deals brokered, so that 'parmi les vices inhérents à tout système fédéral, le plus visible de tous est la complication des moyens qu'il emploie.'[6]

What's more, the 'genetic code' of federations means that they will often be riven with conflict and instability. Part of the conflictual nature of federations is of course desirable, for reasons that we have already touched on: where levels of government vie with one another, the hope is that citizens will be better served. Furthermore, the multiplication of governments can give rise to a more experimental approach to policy-making that can, in principle at least, give rise to better policy. A novel policy can be tried out in a federal unit, and then adopted (or not) by other units and by the federal government, depending on its success. Policy-making initiatives in unitary states are by contrast all-or-nothing affairs, where policies apply to everyone if they apply to anyone. The tension and competition within a federation can thus in certain cases be a 'creative tension.'

But there is no gainsaying the fact that the tensions in federations can be destabilizing. When formerly self-governing people join federations, the motivational hold that the constituent unit will have upon citizens will perforce be felt more intensely than that of the new, larger, and more distant federal government. Alexander Hamilton attempted in *Federalist XVII* to turn this into an advantage of federations. In his view it would serve as a guarantee that citizens would be ever vigilant lest the federal government overstep its legitimate bounds.[7] But the effect of this motivational asymmetry might just as well be to give rise to secessionist politics, to which even federations born of restructuring are not immune. Political units with no pre-existing sense of themselves as distinct might come to acquire a proto-national self-conception as a result of its citizens coming to share political institutions. It will thus be very difficult for federations to have their cake and eat it: the tension that is the political condition of increased political freedom for individual citizens and of innovative policy-making at every moment risks tearing the federation asunder.[8]

Thus far I have stipulated what I take to be fairly uncontroversial conditions that must be met for a form of government to count as federal. I have claimed that these conditions are compatible with both SSF and OF. The basic proposition is that federalism recommends itself as a form of government because it puts in place political conditions for the realization of individual freedom, and it allows for communal self-determination while increasing the scope of principles of distributive justice and allowing for the political expression of complex identities. Those who favour the expansion of federal institutions throughout the world believe that these normative advantages outweigh the disadvantages that the complexity and the instability of federations often occasion.

So the question that must now be posed is this: Is there anything about the spirit of federalism that tells either for SSF or for OF? I would argue that what I take to be the primary advantage of federations – their greater guarantee as opposed to unitary states of individual freedom – tells in favour of OF. When jurisdictional spheres are rigidly demarcated and apportioned exclusively to one or the other level of government, then citizens are not so much living under federal institutions as they are under serial unitary ones. If the functions of government are hermetically sealed off from one another, then it is hard to see how the freedom-enhancing effects of rival levels of government competing with one another can be achieved. Both levels of government would, according to the SSF vision, wield complete authority over citizens with respect to this or that function.

When overlap and redundancy are built into the system, no level of government can claim complete control. Compromises must be made and administrative arrangements must be reached. Each side will vigilantly observe the other for signs that it is overstepping bounds agreed to. They will thus both end up unintentionally promoting the freedom of citizens. When both levels of governments attempt to rein each other in, the effect is that the power of government is limited. And this is a good thing for those who favour individual freedom.

I should emphasize that this argument is being made under a simplifying assumption that in reality never holds, no matter how much partisans of SSF wish that it would. It is assumed that policy domains can be neatly segregated off from one another, but in fact they cannot. Policies in one area have predictable direct effects in others, and this is because the whole idea of a policy 'domain' is a theoretical creation rather than a reflection of reality. Think, to cite just one important example, of the multiple determinants of health. Imagine that an environmental policy is enacted explicitly because of its impact on population health. On the assumption that environment and health are held as exclusive jurisdictions by different levels of government, has there or has there not been encroachment of one level of government on the other? The fluidity that exists between what some think of as discrete policy domains puts paid to this kind of question.

I would argue moreover that the other advantages of federalism that I have tried to delineate are better served by OF than by SSF. First, complex individual identities are not to be thought of on a cookie-cutter model. Imagine an individual whose identity is deeply constituted by an allegiance both to a federal sub-unit (A) and to the federation as a whole (B). The two aspects of his identity are in constant interaction with one another: being an A will colour what it means for him to be a B, and vice versa. Moreover, it is absurd to think that the individual in question is an A when he thinks about, say, the environment, security, and agriculture, and a B when he thinks about health, education, and communications. Rather, the complex, dynamic whole that is constituted by the interacting parts of his political identity will be brought to bear on the way in which he thinks about all of these issues. Thus, a federal politics reflective of the dynamic character of complex identities will look like OF rather than SSF.

Second, the extension of our sympathies required to broaden the reach of principles of distributive justice is, if contemporary defenders of liberal nationalism are right, more likely to occur when we consider those to whom the principles apply as *concitoyens*, but this in turn seems more likely to occur if we have political discussions with citizens from different federal sub-units about issues of common concern. The more sealed of from one another discussions about issues such as health, education, and the like are from one sub-unit to the next, the less likely members of these different sub-units are to think of themselves as joined together in a common political enterprise, and the more difficult it will be in turn to extend the kind of moral concern across the federation that is required to motivate people to act according to their distributive obligations.

Third, learning and innovative policy-making is more likely to occur in federations where sub-units see themselves as sharing concerns on common policy areas. They may be less likely to attempt innovative, adventurous policies if they view themselves as saddled with the entirety of costs in case of failure, than if the other sub-units and the federal government were to ensure some degree of back-up.

Is the self-determination of sub-units substantially diminished in OF as against SSF? At first glance, it appears clear that the answer to this question can only be yes. Indeed, in SSF, sub-units would get to decide certain things on their own, or so it would seem, whereas in OF there is a wide range of issues over which they will have to negotiate and compromise with their federal partners.

But it would be a mistake to overestimate the degree of real autonomy that sub-units would have over the areas over which they have theoretical sovereignty, especially in conditions of globalization. In an increasingly interdependent world, the decisions of other, especially larger and more powerful states, will have to be integrated parametrically into the policy-making process of the sovereign sub-unit. But as opposed to what occurs within federal institutions, no institutionalized dialogue will exist for the sub-unit in question to have an impact on the policy decisions that others make. Federations may make sub-units more interdependent, but they also incorporate a multitude of occasions for deliberation, discussion, and negotiation, so that the interdependence that holds in a federation can aspire to being reflective and deliberative, rather than the result of the causality of brute force and power differentials.

So there are reasons to think that the spirit of federalism favours OF over SSF. It is a mistake, on this view, to build federal institutions on the assumption of exclusive jurisdictional spheres. Such an idea is empirically suspect. And to borrow a phrase from Professor Lajoie, it may also be disruptive of the federal principle and spirit.

174 Daniel M. Weinstock

NOTES

1 See Wayne Norman, 'Toward a Philosophy of Federalism,' in Judith Baker, ed., *Group Rights* (Toronto: University of Toronto Press, 1994).
2 William Riker, 'Federalism,' in Robert E. Goodin and Philip Pettit, eds., *A Companion to Contemporary Political Philosophy* (Oxford: Basil Blackwell, 1993), 508–9.
3 I take up ideas here that I have already discussed in 'Towards a Normative Theory of Federalism,' in *International Social Science Journal* 167 (March 2001) 75–83.
4 John Stuart Mill, *Of Representative Government* (Buffalo, NY: Prometheus Press, 1991), ch. 15.
5 See, for example, David Miller, *On Nationality* (Oxford: Oxford University Press, 1995).
6 Alexis de Tocqueville, *De la démocratie en Amérique*, vol. 1 (Paris: Garnier-Flammarion, 1981), 242.
7 James Madison, Alexander Hamilton and John Jay, *The Federalist Papers* (Harmondsworth: Penguin Books, 1987), 157.
8 Will Kymlicka, 'Is Federalism a Viable Alternative to Secession?' in Percy Lehning, ed., *Citizenship, Democracy and Justice in the New Europe* (London: Routledge, 1998).

Fiscal Federalism: Not Resolvable by Constitutional Law

PETER H. RUSSELL

It is a pleasure to read and have the opportunity to comment on the paper by Andrée Lajoie. As usual it is clear, forceful, and principled, and addresses an issue of fundamental importance in our constitutional life. However, I fear that my comment may be somewhat disappointing to her. For I am the kind of Anglo-Canadian federalist that should be receptive to her arguments. Unlike many constitutional scholars who have taught at the University of Toronto, I was rather partial to the constitutional jurisprudence of the Judicial Committee of the Privy Council – not all of it, but its tendency from the 1890s to the 1930s to protect provincial autonomy. When the Supreme Court began to wrestle with crucial issues of federalism, I found Jean Beetz more appealing than Bora Laskin. And in the 1980s I disagreed with the Court's decision in the *Quebec Veto Reference*. I did not think it constitutionally proper to proceed with patriation without Quebec's consent and was a strong supporter of the Meech Lake Accord. So, if my comments on Andrée's paper are somewhat negative, may I note that they come from a not unfriendly quarter of English Canada.

My comments fall into three parts. First, I will explain why I take a narrower view of the Judicial Committee's 1937 landmark decision on the spending power and a broader view of the constitutional basis for federal legislation in the field of social policy. Second, I will discuss my uneasiness with her view that federalism requires a strict fiscal balance. In the concluding section I will advance my own preference, at this point in Canadian history, for resolving contested issues of fiscal federalism by political agreements rather than through litigation or constitutional amendment.

The 1937 *Unemployment Insurance Reference*

In the 1937 *Unemployment Insurance Reference*, the Privy Council ruled that federal legislation which 'in pith and substance ... invades civil rights within the Province' cannot be saved simply by the fact that the legislation involves the expenditure of money collected through federal taxation.[1] The legislation in question setting up an unemployment insurance fund to which employers and employees were required to make contributions was considered to be an invasion of civil rights within the province because it regulated contracts of employment and thus was legislation falling under the provinces' exclusive power to make laws in relation to property and civil rights in the province. The federal government's lawyer (a future prime minister, Louis St Laurent) offered two arguments in defence of the legislation.[2] The first was an attempt to invoke the federal Parliament's general power to make laws for the peace, order, and good government of Canada (POGG) on the basis that unemployment insurance was a matter of grave national concern not specifically provided for under sections 91 or 92. That argument was rejected on the basis of a series of decisions beginning in 1922 in which the Privy Council had reduced POGG to a power that could be used only to support temporary legislation aimed at dealing with a special emergency. Because the unemployment in-surance legislation was to be permanent legislation, it could not be supported by POGG as it was interpreted at that time. The second argument was an appeal to Parliament's so-called spending power – that is, a power to dispose of money it has collected through any form of taxation. To this, the Law Lords said that legislation disposing of such funds is *ultra vires* if, as in the case at hand, it is properly characterized as legislation that in pith and substance regulates a matter assigned exclusively to the provinces.

Now this is all that was decided in the 1937 *Unemployment Insurance Reference*. However, as I read Professor Lajoie's essay I get the impression that she thinks it decided a good deal more than this. She writes as if the case determined that the entire field of social policy lies under exclusive provincial jurisdiction and that any federal initiative providing funding in the field of social policy is constitutionally suspect. She contends that the fact that the Privy Council decision denying federal competence to enact an unemployment insurance measure prompted a consequent constitutional amendment establishing federal competence in that field confirms 'provincial competence over remaining social policies, even in the field of old age security where, despite constitutional modifications, the provinces retained their paramountcy.'[3] I find it difficult to accept this inference. The array of programs in the field of social policy which has come to constitute the Canadian welfare state is far beyond anything that the Fathers of Confederation could have envisaged. It seems to me a big stretch of the historical evidence to argue that the 1867 constitution must have given the provinces paramount legislative authority over all social policies, because it was necessary, after an adverse judicial decision, to give the federal Parliament exclusive legislative authority in one area of social policy, namely unemployment insurance.

There have been many federal programs in the social policy field that do not regulate private contracts of employment in the way that the unemployment insurance scheme impugned in the 1937 reference did. These programs can take the form of making payments to individuals directly or through tax deductions, or granting money to provincial and territorial governments. In many of these programs individuals and governments must meet certain conditions if they are to be eligible for the payments, but they are not required to participate in the federal program. Occasionally such federal grants, especially to governments, are unconditional. As Sujit Choudhry points out, a federal unemployment insurance scheme funded in this way that was non-contributory and non-mandatory might well have survived judicial scrutiny. Professor Lajoie, however, suggests that federal grants to individuals or governments in the field of social policy, to the extent that their constitutional foundation is 'the federal spending power,' are 'not part of our constitutional law,' especially when they impose conditions 'that are equivalent to the exercise of normative power in fields of provincial jurisdiction.'

I am in full agreement with Lajoie that our constitutional law, as developed by the courts, has not recognized a federal spending power that justifies federal legislative intrusions into spheres of exclusive provincial jurisdiction. What matters in any division of powers dispute is the 'pith and substance' of the legislation at issue. When we consider federal legislation establishing or regulating national social programs, such as family allowances, or the child tax benefit or the Canada Health Act, it seems weird to characterize such legislation as in pith and substance laws for the spending of federal money. Surely such a characterization would be a case of the tail wagging the dog. The spending of money is necessarily incidental to the implementing these programs but is not their pith and substance, their primary legislative intent. The crucial issue is under which head of power in sections 91 and 92 does such legislation most plausibly fall. For most elements of the modern welfare state, the specific heads of power set out in these sections are of little help. Section 7 in the provincial list – 'The Establishment, Maintenance and Management of Asylums, Charities and Eleemosynary Institutions in and for the Province' – is perhaps a little broader than section 11 in the federal list – 'Quarantine and the Maintenance of Marine Hospitals.' But both fall far short of the panoply of state-sponsored social programs in the Canadian version of the welfare state. The main contenders are the general powers in each section: section 16 in the provincial list – 'Generally all Matters of a merely local or private Nature in the Province' and the federal Parliament's power to 'make Laws for the Peace, Order and Good Government of Canada.'

Constitutional jurisprudence on these broad general powers (and here I would include the federal trade and commerce power and the provincial property and civil rights power) has never been, and never will be, fixed and unchanging. When the *Unemployment Insurance Reference* was decided, the scope of POGG, as interpreted by both the Privy Council and the Supreme Court of Canada, was extremely narrow. POGG had been reduced to a power that could be invoked only to deal with short-term crises such as war or famine. The general aspect of the federal trade and commerce power had been reduced to an ancillary power that could be invoked only in support of some other head of power. At the same time, under the sway of a very laissez-faire oriented Privy Council, provincial jurisdiction over property and civil rights had been expanded into a giant of a power capable of sucking in virtually any government regulation interfering with freedom of contract. As we know, none of this jurisprudence stood still. Once the Supreme Court of Canada became truly supreme, it began to move in a more centralist direction, quite boldly in the 1950s and 1960s, more cautiously in the 1970s, then returning to a more centralizing thrust in the 1980s. Sujit Choudhry has provided a detailed account of how these jurisprudential developments provide a stronger constititutional base for federal jurisdiction in the field of social policy.[4] Even if future Supreme Courts are not prepared to follow Professor Choudhry in extending this jurisprudence to the point where it could justify a broad federal power to redistribute income, they are unlikely to repudiate all the new life that the Supreme Court has breathed into POGG and the trade and commerce power. In particular, I think Justice Beetz's majority position in the *Anti-Inflation Reference* acknowledging a residual use of POGG to deal with specific matters of national concern that are not clearly assigned to the provinces is likely to stand, as is the provincial inability test set out by Justice LeDain in *Crown Zellerbach*.[5] In my view, both these uses of POGG provide a far more appropriate constitutional foundation for federal programs in the field of social policy than the so-called federal spending power.

In making this point I am not advocating a federal takeover of social policy. Both levels of government have played and must continue to play major roles in developing and managing the Canadian welfare state: the provinces bringing forward new initiatives in response to local demands and taking the major responsibility for program delivery, the federal government setting national standards and using its predominant fiscal position to support and steer provincial spending in directions favoured by national electorates. If federal involvement in social policy is challenged in the courts, I believe that the POGG doctrines referred to above will provide the best defence of such a federal role, rather than a very dubious spending power. But, as I shall argue, constitutional litigation is not the best way of working out the respective roles of the two levels of government in this field. Before turning to that point, I want to suggest why an acknowledgment of the fluidity of constitutional law in the field of social policy, and other areas of policy, calls for a less rigid approach to the federal fiscal balance than that suggested by Professor Lajoie.

Federal Fiscal Imbalance

The principle of federalism enunciated by Lord Watson in the *Maritime Bank*[6] case cited by Professor Lajoie is one that I can accept as a general normative ideal for a polity that is truly federal. The crux of that principle is that the provinces should not be subordinate to the central government and that the legislative powers of the provinces are constitutionally protected, and are not to be altered 'by the unilateral action of the federal authorities.' While I believe the unilateral federal action Lord Watson had in mind was of a legislative nature, analysts of federalism should recognize that unilateral federal action that so pre-empts the major fields of taxation as to deny provincial governments access to their own revenue sources could violate the federal principle, and in effect convert a federal state, de facto, into a unitary state. Where I differ with Professor Lajoie is her conclusion that Canada has reached that point and has become 'a centralized monist state.'

By Professor Lajoie's standard, virtually every federal state in the world is monist. Among federations, fiscal imbalance, both vertical and horizontal, is the rule, not the exception. In his classic work on comparative federalism, Ronald Watts explains why the revenues of the central government usually exceed what it needs to support its own legislative responsibilities:

> It has usually been found desirable to allocate the major taxing powers to the federal government because these are closely related to the development of the customs union and more broadly to an effective economic union, while some of the most expensive expenditure responsibilities such as health, education and social services have usually been considered best administered on a regional basis where particular regional circumstances can be taken into account.[7]

Certainly this is true of Canada's constitutional arrangements. Section 91 (3) of the Constitution Act, 1867 gives the federal Parliament the power to make laws for 'the raising of Money by any Mode or System of Taxation,' whereas section 92 limits the provinces to raising money by 'Direct Taxation within the Province' and certain specified kinds of licences. Even though the provinces have made ample use of their power of direct taxation, which the courts have interpreted so generously so that it can support provincial sales taxes,[8] from the very beginning, provinces have relied on fiscal transfers from Ottawa to provide a significant portion of their revenues.

Professor Watts gives a second reason for vertical fiscal imbalances in federations:

> No matter how carefully the original designers of the federation may attempt to match the revenue sources and expenditure responsibilities of each order of government, over time the significance of different tax changes (such as income taxes and consumption taxes) and the costs of expenditures vary in unforeseen ways.[9]

This has certainly been the case in Canada, where the founding fathers anticipated neither the costs of the welfare state nor the importance of the central government's use of its instruments of fiscal policy for the economic management of the state.

Despite the growth of federal government revenues and their use to support transfer payments to the provinces, the Canadian federation remains one of the least centralized in fiscal terms. In 1993 federal government revenues before intergovernmental transfers were 47.7 per cent of total (federal-provincial-municipal) government revenues in Canada. The comparable figures for Australia and the United States were 69.1 per cent and 65.8 per cent respectively. And, because Lajoie suggests that the federal imbalance may be most severe in 'classical federations emanating from the British Empire,' let me point out that the comparable figures for Spain, Austria, and Germany were 84.0 per cent, 72.8 per cent and 64.5 per cent respectively. Indeed, the only federations in Watts's tables in which central government revenues constitute a lower percentage of total government spending are Switzerland (44.7 per cent) and the EU (0.9 per cent). The picture does not change substantially when federal expenditures after intergovernmental transfers are compared. In Canada, federal expenditures less intergovernmental transfers constitute 40.6 per cent of all government expenditure in the country as compared with 61.2 per cent in the United States and 53 per cent in Australia. The narrowing of differences on the expenditure side indicates that the constituent units of these other federations are even more dependent on fiscal transfers from the central government for discharging their constitutional responsibilities than are Canada's provinces. Watts's data also show that a significantly larger portion of fiscal transfers in these other federations are of a conditional nature than is the case in Canada.[10]

The sharing of public funds and government responsibilities for the evolving expectations of the welfare state are matters that must be settled primarily at the political level rather than juridically. I do not believe that it is possible or desirable to allocate precisely in constitutional law the shares of the various tax fields that ought to be allocated to each level of government. Nor do I think that by constitutional law we could or should try to define precisely the federal government's role in health, social security, or even in education. To do so would plunge us into a highly divisive constitutional battle between Quebec and the Rest of Canada, arousing competing senses of national identity. The choice is between managing these dimensions of our federalism in a cooperative manner that is respectful of provincial rights or in a highly centralist manner that leaves the provinces with little freedom to mount their own programs. Though I cannot undertake here a detailed comparative study of how Canada compares with other federations in this regard, let me offer two general comments. First, relative to other federations, issues relating to fiscal federalism and coordinating government roles in various fields of social policy have been handled more cooperatively in Canada than in most other federations. Second, however, we could and should improve how we manage these aspects of our federal polity by establishing a process that is more respectful of provincial jurisdiction and policy-making capacity.

Two Cheers for SUFA

The Social Union Framework Agreement (SUFA) signed by the federal government and all of the provinces except Quebec in February 1999 is a good first step in the direction of establishing a process for regulating federal initiatives in health care, post-secondary education, social assistance, and social services in a manner that is more consonant with the federal principle.[11] According to SUFA, any new federal initiatives in these areas that are to be funded by fiscal transfers – whether block-funded or cost-shared – must be approved by a majority of provincial governments, and a government that opts out will receive its share of fiscal compensation for a provincial program that meets 'Canada-wide objectives.' With respect to new programs that make payments directly to citizens or organizations, SUFA requires the federal government to give three months' advance notice and consult with the provinces to identify potential duplication and consider alternative policies. As a means of constraining use of the federal government's spending power in fields primarily under provincial jurisdiction, SUFA goes further than similar provisions in the Meech Lake Accord. The Meech Lake provision did not subject the introduction of new shared-cost programs to a majority vote of the provinces, and did not deal with federal programs distributing funds directly to citizens. It should also be noted that the condition that an opting-out province must meet to qualify for fiscal compensation is 'Canada-wide objectives' rather than the more demanding 'national standards' advocated by social democratic, Canadian nationalist critics of the Meech Lake Accord. SUFA also introduces a dispute resolution process and a ministerial council to facilitate joint planning for the Canadian social union.

Though the Meech Lake Accord was approved by the Quebec government of Robert Bourassa and by Quebec's National Assembly, the government of Bernard Landry refused to sign SUFA, even though it is more respectful of provincial rights than Meech Lake. Premier Charest has made it clear that he is not about to reverse that decision. Professor Lajoie's paper helps us understand the reluctance of the Quebec government to sign an agreement such as SUFA. The language of her paper assumes that federal initiatives in the field of social policy are based on 'the federal spending power.' Quebec's signing SUFA could, as Lajoie suggests, give that dubious concept the strength of a constitutional convention. Moreover, by refusing to sign, Quebec confirms de facto its special status in the Canadian federation, a recognition it is unable to secure through formal constitutional amendment. Despite its incompleteness, SUFA may be the best Canada can do in managing the social union dimension of its federal structure. Quebec's opting out serves as clear signal that, like it or not, the Canadian social union must be adapted to the reality of a multinational state.

What are the alternatives? Attempts were made in both the Meech Lake Accord and the Charlottetown Accord to regulate federal spending in the social policy field by constitutional amendment. In the light of Quebec governments' rejection of SUFA, there would seem little prospect for success in renewing the effort of constitutional amendment. Constitutional litigation may help to clarify the respective roles of the two levels of government in various fields of social policy, though I remain sceptical of solutions emerging from the judicial process that do justice to the practical, policy issues at stake and at the same time satisfy the constitutional beliefs and aspirations of Canadian and Quebec nationalists. So I believe that for the foreseeable future Canada will rely primarily on the political process and informal intergovernmental agreements to improve the management of fiscal federalism and coordinate government policy in areas where both levels of governments have popular mandates.[12] In addition to SUFA, the Council of the Federation and the Canada Health Council have recently emerged as new intergovernmental structures for regularizing the political negotiations that are the best hope for achieving outcomes that are fairer to the rights and interests on both sides of our federation's politics.

NOTES

1 *Attorney General for Canada v. Attorney General for Ontario*, [1937] A.C. 355.
2 For an analysis of the how the federal governments' lawyers argued the case, see W.H. McConnell, 'The Judicial Review of Prime Minister Bennett's "New Deal,"' *Osgoode Hall Law Journal* 6 (1968): 39.

3 Andrée Lajoie, p. 161 in this volume.
4 Sujit Choudhry, 'Recasting Social Canada: A Reconsideration of Federal Jurisdiction over Social Policy,' *University of Toronto Law Journal* 52 (2002): 163.
5 *Reference re Anti-Inflation Act*, [1976] 2 S.C.R. 373. *The Queen v. Crown Zeller-bach Canada*, [1988] 1 S.C.R. 401.
6 *Liquidators of the Maritime Bank of Canada v. Receiver General of New Brunswick*, [1892] A.C. 437 (P.C.).
7 Ronald L. Watts, *Comparing Federal Systems*, 2nd ed. (Kingston: Institute of Intergovernmental Relations, Queen's University, 1999), 45–6.
8 The key case was *Atlantic Smoke Shops Ltd. v. Conlon*, [1943] A.C. 550.
9 Watts, *Company Federal Systems*, 46.
10 Ibid., 46–9.
11 *A Framework to Improve the Social Union for Canadians* (Ottawa: Government of Canada, 4 February 1999). For a commentary on how SUFA is functioning, see Harvey Lazar, 'Managing Interdependencies in the Canadian Federation: Lessons from the Social Union Framework Agreement,' in Douglas Brown, ed., *Constructive and Co-operative Federalism: A Series of Commentaries on the Council of the Federation* (Kingston: Institute of Intergovernmental Relations, Queen's University, 2003).
12 This point is more fully developed in my *Constitutional Odyssey: Can Canadians Become a Sovereign People?* 3rd ed. (Toronto: University of Toronto Press 2004), ch. 12.

The Irreducible Federal Necessity of Jurisdictional Autonomy, and the Irreducibility of Federalism to Jurisdictional Autonomy

JEAN-FRANÇOIS GAUDREAULT-DESBIENS

What is the meaning of jurisdictional autonomy in a federation? Where does jurisdictional autonomy start and where does it end? Does it, alone, define federalism? Andrée Lajoie's contribution to this volume obliquely raises these fundamental questions by analysing the positive law framework applicable to a constitutional problem that has lately drawn a lot of attention. This problem is that of the 'fiscal imbalance,' which allegedly exists between the two orders of government and which permits the federal government to encroach at will on provincial jurisdiction, primarily through its spending power. Lajoie says that a 'fiscal imbalance' occurs when 'there is too great a fiscal gap between the federated entities' own revenue sources and their direct spending, because such a difference threatens to subordinate those entities to the federal government, which is contrary to the federal principle.' It is important to understand that this alleged fiscal imbalance is not per se justiciable – that is, cognizable from a legal standpoint by a judicial authority. What may make it justiciable, however, is an attempt by the federal government to take advantage of it in order to interfere in areas of provincial jurisdiction, generally through its spending power.

I will first comment on the foundational argument underlying Professor Lajoie's analysis of the uses and abuses of the federal spending power – that is, the irreducible federal necessity of jurisdictional autonomy. I will then argue that federalism cannot be reduced to that principle of jurisdictional autonomy, and that, in the context of the political debate on fiscal imbalance and of the juridical debate on the scope of the federal spending power, it should balanced against that of solidarity. My primary goal is to use Lajoie's paper as a springboard to reflect on the doctrine of federalism informing the *judicial* interpretation of the federative division of powers. The central assumption underlying my comment is that the problem of fiscal imbalance, which has a constitutional resonance whenever the federal government seeks to implement policies in provincial jurisdictions, raises fundamental normative questions from the standpoint of federalism.

In this paper, federalism will therefore be treated as an end in itself, as a constitutional good. Admittedly, federalism can also be viewed as a tool for achieving other political, social or economic objectives. However, I think that, in a division of powers case, such objectives should be regarded as fundamentally external to federalism itself, and should only be brought to bear once the court has approached the case from the standpoint of federalism itself – that is, after having examined the text of the constitution and the precedents in light of the core normative, and often implicit, principles underlying federalism. From a juridical perspective, therefore, the very fact that this type of regime is entrenched in the constitution, rather than in a mere statute, should induce interpreters to grant it a pre-eminent normative status and to draw interpretive consequences from it. Hence the importance of treating federalism as a constitutional good in such a context, on par with, say, a constitutional structure of rights protection.

It is moreover arguable, from an instrumental perspective, that the appropriate balance between external objectives is more likely to be struck if core federalism-related arguments and arguments based on these objectives are, to the extent possible, consciously dissociated. Instead of allowing that such external objectives be hidden behind legal arguments, the proposed approach therefore seeks to make them as visible as possible and as debatable as possible in the open.

The Irreducible Federal Necessity of Jurisdictional Autonomy

Professor Lajoie posits that, in Canada as in many other federations, 'centralization is the name of the game.' Although recent political evolutions in countries such as Belgium, Spain, Mexico, or India may point to a different conclusion, it is true that top courts in federations tend to lean towards centralization rather than decentralization.[1] Lajoie argues that such is the case in Canada, a claim that seems plausible when one compares the Supreme Court's nation-building approach to that adopted by the Judicial Committee of the Privy Council when it was Canada's highest appellate court.[2]

Still, all this begs a question: to what extent can the centralization/

decentralization dichotomy be properly used as a criterion on which to ground an evaluation of the success or failure of any federation? My sense is that this dichotomy's heuristic potential is rather limited. First, its use raises a normative problem in that it presupposes that either decentralization or centralization is valuable for its own sake.[3] It is indeed arguable that both mask ideological viewpoints, which, while legitimate, are rooted in other external perspectives, and that both may thus be appropriate in certain circumstances and problematic in others. Moreover, neither can be said to be intrinsically 'progressive' or 'conservative.'[4] Second, on the basis of what criterion should the level of decentralization or centralization in a federation be assessed? Many factors such as legislative or administrative authority, financial capacity, formal constitutional constraints as well as democratic values, and the ability of the system to recognize and accommodate alternative conceptions of nation and community need to be looked at.[5] Without such underlying criteria, claims such as 'more powers to the provinces' or 'more powers to the federal government' risk becoming mere intellectual automatisms which are of little help in understanding complex federative dynamics.

Granted, the Supreme Court of Canada's federalism jurisprudence has often favoured constitutional interpretations supporting the federal government's nation-building ambitions. However, judging the evolution of Canadian federalism from the sole angle of judicial pronouncements seems insufficient to draw a definitive conclusion on the dynamics at play in the federation, or on its health.

First, such an approach equates federalism with its *judicial* expression. I would be the last to deny the importance of the judiciary's role in fostering the adherence to strong federative values. However, the problem is that a reduction of federalism to its judicial expression leads its proponents to ignore relevant and significant data of non-judicial origin without which it is hard to fully appraise any particular expression of federalism, including the Canadian one. Therefore, sweeping statements regarding the failure of a given federal experiment which are made solely on the basis of an appraisal of the evolution of the case law should be viewed with suspicion. Formal law, especially case law, does not, and cannot, exhaust all the meanings of federalism, nor should it be used, from a methodological standpoint, as the sole variable determining the success or failure of a given federal experiment. Furthermore, the strategy of reducing Canadian federalism to its formal legal expression for the purpose of ascertaining its health ends up reducing the law itself to its most formal and rigid expression. Indeed, can one reasonably make a statement as to the success or failure of a given federation by simply looking at rulings interpreting its constitution without examining their concrete consequences in the daily life of the federation?

This raises the question of the actual implementation of such rulings. For example, while it is arguable that the majority's interpretation of the national concern branch of the federal power to legislate for the peace, order, and good government of Canada in the case *R. v. Crown Zellerbach*[6] is conceptually problematic, in addition to giving free rein, at least theoretically, to the federal government to extend its jurisdiction over fields which were until then under provincial jurisdiction,[7] it is a bit of an overstretch to use this jurisprudence as evidence of a broader failure of Canadian federalism. In this example, it bears noting that the ruling of the Supreme Court in *Crown Zellerbach* has *not* triggered a wave of laws asserting federal jurisdiction over provincial matters deemed to have acquired a national dimension. Many other factors will inform federal actions.

This is not to minimize the impact of judicial pronouncements on the constitutional and political cultures of a federation: as much as formal law is influenced by extrinsic variables, it also shapes, to some extent, these variables. Judicial pronouncements that thoroughly address all the fundamental principles relevant to a case can significantly influence the behaviour of political actors by identifying reasonably clear legal parameters beyond which they cannot venture. Conversely, the absence of such judicial pronouncements may allow them to impose their own conception of what is 'right,' and to remain largely unaccountable. This ultimately undermines the rule of law, which requires political actors to act in a manner reflecting a concern for the proportionality of their actions.[8] Indeed, in a federative context, the validity of a law often depends on whether or not the otherwise constitutionally legitimate aims pursued by the enacting government disproportionately encroach on the other level of government's constitutional authority.

By requiring that these actors be mindful of the consequences of their actions for other parties and, therefore, that they show some level of self-restraint, this imperative of proportionality makes it possible to win legitimatization of actions that, while affecting others, are less likely to be perceived as *unduly* affecting them. Such an intersubjective legitimization may of course flow from the free will of the political actors involved, but it may also be achieved when a court of law fully and thoroughly addresses the deep theoretical background of the topic it is adjudicating upon, and speaks to the core values embedded in the legal structure it is dealing with. This goes for the rule of law in general, but this goes as well for what I would call the 'federal rule of law.' In this regard, I have argued elsewhere that these values must be found through a reflection on the core requirements of a federal alliance.[9] In my view, such an alliance necessarily implies a minimum level, first, of trust between the parties, which presupposes that they act in a spirit of *loyalty* toward each other and toward the federal principle itself (at the minimum, it imposes upon them a duty of self-restraint); second, of *equality* between them, understood here in terms of status equality, which renders problematic the *de jure* as well as the *de facto* subordination of one to another and which thus presupposes the relative autonomy of federal actors (and from the principles of equality and autonomy flow the sub-principles of anti-hegemony and non-subordination); third, of *solidarity* between the parties, which raises the questions of distributive justice, interpersonal equality, and meaningful federal citizenship (which, in Canada, is partly realized though a constitutionally entrenched system of financial equalization); and finally, of *federative arbitration* understood as requiring that all intergovernmental disputes concretely affecting the federal division of powers as well as governmental actions potentially threatening the equilibrium of the federation be susceptible of adjudication by an independent and impartial third party, most likely a judicial authority.

For federalism is more than the technical division of powers found in a given constitution. First and foremost, it is also a mode of constitutional apprehension of the political dynamic at play in states sharing some core structural features characterizing a federation, from which stems a particular mode of constitutional justification that is conditioned by the above-mentioned normative principles. Altogether, these principles form a discursive and ethical interval from which interpretive consequences must be drawn.[10] Indeed, in spite of the great variety of federative structures and archetypal dynamics, such as cooperation versus competition, or association versus dissociation, some recurrent patterns of constitutional justification transcend differences between federations, something that reveals 'the deep unity of federal processes.'[11] Thus, to discharge their burden of justification when an action directly affects the equilibrium of federalism, and once again absent an exceptionally 'clear and unambiguous' provision, courts must seek to assess that action in light of the core principles inherent to federalism and use them as optimization precepts.[12]

Returning to the constitutionality of the federal government's conditional spending in provincial areas of jurisdiction, I am of the view that when it imposes conditions on provincial governments which, due to their insufficient revenues, are in dire need of federal money to carry out public policies that fall under their jurisdiction and that their residents forcefully claim, the federal government can be said to use its dominant position to coerce provinces, under the guise of a contract, into regulating in a direction that they might not have taken otherwise. This assumes, first, that a case can be made on the balance of probabilities that such a dominant position exists due to a real fiscal imbalance,[13] and, second, that the 'conditions' imposed by the federal government are prescriptive enough so as to be characterized as unconstitutionally coercing a financially strapped provincial government to act in a way it would not have chosen otherwise.[14]

I have observed elsewhere in this respect that a distinction could be drawn between mere 'standards' (or principles) such as 'accessibility' in the Canada Health Act, which could *prima facie* be constitutional because they leave a substantial margin of appreciation to the recipient provinces, and 'rules,' the meaning, scope, and consequences of which are entirely predetermined and which leave no tangible margin of appreciation to its addressees. Under this approach, an example of an unconstitutional rule would be that of a norm determining the maximum delay to be respected for treatment in an emergency room. All this assumes that the compatibility of provincial programs with such federal standards would be evaluated not by the federal government itself (the spender) but by an impartial third party, this, on the basis of the principle of federative arbitration. This brings us back to federalism's core normative principles and how they can be brought to bear in the constitutional apprehension of the federal spending power. The following remarks can be made in this regard.

First, when it attaches genuinely prescriptive conditions to its transfers to provinces in areas over which they possess jurisdiction, the federal government fails to respect the principle of federal loyalty which, at the minimum, requires that an order of government does not do indirectly what the constitution forbids it to do directly. This directly relates to the principle of constitutionalism and to the corollary idea of a federal rule of law. Federal loyalty also demands that all governments refrain from using tactics that are likely to undermine the equilibrium of the federation, by neglecting to take into account the legitimate interests and expectations of its federal partners.

Second, by taking advantage of its dominant position, the federal government breaches the equality principle in that it reduces provinces to mere subordinates even in areas in which they have jurisdiction. *De jure* equality must be understood in a substantive rather than in a purely formal manner. This means that factors that prevent one order of government, supposedly equal to the other, from freely exercising its powers, must be taken into account from a legal point of view.

Third, it follows that the federal government, by so acting, breaches the autonomy principle, which posits that federated entities must have the power to *freely* determine their policies within their own spheres of jurisdiction,[15] so long as they do not negatively affect their federal partners' interests and that they acknowledge the necessity of some minimum level of cooperation between each order of government. In that sense, the interplay of the autonomy and the loyalty principles may lead to the reformulation of the principle of autonomy as emphasizing the inherent 'heteronomy' of federative actors.[16] The principle of autonomy also implies that each order of government is presumed to act legitimately within its jurisdiction, but is at the same time accountable to its own electorate. In that sense, it is linked to the democratic principle. It further requires that no government should be placed, through the wilful or careless actions of the other order of government, in a position where its legitimacy could be unduly undermined. Refusing to abide by federal conditions could undermine the legitimacy of provincial governments since their residents could be submitted to federal taxation without receiving the services resulting from that taxation. The non-delivery of services due to a lack of funds caused by the withholding of federal monies, if this action cannot be justified on the basis of an otherwise valid federal reason, would force provincial governments to assume full responsibility for decisions that could not be characterized as having been freely taken. Living in a state of coercion, it bears remembering, is antithetical to living in a state of real autonomy, albeit relative. As Friedrich Hayek correctly observed:

> By coercion we mean such control of the environment or circumstances of a person by another that, in order to avoid greater evil, he is forced to act not according to a coherent plan of his own but to serve the ends of

another. Except in the sense of choosing the lesser evil in a situation forced on him by another, he is unable either to use his own intelligence or knowledge or to follow his own aims and beliefs.[17]

Having to settle for the lesser evil – that is, accepting both the federal monies and prescriptive conditions on a question over which a given level of government possesses exclusive constitutional jurisdiction – cannot be viewed, in my opinion, as a proportionate and legitimate encroachment on that government's autonomy.

Even more problematic is the fact that, under the guise of the federal spending power, 'national majorities [are allowed] to set priorities and to determine policy within spheres of influences allocated under the Constitution to regional majorities.'[18] I may not, as a member of a national majority, like what a particular province does, but, absent any unconstitutional encroachment on federal prerogatives or neglect of federal loyalty, or any unconstitutional restriction of individual rights and freedoms, I fail to see why my will should prevail over the will expressed by that provincial majority. This point is important: federalism is encoded in Canada's model of democracy,[19] and reinforcing the pan-Canadian democracy should not be done at the expense of the sub-state democracies constituted by the provinces. Following Dicey, Vernon Bogdanor recently reminded us that federated entities 'desire union without seeking unity.'[20] I take it to mean that, classically, 'unity' should *always* be in a dialectical tension with 'diversity' (and vice-versa). Federalism does not require uniformity; that is a feature of unitary states. This explains why policy-based or efficacy-based arguments emphasizing a possible 'race to the bottom' in fields under provincial jurisdiction should not, as a matter of principle, lead to a conclusion that Parliament is justified in interfering.[21] The autonomy that states or provinces enjoy under a federal constitution may lead to different social choices – 'experiments' – and these choices must be respected unless they encroach in a significant manner on a core federal principle.

Subject to this caveat, I would go as far as to argue that meaningful autonomy implies, in a federation, a *right* to experiment,[22] which necessarily presupposes the recognition of some margin of appreciation to the experimenting government. In any event, it must be noted that in Canada, the focus of a division of powers inquiry has to be placed on the subject matter of the impugned legislation, rather than on the 'practical purpose that inspires the legislation and the implications that [the legislative] body must consider in making its decision.'[23] As a result, ideological preferences or efficacy-based concerns inspiring the enactment of a statute are generally immaterial for the purpose of assessing its constitutional validity. To be given some bearing, such preferences or concerns should be based on one of federalism's core principles, such as solidarity, in addition to being addressed in the context of a broader reflection on subsidiarity, which points to the other order of government's incapacity to effectively regulate. For example, under this view, the normative foundation of an argument supporting federal intervention in health care for fear of a race to the bottom would likely be stronger than that of an argument justifying uniform, federally enacted securities legislation inspired by concerns for mere efficacy or competitiveness. Indeed, the former hypothesis speaks to the principle of federal solidarity and the corollary idea of a meaningful federal citizenship, which the latter hardly does.[24]

Thus, Professor Lajoie is, in my opinion, generally correct in characterizing the judicial discourse on the federal spending power as inconclusive and not determinative of the question as to whether the federal government can freely spend in areas that are under provincial jurisdiction, and attach conditions to its expenditures. As she demonstrates, the proponents of an unfettered federal spending power can hardly find comfort in a case law where a clear *ratio* on the question is conspicuously absent. More important, however, is the fact that, even if the present mosaic of cryptic pronouncements resting on unarticulated assumptions were considered conclusive, the case law would remain entirely unpersuasive by failing to address the spending power from the angle of federalism, even though some exercises of that power are arguably antithetical to federalism. Opinions may legitimately vary on this issue, but it seems to me that courts responsible for upholding the constitution bear a specific and heightened burden of justification when an action undertaken by a political actor directly impacts on a central feature of our constitutional structure, be it federalism or the Charter. In conclusion, with some caveats that I have suggested, Professor Lajoie wins the draw when it comes to conditional spending. This analysis, however, has been applied to federal transfers to provinces. What about direct grants to individuals or organizations? In this area, the indeterminacy of the case law, the silence of the constitution, and the principle of federal solidarity, militate in favour of a slightly more nuanced analysis than that proposed by Lajoie.

The Irreducibility of Federalism to Jurisdictional Autonomy

As fundamental as it may be, the principle of jurisdictional autonomy cannot alone define federalism. Professor Lajoie herself recognizes that 'the concept of federalism is not completely univocal.' One of the principles that may counterbalance that of jurisdictional autonomy, and that ranks alongside those of loyalty, equality, autonomy, and federative arbitration, is the principle of *federal solidarity*, which stems from the very nature of a federal alliance, in contrast to looser forms of associations of states such as confederations. Indeed, such an alliance arguably requires a minimal commitment to the principle that a certain redistribution of wealth and some basic level of services are needed to give a tangible meaning to the idea of a *common federal citizenship*, independent of where citizens actually reside.

Why emphasize the importance of the idea of a common federal citizenship? Merely answering that a federation presupposes the existence of a political community – and thus of a mutual solidarity – is insufficient. A federation, unlike a confederation, also constitutes a juridical order that is distinct and autonomous from its constituent states or provinces. Being more than the sum of its parts, it cannot *juridically* be treated as their creature. This means that states or provinces cannot subordinate the federation in such a way that it becomes a tool for achieving their ends: the federation is a legal subject in its own right, and not a mere object belonging to third parties. Thus, the federation as a whole and the federal government in its jurisdictional spheres benefit from the principle of autonomy as much as states or provinces do. The autonomy of the federation vis-à-vis both orders of government not only forbids them to instrumentalize it for their own ends, but also precludes any legal or political characterization of the federation as merely reflecting a constitutional contract founded on the reciprocity of obligations of the parties. Granted, such a contract may be at the origin of the federation, and there arguably exists a duty of constitutional memory not to lose sight of that, even in adjudicative contexts.[25] Moreover, further intergovernmental relationships of a contractual nature generally arise in the course of the federation's existence, to such an extent that a federation can accurately be characterized as a particular form of 'relational contract.'[26] Characterized, for sure, but not reduced to such a characterization. Indeed, given its juridical nature, a federation can be said to be founded on an aspiration to transcend mere relations of reciprocity so that they become relations of solidarity. The very recognition of the federation as an autonomous legal order, whose norms have a direct effect on the citizens of all states or provinces, enjoins both constitutionally recognized institutional actors and citizens to acknowledge that there is such a thing as a greater federative common good. As was observed by comparative constitutional law scholar Manuel Garcia-Pelayo, a federation implies a dialectical synthesis between a central power and a plurality of other powers, and the juridical expression of that synthesis is the creation of a global entity that transcends its constituent ones without absorbing them.[27] Hence the fundamentally heteronomous nature of the relationship that links federated entities between themselves and these entities with the central government. Such a heteronomous relationship in one global juridical order arguably implies a minimum degree of solidarity. This in no way prevents each order of government from legitimately advancing or defending its particular interests and aspirations, but it does point to the antithetical nature of federalism, on one hand, and radical constitutional isolationism or egoism, on the other. Positing the principle of solidarity as inherent, rather than foreign, to federalism might seem idealistic and even counter-intuitive, but law, it bears remembering, is not only about rules, it is also about aspirations.

That solidarity is not infinite, obviously, but acknowledging its overarching importance as a core principle of legal federalism may allow us to look differently at the federal spending power, the constitutional basis or scope of which is not entirely clear. Indeed, while the expression of the principle of solidarity may take many forms, the federal government clearly has a legitimate constitutional interest in its implementation. That role may be expressly mentioned in the constitution, as in section 36 of the Constitution Act, 1982, which provides for equalization payments. But it would be unduly reductive to confine the impact of federal solidarity to that provision alone. In my view, that normative impact should focus on the interpretation given to the principle of equality in a federal setting, and on the federal actions purporting to implement this principle. This involves both the equality of provinces, and an element of interpersonal equality. But, as Ossipow notes, to the extent that interpersonal equality requires uniformity in the whole country, federalism may conflict with this ideal, as it allows for variations in the treatment of individuals, especially in socio-economic areas.[28] However, if solidarity is deemed inherent to federalism, it entails that federal citizenship, while not reducible to social citizenship, may be said to encompass some measure of social citizenship. Thus, being what it is, and considering what it is not – that is, a confederation – a federation can hardly tolerate blatant discrepancies in the delivery and accessibility of basic social services.

This does not mean that every discrepancy offends the principles of solidarity and equality, as defined here. For instance, differences in the manner in which these services are delivered should not be presumed to offend these principles. The idea here that some core social services should be *broadly* accessible does not imply that *specific* policies or practices should be uniformly implemented across the federation. Interpersonal equality in a federation should be conceived of as demanding equivalent rather than identical services.[29] A perfect, symmetrical, equality of results or outcomes is neither possible nor even desirable. As Føllesdal has argued, the citizens of certain provinces may choose to renounce a higher level of individual equality in order to benefit from the collective advantage afforded by jurisdictional autonomy. Such arrangements remain legitimate provided they do not generate misery or domination, and provided all federated units have access to minimal resources that allow them to offer basic services (such as health and education).[30] Indeed, these citizens may privilege a higher level of collective self-determination to further distinctive social and cultural objectives over the optimal level of social services potentially available in the federation, or they may choose to prioritize some services over others; but I fail to see why, from the standpoint of federalism, this should be seen as problematic. Furthermore, by no means does federalism make such a trade-off between social benefits and collective identity inevitable or necessary.

Since the principle of solidarity may be used to justify federal actions that could undermine the autonomy of provinces, it must be treated as a principle of interpretation that does not per se give rise to positive obligations. It bears remembering that the individuation of principles does not dictate any specific or predetermined outcome and presupposes, by definition, the recognition of a margin of appreciation to those responsible for individuating them. Thus, in order for the principle of solidarity to give rise to positive obligations, explicit and unambiguous support should be sought and found in the constitutional text. For example, the German constitution clearly provides that Germany is not only a democratic federal state, but also a social one. As Orban points out, this imposes upon the state the duty 'to respond to the requirements of social justice understood in its collective dimension.'[31]

Without such a specific positive obligation, the principle of solidarity conceived as a foundation for some minimal level of redistribution orchestrated by the federal government should therefore be treated as a 'default interpretive principle,' unless this possibility is itself expressly eliminated or unambiguously circumscribed.

That being said, Richard Simeon and Alain Noël have correctly observed in their respective chapters that the concepts of social citizenship and solidarity are understood differently depending on the socioeconomic circumstances and political culture of each federation. For example, some federations, such as the United States, do not consider that a significant governmental intervention is justified in that field because other social actors and forces are deemed to take care of redistribution more efficiently. The variety of federative experiments thus begs the question of how the recognition of a default principle of solidarity would affect the adjudication of division-of-powers cases. As mentioned, it would not dictate any specific, predetermined outcome, but it would somehow force courts of law, and federative actors pleading before them, to speak explicitly to the question of redistributive justice. In practice, instead of formulating their claims as if solidarity was exogenous to federalism, those arguing against a 'pro-solidarity' interpretation of the constitution would have to demonstrate on the balance of probabilities that the constitution precludes such an interpretation and how it does so. This would amount to a reversal of the burden of proof, which, in most federations where no explicit pro-solidarity obligation can be found in the constitution, falls rather on those who argue in favour of solidarity, often as a result of a legitimate concern for the autonomy of states or provinces. This is why solidarity, as I understand it, acts as both an interpretive and a default principle. Moreover, through this reversal of the burden of proof, this principle would appropriately fulfill its role as an optimization precept, by heightening awareness about pan-federal solidarity, elevating it to the status of a reversible constitutional presumption and thus optimizing its potential effectiveness in a federative context. However, the principle's interpretive status would mean that in the case of a direct conflict between this principle and that of autonomy, the former, and not the latter, should yield.[32]

As to the interplay between the principle of solidarity, the idea of meaningful federal citizenship, and the potential implementation of these goals through the federal spending power, the discussion above leads me to conclude that these goals can be met only if the federal government has enough fiscal room and juridical leverage. Therefore, it would be a mistake to limit its fiscal space to areas that are specifically assigned in the constitution. Does that mean, however, that the federal government has free rein to encroach upon provincial jurisdictions, whether by direct grants to private actors or by constitutionally dubious conditional grants to governments? I do not think so. But the problem is that the constitutional analytical framework applicable in Canada to federalism-related disputes does not provide us with the necessary tools to grasp the practice of direct grants in a manner that is mindful of federalism's core principles. The courts need to refine the conflict rules applicable in division-of-powers cases. As it is, there is only one, hegemonic rule that applies. The rule is that in case of conflict between overlapping federal and provincial legislation, the former prevails: this is called the federal paramountcy doctrine.[33] This rule should be refined to take stock of the complexity of twenty-first-century federalism in Canada. It would thus be appropriate to consider the elaboration of a new conflict rule, loosely based on the one recently formulated in *Rothmans, Benson & Hedges Inc. v. Saskatchewan*. In a nutshell, the Supreme Court clarified in that case that a 'conflict' exists whenever there is an actual impossibility to comply with both the federal and provincial enactments, and, most importantly for the sake of my argument, when that provincial enactment frustrates the purpose of the federal one. Thus, the conflict rule I am suggesting could be formulated as follows: when an order of government spends, through direct grants to private parties, in a field that is constitutionally allocated to the other, that spending should be constitutionally allowed so long as it does not substantially undermine a policy or program promulgated by the order of government which does possess primary constitutional jurisdiction over the matter, or conflicts with its purpose. This rule would apply both to federal and provincial spending, and would temporarily legitimize the occupation by one government, through spending and only through spending, of fields that are not occupied yet by the government with formal jurisdiction over them.

Granted, this conflict rule, like some other normative ideas suggested in this comment, is a 'proposition of law,'[34] in that it advocates a reconsideration and reform, from an external point of view, of the positive law framework presently applicable to the spending power. But it does not necessarily amount to wishful thinking, since the common law tradition's requirement of 'fit' with past precedent does not preclude the reconsideration and reversal of those precedents. It only ensures that these precedents be brought to bear in the case at bar and examined on their merits. However, as far as the federal spending power is concerned when it is used to regulate areas of provincial jurisdiction, precedents that barely address the core federalism-related issues raised by this practice hardly deserve respect.

Conclusion

It is striking to observe how political and legal debates over the uses of the federal spending power have been, and still are, Manichean. I am afraid, however, that both the proponents of an unfettered federal spending power, who constantly seek to legitimize what has been characterized as Ottawa's 'centralizing *habitus*',[35] and those who wish the spending power to be strictly confined to constitutionally-allocated exclusive jurisdictions fall into the trap of instrumentalizing federalism to further causes they may legitimately care about. But that provides little insight as to how better to construe a federal constitution such as that of Canada. This is why I ultimately conclude that Andrée Lajoie is correct in reminding us of the irreducible federal necessity of jurisdictional autonomy, but is open to criticism when she overlooks that federalism is irreducible to jurisdictional autonomy. Federalism is a specific type of union that calls for both autonomy and solidarity, principles that should be reconciled to the extent possible rather than systematically opposed.

The types of arguments raised in both camps may account for the prevalence of zero-sum logics. Indeed, it is fascinating to see how they rely on positivist arguments to legitimize their claims about either the meaning of the constitutional text or the meaning of constitutional silences, thereby showing the usefulness of legal positivism as a 'self-service' paradigm.[36] Fundamentally, however, what lies behind these positivist arguments on both sides of the debate is a worldview, a conception of what Canada is, or of what it should be – be it a community of association, project, or fate, or, as I would rather see it, a more modest community of comfort.[37] Thus, one cannot understand Andrée Lajoie's emphasis on jurisdictional autonomy, or her opponents' support for a greater federal role in socio-economic policy, whatever the means, without considering that their respective discourses reflect two different *national* logics: one that posits that Quebec – and Quebec City – is the primary locus of the nation, and one that posits the same in respect of Canada – and Ottawa.

I insist that, contrary to what is often heard outside Quebec, by no means do Quebec French-speaking scholars have a monopoly on such a nationalist logic. For instance, in the best defence in years of the constitutionality of a broad federal spending power paired to a broad federal jurisdiction over social policy, my colleague Sujit Choudhry makes it clear that he grasps that question assuming that there is 'a truly Canadian political identity, one that both encompasses and transcends our linguistic and regional diversity' and that '[s]ocial Canada is the cement of that political identity, both acknowledging the existence of and giving effect to obligations of distributive justice between the citizens of the constituent units of the federation, bound together in a community of fate.'[38] From a Quebecker's perspective, this is a genuinely nationalist discourse since social programs and particularly healthcare-related ones are strong identity markers outside Quebec, while they do not play any such role in Quebec. If most Quebeckers happen to support the existence of such programs, it is because of their social-democratic leanings, and not because they see them as pillars of the Canadian identity. Actually, those who would vest them with an identity load would probably refer to them as pillars of the *modèle québécois*.

The fact that Quebec is for a majority of them the primary, but not necessarily the exclusive, locus of national identification explains why their 'constitutional patriotism' is centred neither around the Canadian Charter of Rights and Freedoms nor around an interpretation of federalism where Ottawa can pretend to act as the sole 'national' government, but around an interpretation of federalism where the jurisdictions allocated to their provincial government guarantee the flourishing of their distinct sub-state national identity. While not being constitutive of that identity, a federalism based on a stringent conception of jurisdictional exclusiveness is seen as a means to ensure control over that identity. This explains why jurisdictional disagreements as to which level of government should exercise responsibility over certain types of programs are often perceived differently in Quebec than they are in other provinces. Issues that seem to appeal first and foremost to functional concerns, or that do not *prima facie* carry any identity load, soon become 'identitized' in Quebec as they mutate into fundamental, 'national' ones. Such processes are evidenced by the positions taken over the years by successive Quebec governments, sometimes to the point of revealing – let us call a spade a spade – a form of narcissism of small differences. But what bears remembering here is that while Canadians outside Quebec tend to have an existential rapport to the Charter and a more functional one to federalism as English-speaking Canada more and more constructs itself as both a nation-state and an ethnicity,[39] it is clearly the opposite for a significant number of Quebeckers. That being said, from the perspective of most federalist Quebeckers, claiming at the same time two political identities (both defined around the idea of nationhood, and recognizing that one may temporarily prevail over the other depending on the circumstances, even though the primary locus of identification generally remains Quebec) is not problematic either in theory or in practice. However, this whole intellectual edifice relies on the assumption that the broader Canadian national identity is effectively able to acknowledge the legitimacy of their sub-state's national – rather than merely provincial – identity, and to understand that this sentiment of sharing a sub-state nationality influences attitudes vis-à-vis the interpretation to be given to Canadian federalism. The same is true for those who define their nationality as being solely Canadian and who may sometimes be inclined to view provinces as mere administrative impediments. What is important to note here is that although we hear more and more that identity issues do not matter as much as in the past in the relation between Quebec and the rest of Canada, and that what now counts is how the different communities that exist in Canada actually manage their shared objective of wealth redistribution, the primordial identification to one political community rather than to another still explains why a given level of government will be perceived as the main operator of social solidarity instead of the other.

While such logics cannot be compressed into neat little constitutional boxes, and while no theory of federalism can obliterate them, ways must be found to funnel them into constitutional discourse in such a way that they will not always oppose each other. In that sense, maybe a deeper reflection on federalism itself, on the values it underlies, can serve as a start for this noble mission.

In light of the above considerations and despite certain shortcomings, Professor Lajoie's chapter represents a useful reminder that sooner or later Canadians will have to contemplate again the possibility of enshrining in their constitution some form of asymmetric federalism for Quebec and maybe for other provinces as well – something they might eventually accept if all federated units willingly subscribe to a core set of basic values. Granted, this may not be a popular view to hold at a moment when so many politicians say that we should not 'talk about the constitution.' However, one should not lose sight of the fact that talking about the constitution is essentially talking about who we are, what we want to become, and where we want to go. As difficult as such a dialogue may be, the mere fact of participating in it may indeed indicate that Canadians actually consider themselves bound by a community of fate. Conversely, a staunch refusal to participate in that kind of dialogue could also indicate that if there ever was a community of fate, it has all but gone up in smoke. In that respect, what is presently being accomplished in the European Union teaches us Canadians that being constitutionally proactive could still be a promising path, whether or not the constitutional process under way in Europe leads to the adoption of a formal constitution.

NOTES

1　André Bzedra, 'Comparative Analysis of Federal High Courts: A Political Theory of Judicial Review,' *Canadian Journal of Political Science* 26, no. 1 (1993):3.
2　See John T. Saywell, *The Lawmakers: Judicial Powers and the Shaping of Canadian Federalism* (Toronto: Osgoode Society, 2002).
3　Robert Howse has correctly argued that the claim that decentralization is intrinsically good is indefensible. See Robert Howse, 'Federalism, Democracy, and Regulatory Reform: A Skeptical View of the Case for Decentralization,' in Karen Knop et al., eds., *Rethinking Federalism: Citizens, Markets, and Governments in a Changing World* (Vancouver: UBC Press, 1995), 273. The argument goes as well for a-contextual valorizations of centralization.
4　Alain Noël, 'Is Decentralization Conservative? Federalism and the Contemporary Debate on the Canadian Welfare State,' in Robert Young, ed., *Stretching the Federation: The Art of State in Canada* (Kingston: Institute of Intergovernmental Relations, 1999), 195.
5　Ronald W. Watts, 'Comments on Michael Keating's Paper,' ibid., 32.
6　*R. v. Crown Zellerbach Canada Ltd*, [1988] 1 S.C.R. 401.
7　Henri Brun and Guy Tremblay, *Droit constitutionnel*, 4th ed. (Cowansville, QC: Éditions Yvon Blais, 2002), 556–9.
8　On the connection between proportionality and the rule of law, see generally David M. Beatty, *The Ultimate Rule of Law* (Oxford: Oxford University Press, 2004).
9　I have elaborated on the genesis of these principles in Jean-François Gaudreault-DesBiens, 'The Canadian Federal Experiment, or Legalism without Federalism? Toward a Legal Theory of Federalism,' in Manuel Calvo-Garcia and William Felstiner, eds., *Federalismo/Federalism* (Madrid:

Dyckinson, 2004), 81. The present chapter, especially its first part, draws on this article.

10 *Re Reference Secession of Quebec*, [1998] 2 S.C.R. 817.

11 Elisabeth Zoller, 'Aspects internationaux du droit constitutionnel. Contribution à la théorie de la fédération d'États,' *Recueil de cours de l'Académie de droit international* 294 (2002): 39, 51 (translation of 'l'unité profonde des processus fédéraux').

12 A good example of the type of reasoning I have in mind is to be found in Justice Iacobucci's opinion in *Ontario Hydro v. Ontario*, [1993] 3 S.C.R. 327. On principles as optimization precepts, see: Robert Alexy, *A Theory of Constitutional Rights* (Oxford: Oxford University Press, 2002).

13 It is assumed here that parties negotiating in a context of a substantial power imbalance are placed in a situation of pseudo-equality rather than one of genuine equality. See Ching Lai Sheng, 'On Equality and Some Situations of Pseudo-Equality in Law,' *Ratio Juris* 15 (2002): 97.

14 We cannot assume that a province in a situation of fiscal imbalance cannot give its assent to conditions imposed by the federal government, but nor can we assume that the mere use of a contract-like mechanism implies a genuine assent.

15 Johanne Poirier, 'Pouvoir normatif et protection sociale dans les fédérations multinationales,' *Canadian Journal of Law and Society* 16, no. 2 (2001): 155.

16 At the risk of oversimplifying its content and scope, the concept of heteronomy has been used by philosopher Emmanuel Lévinas in the context of a reflection on the genesis of the ethical experience, which finds its roots in the meeting of the other, of his or her visage. It is by meeting with this other that one feels responsible for him or her, thereby forging one's own subjectivity with this other. See Emmanuel Lévinas, *Totalité et Infini: Essai sur l'extériorité* (The Hague : Martinus Nijhoff, 1961).

17 Friedrich A. Hayek, *The Constitution of Liberty* (Chicago: University of Chicago Press, 1960), 20–1.

18 Andrew Petter, 'Federalism and the Myth of the Federal Spending Power,' *Canadian Bar Review* 68 (1989): 465.

19 *Figueroa v. Canada (A.G.)*, [2003] 1 S.C.R. 912, at par. 168 (LeBel J.).

20 Vernon Bogdanor, 'Federalism and the Nature of the European Union,' in Kalypso Nicolaidis and Stephen Weatherill, (eds., *Whose Europe? National Models and the Constitution of the European Union* (Oxford: European Studies at Oxford, 2003), 49.

21 For another view, see Sujit Choudhry, 'Recasting Social Canada: A Reconsideration of Federal Jurisdiction over Social Policy,' *University of Toronto Law Journal* 52 (2002): 163.

22 In order to better understand the claim that federalism's core principle of autonomy implies a right to experiment, it is interesting to contrast the situation of a federation such as Canada with that of an archetypal unitary state such as France, where a mere faculty to experiment granted in the context of a project of administrative decentralization was vigorously criticized as legitimizing breaches of the constitutional principle of equality before the law. See Isabelle Domergue, 'Pour ou contre le droit à l'expérimentation,' *Regards sur l'actualité* 286 (December 2002), 17.

23 *Friends of the Oldman River Society v. Canada (Minister of Transport)*, [1992] 1 S.C.R. 3, at 69 (La Forest J.).

24 Mere economic inefficiencies created by the presence of several provincial legislative frameworks should not alone be equated as breaching the principle of loyalty.

25 In the Canadian context, this points, in my view, to the incorrectness of a-historical and presumptively a-political conceptions of the federation such as the one reducing it to a mere statutory creation of the British Parliament. For an illustration of such an approach, see: *Re Resolution to Amend the Constitution of Canada*, [1981] 1 S.C.R. 753 at 803. It is arguable, however, that it would be much more difficult to uphold that type of conception after *Reference re Secession of Quebec*, [1998] 2 S.C.R. 217.

26 On the theory of relational contracts, see Ian R. MacNeil, 'Relational Contract: What We Do and Do Not Know,' *Wisconsin Law Rewiew* (1985): 483.

27 Manuel Garcia-Pelayo, *Derecho constitucional comparado* (Madrid: Allianza Editorial, 2000), 239.

28 William Ossipow, 'Architecture fédéraliste et exigence de la justice,' *Philosophie politique* 9 (1998): 118.

29 On that distinction, see André Burelle, *Le mal canadien: Essai de diagnostic et esquisse d'une thérapie* (Montreal: Fides, 1995).

30 Andreas Føllesdal, 'Federal Inequality among Equals: A Contractualist Defence,' *Metaphilosophy* 32 (2001): 236.

31 Edmond Orban, 'La Cour constitutionnelle fédérale et l'autonomie des Länder en République fédérale d'Allemagne,' *Revue juridique Thémis* 22 (1988): 42 (my translation).

32 See, for a similar conclusion, Alain Noël, 'Le principe fédéral, la solidarité et le partenariat,' in Guy Laforest and Roger Gibbins, eds., *Sortir de l'impasse: Les voies de la réconciliation* (Montreal: IRPP, 1998), 263.

33 The paramountcy doctrine presupposes that an inconsistency must be found between the federal and provincial legislation. The Supreme Court's case law provides in this respect two different definitions of what constitutes an inconsistency. The first conceives of an inconsistency as the impos-

sibility to comply simultaneously with both legislations. In this view, the conflict must thus be direct and actual. See *Multiple Access Ltd. v. McCutcheon*, [1982] 2 S.C.R. 161. For its part, the second, more lenient, definition envisages the notion of inconsistency as the potential frustration by the provincial legislation of the federal legislative purpose. See *Bank of Montreal v. Hall*, [1990] 1 S.C.R. 121. In a recent case, *Rothmans, Benson and Hedges Inc. v. Saskatchewan*, [2005] 1 S.C.R. 188, at para. 15, a unanimous Supreme Court clarified that the two definitions are not mutually exclusive and came up with the following test: Is it possible to simultaneously comply with both the federal and provincial enactments? and Does the provincial enactment frustrate Parliament's purpose in enacting its own legislation?

34 Hans Kelsen, *Théorie pure du droit* (Paris and Brussels : L.G.D.J. and Bruylant, 1999), 69.

35 Gilles Paquet, *Oublier la Révolution tranquille: Pour une nouvelle socialité* (Montreal: Liber, 1999), at 105–110.

36 I have commented on this phenomenon in my article, 'Les Chartes des droits et libertés comme louves dans la bergerie du positivisme? Quelques hypothèses sur l'impact de la culture des droits sur la psyché juridique québécoise,' in Bjarne Melkevik and Pierre Issalys, eds., *Transformation de la culture juridique québécoise: Est-ce la fin de l'hégémonie positiviste?* (Quebec : Presses de l'Université Laval, 1998), 83.

37 I have raised this idea in 'The Challenge of Maintaining a Federal (or Quasi-federal) Culture: Canadian Musings on the Legal and Political Dynamic of the European Constitutional Project,' in *Towards a New European Constitution Conference* (2004) The Federal Trust (U.K.), available on line at www.fedtrust.co.uk/uploads/constitution/desbiens.pdf

38 Choudhry, 'Recasting Social Canada,' 163.

39 Rhoda E. Howard, '"Canadian" as an Ethnic Category: Implications for Multiculturalism and National Unity,' *Canadian Public Policy* 25 (1999): 523.

Afterword: Solidarity as the Boldness of Modesty

SUJIT CHOUDHRY, JEAN-FRANÇOIS GAUDREAULT-DESBIENS,
AND LORNE SOSSIN

The individuals who drafted Canada's federal constitution in the nineteenth century, were trying to respond to a set of preoccupations that were common to the different societal and cultural experiences and interests of their constituents. They were joining together North American British colonies that, prior to Confederation, had not had extensive political or economic ties with each other (with the possible exception of the two parts of the United Province of Canada, which later became Ontario and Quebec). These individuals, the so-called Fathers of Confederation, were working to unite colonies that were either functionally foreign to one another or had been involved in relations where distrust was as much part of the picture as trust. From what was arguably a community of strangers in 1867, they sought to create a lasting community of fate. In spite of their often conflicting views on the future orientations of this new federation called Canada, they compromised and drafted a constitution that took into account the socio-cultural constraints flowing from the presence of pre-existing political entities with well-entrenched identities, while allowing for the creation, by and large incremental, of the desired community of fate.

These constitutional framers spoke to both the past and the future, even though the contours of that future remained ambiguous. The silences of the Constitution Act, 1867 somehow reveal this ambiguity. But this did not prevent them from assigning ambitions to the new country – for example, the creation of a common market, the country's eventual expansion to the West, or the lasting union of a population mainly composed of French Catholics and English Protestants.[1] They soon acknowledged, however, that these ambitions could be achieved only if all constitutional actors were given a tangible comfort zone, through the creation of a federal structure. Most importantly, the constitutional framers shied away from grand declarations about who Canadians were, or were to be. It has often been noted in this respect that, when compared to other constitutions, for example that of the United States of America, the Constitution Act, 1867 is a rather conservative, if not uninspiring, document. This is probably correct in many respects. But could anything else have been done in a federation that overlaps with a truly federal society?[2] Weren't the framers showing some prescience about the possibilities, but also the limits, of that type of federation? In that sense, while their decisions evinced the pragmatism ordinarily associated with the British constitutional law tradition, they may also have been informed by a more principled vision of the Canadian federation and of its federal society, albeit an implicit one. Viewed from this angle, the alleged conservatism of the Constitution Act, 1867 as well as its intriguingly non-nationalist silences in an era where nationalism was triumphing everywhere else, may be construed as a manifestation of boldness – the boldness of modesty.

Such modesty was mandated because the evolution of the Canadian federation would inevitably be evaluated by Canadians from very different, and often conflicting, perspectives – what Richard Simeon called the 'criteria for choice' in federations. In a nutshell, these perspectives revolve around various conceptions of community, democracy and functionality.[3] While they inform attitudes about federalism everywhere, they are particularly relevant to Canada. Indeed, the relatively open texture of the Constitution Act, 1867, which not only allows for all sorts of political appropriations and judicial interpretations, but also for their permanent contestation, inevitably calls for an incessant balancing of these perspectives in both the political and juridical realms.

This was the case when Canada's federal constitution was drafted, and it is still the case today. Contemporary debates about fiscal federalism and redistribution continue to raise more or less the same questions, and all the contributors to this volume approach these problems from either one or many of these perspectives. More specifically, however, they draw our attention to the hurdles upon which *conversations about solidarity* may stumble, and upon which *solidarity* itself may trip. For if the questions themselves have not changed that much, the manner and the circumstances in which they are posed have changed dramatically.

Starting with the hurdles facing conversations about solidarity, we are reminded that if redistribution constitutes, to some extent, a norm in the Canadian federation, well-entrenched preconceptions about that federation may actually prevent us from grasping in a complex manner the impact of recent social, political, and economic changes on the implementation of that norm in contemporary Canada. These preconceptions may be about Canada itself, about the identity, contours, cohesion, and political relevance of the different communities forming Canada, about the efficiency of particular modes of governance, or about the way democracy operates in a highly regionalized, multinational, and multicultural federation. As they related to conversations about solidarity, such preconceptions may actually constitute 'epistemological obstacles,' a concept that, according to French philosopher Gaston Bachelard, designates causes of inertia, stagnation or setback in knowledge.[4] An epistemological obstacle prevents the rigorous intellectual construction that is required in order to grasp realities and concepts in a complex manner. Since an epistemological obstacle does not have any particular, well-defined, identity, this allows it to operate an intellectual closure that facilitates the perpetuation of debatable certainties and received ideas. It may thus elevate 'ideal realities' from the status of contestable constructs to that of unchallenged givens.[5] In debates about redistribution in a federation as diverse as Canada, epistemological obstacles could, for example, take the form of untested assumptions such as depicting federalism as being inherently opposed to social justice, or the uncritical acceptance of monolithic understanding of the political, financial, and juridical relations inherent to federalism, such as apprehending fiscal federalism solely from the perspective of vertical fiscal imbalance.

The implementation of the norm of solidarity in Canada through practices of redistribution seems particularly susceptible to stumbling upon such obstacles. Several contributors to this volume have, in this respect, directly or indirectly alluded to the impact on pan-Canadian solidarity of existing, emerging, and potentially competing, communities of solidarity. Solidarity can indeed play out at different levels. Acknowledging that inevitably leads one to recognize that the prioritization or ranking of communities of solidarity may vary depending on the primary identification of Canadians with one particular community or another. For some, it can be Canada as a whole, for others it can be their provincial or Aboriginal community, for others still it can be a municipal community or a transnational one. Moreover, the intensity and duration of their commitment may vary widely. More than ever, communities of belonging, and of solidarity, are contingent and ever-shifting entities. Thus, at the very moment several groups are challenging the hegemony of state-centred identities, be they federal or provincial, the very cohesion of these sub-state groups is itself being undermined by the emergence of competing, and sometimes ephemeral, social communities of interests. As was observed by legal sociologist Jean-Guy Belley, 'the mystical experience shared by the members of a religious cult or the psychedelic ecstasy of a *rave* provide good illustrations of a social marginality that appears impossible to connect with current regimes of legal pluralism. The sociability of communion, in the first case, and the sociability of mass, in the second, indeed reaches an intensity that annihilates the spirit of community needed for any form of juridical rationality or impulse for the law to emerge, or for them to attain any cognizable consistence.'[6] This quotation not only points to the growing individualism that characterizes advanced societies such as Canada, and which co-exists with another, paradoxical, phenomenon of communitarian affirmation or retrenchment, but also to the mutation of the citizen into a consumer of identities and, possibly, of solidarities. In such a context, it is difficult not to surmise that patterns of solidarity are likely to follow patterns of social identification.

But even if one charitably assumes that these shifts in social identification do not necessarily affect citizens' commitment to solidarity, one is nevertheless forced to examine at which level they are willing to express that solidarity, what costs they are ready to bear for that purpose, and for whom they are ready to incur these costs. There is a need to re-problematize the very concept of solidarity in federations, which seems particularly *à propos* in Canada. The socio-political diversity inherent to such a regionalized, multinational, and multicultural federation, where a genuinely federal society overlaps with the existing federal structure, prevents the emergence of a solidarity based on resemblance – the type that Durkheim labelled 'mechanical solidarity.' But if the form of solidarity that is more likely to appear in such a federal society is one based on interdependence – Durkheim's 'organic solidarity' – it is not even sure that this solidarity can be taken for granted.[7] This is where assuming the existence and the perennial nature of pan-Canadian solidarity risks becoming an epistemological obstacle, as is assuming that no genuine solidarity is possible in such a context. In this respect, not only is socio-political diversity susceptible of affecting attitudes toward solidarity, but so is the plurality of values informing the adherence to one or another 'criterion for choice' in the federation.

Thus, it may well be that solidarity cannot be taken for granted any more in Canada. Digging deeper, it is not even clear that mutual trust should be assumed. Arguably, the very existence of a federation, with the constitutionally-entrenched division of powers that it presupposes, seems to indicate that, on the basis of the principle 'good fences make good friends,'[8] a certain level of distrust existed at the outset, even if the constituent parties were willing to look beyond their relative distrust of each other to build a larger, and distinct, legal order. If one defines trust as 'the willingness to make oneself vulnerable to another without costly external constraints,' it is far from clear that any formal constitutional actor is ready to make oneself vulnerable to the others in today's Canada.[9] Actually, the exact opposite seems to be true. It can be argued that such a definition of trust first and foremost applies to individuals and that it would be naïve to imagine that institutionalized political actors could even consider making themselves vulnerable to others. Still, it is hard to deny that this idea of vulnerability, or of abandonment, captures something essential about trust, whatever the context. Even if we adopt a narrow yet strong, conception of trust as 'encapsulated interest,'[10] resting on the idea that the entity in whom trust is placed will take the interests of those who place such trust into account, vulnerability and thus asymmetry remain central features of trust relationships, even when dealing with institutionalized political actors.

If trust is highly desirable in a federation where solidarity is said to be a norm, it may also be seen as indirectly fostering the unity of that federation. And assuming that unity refers to 'the continuing desire on the part of a population to continue living under the same political institutions, or, perhaps, more precisely, with the *absence* of any desire to sever the existing bonds of political association,'[11] a possibly waning desire of one or more parts of the population of the federation 'to continue living under the same political institutions' will arguably undermine federal solidarity. Thus, while it would be equally problematic to assume that trust, unity, and solidarity cannot exist in Canada, or will inevitably disappear from it, presuming that these properties are necessarily present in the federation, cannot vary in intensity, and are perennial by nature, probably constitutes an even more significant problem as far as conversations about solidarity are concerned.

These presumptions may further hide a refusal to acknowledge the socio-political reality of Canada, where, for a host of reasons, solidarity as a norm and redistribution as a practice seem more contentious than ever. Solidarity, and particularly the type of organic solidarity that characterizes multinational federations, is not a given; it demands work, a work that must take place both at the level of values and at the level of the mechanisms used to implement the norm of solidarity. Suffice it to say here that different types of actors share a responsibility in creating an environment where values conducive to solidarity are fostered. And although the contribution of political actors is absolutely central and invaluable in this respect, judicial actors are important as well. Because most of the debates about solidarity and redistribution in Canada take place in the political realm, it is often thought that the role that courts can play in fostering solidarity and redistribution is marginal at best. While it is certainly true that they cannot implement policies of redistribution, they can nevertheless use their powers to interpret the constitution in a manner that will be more or less conducive to the development of all types of solidarity in the federation. Two examples come to mind here, one that on the whole furthers the agenda of pan-Canadian solidarity, and one that does not.

The recent opinion of the Supreme Court of Canada in *Reference re Employment Insurance Act (Can.)*, ss. 22 and 23, arguably promotes pan-Canadian solidarity. In that case, the court confirmed the constitutional validity of federal statutory provisions providing employment insurance benefits to women not working because of pregnancy, as well as other persons not working because they care for a newborn or an adopted child. The court found that these provisions, which essentially provide for benefits replacing the employment income of insured workers in such circumstances, did not encroach upon the provinces' jurisdiction over property and civil rights, even though one of their effects was to facilitate support for families and the ability to care for children.[12] This case is interesting because it fosters interpersonal solidarity at a pan-Canadian level – an important dimension of solidarity, but perhaps not the most significant one from the perspective of federalism – by recognizing the federal Parliament's power to use its jurisdiction over unemployment insurance to launch narrowly tailored social programs which provide for income security in the event of non-participation in the paid labour market.

The evolving interpretation given by the Supreme Court to that particular federal head of power could be viewed by some as another illustration of the Court's preference for what Daniel Weinstock calls in this volume overlapping federalism at the expense of a strong, watertight conception of jurisdictional exclusiveness. But in our view, the case can hardly be construed as opening the floodgates to massive federal interventions in the area of social policy, even if one considers the broad and dynamic understanding of the labour markets adopted by the Supreme Court.[13] It remains to be seen, however, how the federal government will devise its interventions in that field, and more particularly, how sensitive and responsive it will be to regional differences across Canada. Indeed, it bears remembering that prior to the Supreme Court's decision in the *Employment Insurance Act Reference*, the federal government had negotiated in 2004 a deal with Quebec, in which it had agreed to contribute to the funding of Quebec's pioneering parental leave program, which is more generous than its federal counterpart. However, that deal was struck after a judgment of the Quebec Court of Appeal, which found that federal jurisdiction over unemployment only extended to wage replacement measures for individuals having lost their jobs for economic, rather than personal, reasons. This is the very judgment that was overturned by the Supreme Court. This begs the following question: Would the agreement signed by Quebec and Ottawa on parental leaves have been possible without that Court of Appeal decision? Or, put differently, would such an agreement have been possible after the Supreme Court's decision? We can only conjecture the answer to that question, but a no would certainly have reinforced negative attitudes about federalism in Quebec, thereby undermining the commitment of its citizens to pan-Canadian ideals, including solidarity.

All of this to say that the manner in which a given level of government that is acting within its constitutional prerogatives implements its policies may have an effect on trust, unity and, ultimately, solidarity. In some cases, flexibility and asymmetry may indeed represent a more appropriate way to promote these values than a one-size-fits-all approach, which calls for the need for possibly more, and not less, collaborative intergovernmental endeavours to tackle complex social issues that pertain to solidarity and redistribution.

One of the problems that such collaborative endeavours face, however, is the arguably defective constitutional framework applicable to intergovernmental agreements in Canada. At the very least, this framework can hardly be characterized as trust-enhancing, as is illustrated by the Supreme Court's opinion in *Reference re Canada Assistance Plan (B.C.)*, where a challenge to the legality of the federal government's unilateral decision to cap the Canada Assistance Plan was rejected.[14] The problem in this case lies in the Court's refusal to constitutionally preclude a federal unilateral decision that had the effect of drastically upsetting the finances of the recipient provinces, with the ensuing results on how these provinces could exercise their own constitutional powers and deliver the services their citizens expected. The acceptance of the constitutionality of the unilateral repudiation of intergovernmental agreements was, in essence, grounded in the non-legally binding nature of these agreements in Canadian constitutional law and on the principle of parliamentary supremacy. Nothing, or very little, was said about the particular role intergovernmental agreements play in a federation such as Canada, the impact of breaches of such agreements on the equilibrium of the federation, the legitimate governmental expectations arising out of these agreements, or a possible reconceptualization of parliamentary supremacy in light of the particular imperatives of a federal structure. We are not saying here that all intergovernmental agreements should automatically be characterized as legally binding. We are merely saying that it would be appropriate to consider the possibility that those which somehow affect the very capacity of constitutional actors to exercise their powers meaningfully be granted that status. While arguing in favour of an automatic recognition of a legal status to all intergovernmental agreements might stumble upon an epistemological obstacle, it appears equally problematic to systematically refuse them that status. It is one thing to say that most federalism-related disputes can, and should ideally, be resolved in the political realm, but it is quite another to elevate this prudential principle into a fully fledged constitutional principle. Since these disputes sometimes involve significant power imbalances, which may allow one particular constitutional actor to disregard the legitimate interests and aspirations of other constitutional actors entirely, a judicial policy of systematic non-intervention risks amounting to a refusal to uphold the constitution.

As far as intergovernmental agreements are concerned, a legal framework such as the one we have in Canada raises concerns as to the stability and predictability of governmental decision-making processes and of revenue-sharing mechanisms. And if we turn to solidarity as a broader value-norm, this legal framework seems even more problematic. To the extent that, in a complex federation such as Canada, solidarity is arguably more likely to blossom if a solid capital of trust is maintained, any policy, judicial or otherwise, that can reasonably be characterized as reducing that capital, or as allowing constitutional actors to breach the trust others have placed in them, is worrisome. Thus, reflecting on how such policies could be reformed might be warranted, and could certainly benefit from examining how things are done in other federations, even those whose federal culture and legal tradition is different from ours.[15] Whether topics such as solidarity, redistribution or fiscal federalism are approached from a philosophical, juridical, political, or economic angle, conversations about these topics should always involve prior reflection on the assumptions informing how these topics are grasped. Political debates tend to demonstrate that such a reflective attitude unfortunately represents the exception rather than the rule. Indeed, too many political actors seem content to reiterate constantly their favourite ideological mantras, instead of verifying whether the values they assume to exist, or the objectives they seek to achieve, actually exist or are achievable. If anything, this volume emphasizes that we might need to revisit the ways we converse about solidarity to recast the ways we can concretely achieve it.

As we were finalizing the edition of this volume, an event of significant importance took place in Quebec. A group of prominent citizens, federalists and sovereigntists alike, tabled a manifesto for a 'clear-eyed vision of Quebec' ('Québec lucide'), in which they essentially argued that Quebec society was acting like an ostrich with its head in the sand, and acknowledged that it is facing problems that could drastically undermine its ability to sustain its fabled, solidarity-based, Quebec model.[16] A group of equally prominent citizens, concerned by what they perceived as the right-wing bias of their 'lucid' counterparts, issued a counter-manifesto calling for a Quebec based on solidarity, in which they more or less defended the status quo while calling for more sustainable forms of development.[17] Despite their significant divergences, both groups seem to recognize that solidarity is a work in progress. We hope that a similar debate arises at a pan-Canadian level. However, we would add that, far from being opposed to solidarity, lucidity may be a precondition for it. Indeed, as exemplified in the compromise reached in 1867 by the framers of Canada's federal constitution, while lucidity may compel constitutional actors to formulate their nation-building aspirations in more modest terms, modesty itself does not preclude ambitions: it only induces us to mobilize our energies around ambitions that are realistically achievable. This, alone, may be a bold choice to make when it comes to (re)designing the central policies of a federation like Canada.

NOTES

1 The Aboriginal peoples of Canada were conspicuously left out of the deal, since the were then perceived as mere 'objects' of legislation.

2 A federal society is one where there is a relatively deep level of ethno-linguistic diversity and where that diversity is territorialized. See William S. Livingstone, 'A Note on the Nature of Federalism,' *Political Science Quarterly* 67 (1952): 81.

3 Richard Simeon, 'Criteria for Choice in Federal Systems,' *Queen's Law Journal* 8 (1981): 131.

4 Gaston Bachelard, *La formation de l'esprit scientifique: Contribution à une psychanalyse de la connaissance objective* (Paris: Vrin, 1938), 14.

5 On the anthropological concept of 'ideal reality,' see Maurice Godelier, *L'idéel et le matériel. Pensée, économies, sociétés* (Paris: Fayard, 1984), 198.

6 Jean-Guy Belley, 'Le pluralisme juridique comme doctrine de la science du droit,' in Jean Kellerhals, Dominique Manaï, and Robert Roth, eds., *Pour un droit pluriel: Études offertes au professeur Jean-François Perrin* (Bâle: Helbing & Lichtenhahn, 2002), p. 161 (our translation).

7 On these two types of solidarity, see Émile Durkheim, *De la division du travail social* (Paris: Alcan, 1926).

8 Antoine N. Messara, *Théorie générale du système politique libanais: Essai comparé sur les fondements et les perspectives d'évolution d'un système consensuel de gouvernement* (Paris: Cariscript, 1994), 63.

9 Larry E. Ribstein, 'Law v. Trust,' *Boston University Law Review* 81 (2001): 555.

10 Russell Hardin, 'Trust and Society,' in Gianluigi Galeotti, Pierre Salmon, and Ronald Winthrobe, eds., *Competitition and Structure. The Political Economy of Collective Decisions: Essays in honour of Albert Breton* (Cambridge: Cambridge University Press, 2000) 20.

11 Daniel Weinstock, 'Building Trust in Divided Societies,' *Journal of Political Philosophy* 7 (1999): 289.

12 [2005] S.C.C. 56, at para. 35.

13 On the evolution of the concept of work and on its impact on the law, see generally Alain Supiot, ed., *Au-delà de l'emploi: Transformations du travail et devenir du droit du travail en Europe* (Paris: Flammarion, 1999). On the conciliation of work and family life envisaged from a legal standpoint, see Joanne Conaghan and Kerry Rittich, eds., *Labour Law, Work, and Family* (Oxford: Oxford University Press, 2005).

14 *Reference Re Canada Assistance Plan (B.C.)*, [1991] 2 S.C.R. 525.

15 For example, examining the status of intergovernmental agreements in the constitutional law of other federations could prove extremely fruitful. On

this question, and on the variables influencing the legal or non-legal status of such agreements, see Johanne Poirier, 'Les ententes intergouvernemen- tales et la gouvernance fédérale: aux confins du droit et du non-droit,' in Jean-François Gaudreault-DesBiens and Fabien Gélinas, eds., *The Moods and States of Federalism: Governance, Identity, and Methodology / Le fédéralisme dans tous ses états: Gouvernance, identité et méthodologie,* (Brussels and Cowans- ville: Bruylant and Éditions Yvon Blais, 2005), 441.

16 On line at http://www.pourunquebeclucide.com/cgi-cs/ cs.waframe.index?lang=2

17 On line at http://www.pourunquebecsolidaire.info/index.php?manifeste#

Contributors

Katherine Boothe is a PhD candidate in the Department of Political Science, University of British Columbia.

Paul Boothe is Professor of Economics and Fellow, Institute for Public Economics at the University of Alberta.

Sujit Choudhry is an Associate Professor at the Faculty of Law and the Department of Political Science in the Faculty of Arts and Science, University of Toronto.

David Duff is an Associate Professor of Law at the University of Toronto.

Jean-François Gaudreault-DesBiens is Canada Research Chair in North American and Comparative Juridical and Cultural Identities, and is Associate Professor of Law at the Université de Montréal.

Andrée Lajoie is Professor of Law and Researcher at the Centre de Recherche en Droit Public (CRDP) at the Université de Montréal.

Alain Noël is Professor of Political Science at the Université de Montréal. He was a member of Québec's Commission on Fiscal Imbalance.

Peter H. Russell is University Professor Emeritus of Political Science at the University of Toronto.

Richard Simeon is Professor of Political Science and Law at the University of Toronto.

Lorne Sossin is an Associate Professor at the Faculty of Law and the Department of Political Science in the Faculty of Arts and Science, University of Toronto.

François Vaillancourt is Professor of Economics at the Université de Montréal, and is Research Director at the Centre de recherche et développement en économique.

Daniel Weinstock is Canada Research Chair in Ethics and Political Philosophy, and is Director of the Ethics Research Centre at the University of Montreal.

www.ingramcontent.com/pod-product-compliance
Lightning Source LLC
Chambersburg PA
CBHW021902020426
42334CB00013B/442